MODERN SPORTS
OFFICIATING

MODERN SPORTS OFFICIATING

A PRACTICAL GUIDE

Third Edition

RICHARD CLEGG
Scottsdale Public Schools
Scottsdale, Arizona

WILLIAM A. THOMPSON
Long Beach City College
Long Beach, California

wcb

Wm. C. Brown Publishers
Dubuque, Iowa

Copyright © 1974, 1979, 1985 by
Wm. C. Brown Company Publishers. All rights reserved

Library of Congress Catalog Card Number: 84-72660

ISBN 0-697-00464-3

Printed in the United States of America
10 9 8 7 6 5 4 3

This book is lovingly dedicated to the "subtle influence" of our wives, Nancy and Sally—without whose qualities of "judgment," "hustle," "poise," "consistency," and "rapport" this book would not have been written.

Contents

Preface

Organized sports have enjoyed another decade of growth and progress. But has the art of sports officiating kept pace? An obvious weakness in the preparation of sports officials is the lack of contemporary publications on the subject. *Modern Sports Officiating* represents an attempt to bridge this gap.

This guide is designed for college courses in sports officiating, for supervisors of school sports, community recreation programs, and individuals preparing to enter the sports officiating field. In addition, the book is intended to provide special direction for physical education and recreation major students and prospective coaches.

The approach presents a current, understandable and practical framework beneficial to both prospective and experienced sports officials. The emphasis is on *what to do* and how and why to do it. It was not possible nor was it the desire of the authors to cover all the playing rules and officiating mechanics of each sport. The reader is referred to instructional literature from the National Federation of State High School Associations and the National Collegiate Athletic Association.

Chapter One serves as an introduction to sports officiating. Special emphasis is given to the development of a sound philosophy of officiating and to clarification of the personal requirements of an official and of the roles played by a sports official. Chapter Two presents practical advice for the beginning official. Chapters Three through Ten deal specifically with selected sports—baseball and softball, basketball, football, soccer, swimming, track and field, volleyball and wresting. The format for the sports chapters includes sections on *the game, officials and their responsibilities, basic penalties and rulings, mechanics, problem calls,* and *miscellaneous considerations.* Chapters One, Two, Three, Four, Five and Nine, and final editing were the responsibilities of Richard Clegg. Chapters Six, Seven, Eight and Ten were the responsibilities of William A. Thompson.

This edition reflects important additions and revisions. All chapters have been updated regarding recent changes in rules and mechanics. The soccer chapter has been expanded.

The production of the first, second and third editions of Modern Sports Officiating has been greatly enhanced by the assistance of many people who have offered general and specific suggestions, critiqued manuscript drafts and done the typing. The authors wish to acknowledge their indebtedness to all those who assisted in the preparation of this book.

Richard Clegg
William A. Thompson

MODERN SPORTS
OFFICIATING

1

Officiating Requirements

Welcome to the challenging but rewarding job of sports officiating. If you love sports and are willing to work, you can develop a skill which is personally satisfying and beneficial to the American sports scene. There are no shortcuts to true officiating success any more than there are to true athletic success, but enthusiastic effort on your part can lead to a stimulating addition to your life.

The Officiating Scene Today

The continuous and phenomenal growth of sports programs in this country has produced a great need for qualified sports officials. There is virtually no ceiling to the prospects for advancement of officials who are gifted and eager to learn. Athletic coaches, administrators and recreation personnel at all levels of competition are constantly seeking competent officials. They know that good officiating helps to produce a healthy, educational, and sportsmanlike environment associated with a fair determination of the winner. They wish to hire officials who will be effective in reaching these goals. The same leaders know, on the other hand, that poorly trained, incompetent sports officials create tensions and generate frustration among players, coaches and spectators— sometimes with serious consequences. They prefer not to hire such officials.

To put it simply, the official is the essential *third dimension* of an athletic contest. The player, the coach and the official interact.

Photo by Barb Urbanek.

Depending upon their abilities and attitudes, they produce a variety of possible results—not merely a winner and a loser, but also satisfaction or disappointment, thrills or mediocrity, cooperative teamwork or antagonism, mutual respect or distrust. Any sports expert will acknowledge the contribution of this *third dimension* to the quality of athletic competition.

The challenge for the prospective official is to develop experience-based capabilities to the point where that which is expected of a sports official can in fact be produced in game situations, regardless of the difficulties presented. Achieving a high degree of competence is chiefly the result of concentrated study and game experience, supplemented by continuous evaluation and efforts to improve.

Officiating is not a simple or easy avocation. It is a challenging task. New officials should prepare themselves thoroughly if they contemplate a continuing career in officiating. By the same token, a new official would be mistaken if he or she were to enter into officiating casually or for the sole purpose of financial gain. Officials should direct themselves toward meaningful developmental goals if they expect to be successful.

Our purpose in this chapter is to establish a clear and comprehensive concept of sports officiating. The goal of the reader might be to develop an intelligent, realistic understanding of what competent sports officiating is and what it demands. Consider the following questions:

1. What is the fundamental aim of sports officiating?
2. What are the essential ingredients for effective sports officiating?
3. What qualities should a competent sports official possess?
4. What various roles should be played while officiating?

The Fundamental Aim: To Cause the Game to Progress Smoothly within the Rules

The official's overriding goal is to promote the normal progress of a contest, as it was meant to proceed, with as little interference as possible. This is *not* to say that rule enforcement should be neglected to the slightest degree, but rather that the competent official should not merely be concerned about penalizing rule infractions. *Preventing* rule infractions before they occur is also an important concern. Infractions can be prevented in two general ways: (1) by establishing a subtle but unquestioned influence over the game; and (2) by actively preventing specific infractions.

A contest which is frequently and unnecessarily interrupted by the official's whistle leaves no one satisfied. Under such circumstances, the official rather than the players becomes the dominant factor. Players and coaches alike respect the official who, within the playing rules, provides for continuous and uninterrupted action.

Establishing a Subtle Influence

In almost all cases, players wish to avoid rule infractions because penalties hurt. Players—especially well-trained players—will avoid many rule violations when they have cause to avoid them. The competent official capitalizes on the desires and abilities of the players by establishing a controlling influence over the contest *early in the contest.* For example, in the first two to four minutes of a basketball game.

In order to accomplish this, the effective sports official must be completely "warmed up" on the first play of the game in order to make *any* necessary ruling without hesitation. The quality of "early control" established, or not established, can influence the entire game. When the official's influence is felt from the start, the game progresses as it was meant to progress. Two important ways in which you as an official can establish this influence are:

1. *By being in a position* to call the play at all times, so that the players are constantly aware of your presence.
2. *By reacting immediately* to rule infractions, especially early in the contest.

When opponents, *on their own,* try to compete in accordance with the spirit and letter of the rules, the result is satisfying and rewarding to all concerned. Such a situation is not always found in athletic competition, but the dedicated official constantly seeks it. Athletics benefits from officials' efforts to produce this type of competitive environment.

Active Prevention

Obviously, more than just a subtle officiating influence is needed in athletic competition. On these occasions the usual result is a decision by the official and the enforcement of the prescribed penalty. At other times, however, it is appropriate and advisable for the official to anticipate the impending infraction and to "talk the athletes out of" committing it. Direct action can and should be preventive as well as punitive.

Considerable experience and background in the particular sport are necessary in order to know when and when not to issue warnings. Generally, in the higher levels of competition fewer warnings and less preventive officiating are appropriate. Nevertheless, there are moments in all sports and at all levels of play when this type of preventive officiating can be accomplished appropriately and unobtrusively. Here are a few examples:

1. In football the head linesman cautions a lineman who has been lining up in a position very close to "offsides". Before a kick-off the umpire reminds members of the receiving team, "no blocking below the belt."
2. In basketball post play, the "lead" official warns opposing centers to "watch your hands" in order to prevent pushing for position. Before free throws the trailing official issues explicit warnings to "watch the lines."
3. In baseball, the plate umpire warns the batter about stepping out of the batter's box. While dusting off the pitcher's plate, the base umpire informs the pitcher with a "near-balk move" just what balk he is in danger of committing.
4. In track, the starter forewarns sprinters to avoid "rolling starts." The relay land judges show the athletes the exact areas within which the baton must be passed.

Such warnings not only help to eliminate needless and unwanted infractions but they also can establish a positive player-official relationship.

To summarize, the primary aim of the competent official is to cause the game to progress smoothly and with as little interference as possible. Preventive officiating is superior to "whistle-happy" officiating, but *does not* eliminate the responsibility for unhesitatingly enforcing the rules.

The Essential Ingredients

Regardless of the sport in which you are involved, you must meet four fundamental requirements if you wish to be considered a successful official:

1. You must enforce the rules intelligently.
2. You must show integrity.
3. You must build sound human relations.
4. You must show primary concern for the individual athlete.

Intelligent Rule Enforcement

The rules of American sports have evolved through the concentrated attention of many experts over a period of many years. As such, the rules *command respect and demand enforcement.* The athletes are not adequate or appropriate rule enforcers. The official is there to enforce the rules—to show respect for the sport and for the players by *knowing* the rules and *enforcing* them. To do otherwise usually brings the unwanted consequences of disorganized games, unsportsmanlike acts, and even the danger of injury.

Applying the rules requires the use of judgment on the part of the master official. In particular instances apparent rule violations will be ignored, while in other instances virtually invisible acts will be ruled upon immediately. Preserving the ideal of the sport through rule enforcement is the chief concern.

Judgment by the official in applying the rules is commonly based upon the wisdom of Oswald Tower, former member of the basketball National Rules Committee. Tower said, in effect, that *the purpose of the playing rules is to penalize a player who, by reason of an illegal act, places an opponent at a disadvantage.* Thus, in rulings where judgment is permissible, the competent official is more concerned about the *effect* of an illegal act than about the act itself. For example, the slightest push of a shooter in basketball can affect his shot; if it does, an infraction has occurred and should be ruled. There are many other examples, some of which are specified in subsequent chapters.

Authorities agree that the Tower philosophy is essentially correct, because when properly employed, it assures that the spirit of the game prevails rather than exact or petty enforcement. Two cautions should be noted:

1. The philosophy does not apply to all rules or even to most rules. A player is in bounds or out of bounds, a swimmer did touch or did not touch, the throw did or did not beat the base runner on a force play at second base, and so forth. In most cases, the official is asked, not to exercise judgment, but *to call immediately* what has been seen.
2. When the philosophy *does* apply, the official must know and understand the correct rule interpretation so that the decisions rendered are as consistent as possible. The philosophy permits flexibility, but inconsistency *and* flexibility would soon bring trouble.

The concept of consistency leads us to the second essential ingredient of effective sports officiating.

Absolute Integrity

The official wants to see the game progress correctly, without bias or inconsistency. In spite of pressures, the official should not be unduly influenced by the score, the time remaining, or the reactions of players, coaches or spectators, nor be influenced by the direction of previous decisions. To a considerable degree, the capable official sees each movement of the competition as a moment in itself, unconnected with what has happened previously.

In certain instances, great courage and personal confidence are required in order for an official to rule with absolute integrity. No one, not even the home coach, admires a "homer" official. Regardless of the circumstances, the sports official must be completely honest in all phases of the job, especially in applying the rules, and also in relationships with fellow officials, players and coaches.

Personal integrity can also be shown by what officiating assignments you *do not accept.* An official should never accept an assignment which creates a compromising situation. Contests should not be worked in which an official has a close relationship with the involved schools, players, or coaches. Those who hire officials actively avoid making such assignments, but in many instances only the official is able to sense a potentially compromising assignment.

Personal integrity can be shown by your relationship with officiating associations, coaches, and players. Generally, these relationships should be businesslike—not political. So-called "preferred assignments" will eventually come to the qualified official, regardless of political maneuverings. The official who is not gifted is merely baiting his or her own trap when assignments are attained for which he or she is not qualified. Unfortunately, large officiating associations, because of the official's anonymity, frequently create the impression that influence is more important than ability. Ultimately, such an impression is false.

Finally, personal integrity can be shown through reliability in meeting all accepted assignments and meeting them on time. The only officiating "sin" more serious than arriving late is not arriving at all.

In retrospect it is evident that officiating integrity is a product of personal honesty and reliability. A potentially outstanding official can rise or fall according to the integrity demonstrated.

Sound Human Relations

It has been said with considerable truth that officiating is more like an art than a science. Building sound relationships with fellow officials, players, coaches and spectators while under the fire of intense athletic rivalry calls for "an artist's touch."

Relationship with fellow officials. For the most part, officials are on their own at the contest. If their mutual support and teamwork break down, problems in other relationships will certainly increase. Here are a few specific suggestions which indicate what is needed in order to produce real teamwork among officials.

1. *Always* arrive early enough to consult with your fellow officials before the game so that you can agree on mechanics and rule interpretations and begin to become acquainted with one another.
2. *Never* argue with a fellow official.
3. Agree in advance about who will call what (and who will not call what).
4. Agree in advance about how you may assist one another in making decisions which require assistance.
5. Decide in advance the circumstances, if any exist, in which one official may overrule or cancel the decision of another. This practice is permissible in a few sports—although it is to be avoided. Nonetheless, such a potentially sensitive issue should be agreed upon in advance.
6. Avoid the temptation to "explain" your fellow official's decision. Assuming such a responsibility has the potential for damaging relationships at several levels, including those within the officiating team.
7. The more experienced officials should take the initiative to advise inexperienced officials. Suggestions may be given *before* and *after* the contest, but seldom *during* the contest.

Relationships with players. Good relationships between players and officials are of fundamental importance to effective officiating. Coaches and spectators can sense the quality of player-official relationships, and this influences their evaluation of the official. Officials should be neither overly friendly nor aloof in their dealings with players. Players tend to mistrust an official who seems to be trying to win a popularity contest with both teams. They prefer an official to act like an official who has an important job to do.

The degree to which an official should try to be helpful varies considerably according to the sport and the level of play. In professional sports a particularly helpful official would be treated with amazement, amusement or scorn; whereas, in youth contests a competent official will not hesitate to actually teach the rules at appropriate moments.

A domineering or dictatorial official upsets the players. Officials must be, or at least act, humane and approachable. An official must show respect for the players in order to gain respect. Hustle and enthusiasm also increase player respect.

When unsportsmanlike acts occur, whether directly involving the official or not, these acts should be penalized immediately, but in as calm a manner as possible. Unsportsmanlike acts usually create excitement and emotional reactions in players, coaches and spectators alike. What is especially needed under such circumstances is not anger or revenge but an accurate and efficient penalty enforced confidently and calmly.

Relationships with coaches. As implied by the rules of most sports, contact between the coaches and official should be businesslike, friendly, respectful and *limited.* The coach is concerned about an official's mechanics and judgment and is not likely to be concerned about whether or not an official wishes to be a friend. Occasionally, coaches become extremely upset with officials. Under such circumstances, considerable tact is needed. Often the upset coach is the type who can be calmed down almost as easily as he or she became excited. A brief, businesslike, but not unfriendly explanation of the decision may prevent serious consequences.

The sports official should always remember the importance of a game to the coach—the time and dedication that has been applied towards a successful effort. Most coaches accept highly underpaid positions for the sake of athletes. Emotional reactions to an official's decisions exemplify loyalty to their athletes and their "cause" rather than a personal vendetta against the official. The official should not overreact to the excited coach, but he or she *must not* neglect obvious infractions by the coach. If there is a choice between protecting the coach or the game, the game comes first.

Relationships with spectators. "Crowd control" is the chief responsibility of the host school or organization, but the official also bears an indirect responsibility and exerts considerable influence. While the official's attention is directed principally to the game and the players and partially to the coaches, he or she cannot ignore the presence of spectators, in all reality the *fourth* dimension of sports (players first, coaches second, officials third, spectators fourth.)

The trend of an athletic event can be harmed by intense spectator reactions. An obviously upset official unintentionally adds fuel to the fire. A hustling, efficient, and calm official can do much to neutralize potentially explosive circumstances.

In summary, sound public relations must be a part of competent officiating because sports involve human beings with opposing goals and loyalties. These human beings possess different backgrounds, abilities and emotional responses. In fact, some of them do not like officials. The sports official can seldom satisfy everyone, nor should this be the aim. You should show respect for others, avoid antagonizing anyone and *be approachable.* Primary attention should be directed toward the best officiating job you can produce. When, in part because of high-quality officiating, the contest is played skillfully and fairly, the basis for common good will has been established.

Your Foremost Concern: The Individual Athlete
The capable official has a primary concern for the protection of the players. In many instances his or her actions are based on this concern. The master official:

1. Wants to prevent injuries and knows that in many sports good officiating can prevent damaging and unnecessary accidents.
2. Wants to encourage sportsmanlike behavior and understands the importance of officiating to this end.
3. Knows that correct rulings can motivate player improvement through the trial-and-error learning process.
4. Does not discourage questions on the rules, because he or she knows that players don't know all the rules.
5. Wants to keep all the players in the game and knows that in many cases the disqualification or ejection of a player can be prevented.
6. Is willing to eject or disqualify a player when the rules and spirit of the game demand such action, because the development of the given player, the protection of other players, and the quality of the game itself are involved.

The official who is able and willing to use "protection of the players" as a guide will be amazed at its effectiveness, especially in making difficult decisions. To test this theory, try it against any seemingly hopeless officiating situation that you can imagine. Ask yourself in this imaginary situation, what should be done for the players' protection? Perhaps the indicated decision will not be completely acceptable to all people, but it will be the *best* decision available if it is based upon concern for the individual athlete. The beginning official should be constantly reminded of this responsibility to the players.

Qualities of a Competent Official

If one hundred different sports officiating experts submitted their own lists of the essential qualifications of a master official, one might expect one hundred different listings. If asked to place a given set of qualifications in order of their importance, the same experts might again be expected to differ in their opinions. Thus, the qualities selected by the authors and the following list bear no claim of infallibility or even comprehensiveness. The selected qualities are meant to clarify the game-by-game requirements of successful sports officiating.

The qualities were derived from survey and interview responses from scores of recognized officials and coaches, as well as the personal experiences of the authors. The purposes of the list are (1) to specify the requirements of effective officiating; (2) to guide and motivate improvement; and (3) to suggest guidelines for the evaluation of officials (either self-evaluation or evaluation by those who hire officials). *Good eyesight* was not included, although its importance cannot be questioned.

I. Precise Knowledge of Playing Rules
The rules of any game provide the direction for play. Officials are expected to see that the game is played according to those rules. Mastery of game rules is a continuing effort. Early in their training prospective officials study rule and case books, discuss rules in detail in the officiating association class meetings, and are tested on their knowledge of the rules. The most effective means of resolving confusion and promoting understanding of complex sections of the rules is to participate in smaller study groups. Many competent officials make it a practice to review briefly the total rulebook the night before an assignment. The official finds it helpful to analyze carefully difficult sections of the rules on the day of the game. Following the game, officials should critique their individual effort and the performance of the officiating unit. This will allow for immediate attention to deficiencies in the understanding of the rules while situations are still fresh in the mind. Finally, officiating associations in many areas of the country meet socially during the off-season in an effort to keep their officials posted on rule changes for the coming season.

II. Judgment
Judgment in an individual contest should be based primarily upon a thorough knowledge and understanding of the playing rules. No official ever has said or probably ever will be able to say, "My judgment is complete and perfect." Development of good judgment is a never-ending process. The official who *continues* to study the rules and to apply officiating experiences to personal improvement is the official who will succeed. Good judgment is a foremost qualification of the top-notch official, because it permits correct, unhesitating decision-making under

any game circumstances. It also develops the respect and approval of players and coaches alike.

When an official is able to make one sound decision after another, control of the game becomes evident. The game progresses as it was meant to progress, with the players and the action rather than the official in the spotlight. Competitive playing or coaching experience in a given sport greatly helps the judgment of a new official, but such experience is certainly not enough in itself.

III. Good Mechanics

Officiating mechanics refer to the routine procedures surrounding what the official does. The two primary areas of mechanics are "signaling" and "positioning." When more than one official is involved, "teamwork" becomes a third category, and additional signaling and positioning responsibilities are then necessary. The mechanics of signaling, positioning and teamwork are each of essential importance to assure a professional performance.

Signals may be executed by mechanical device, voice or gesture, depending upon the sport and the circumstance. Sharp, unhesitating and unhurried signals are necessary both to communicate decisions and to build the confidence of participants and observers in your abilities. Correct positioning is necessary to permit you to see (rather than guess) what you are hired to see. Teamwork procedures are necessary (1) to provide balanced coverage of all conceivable actions and (2) to minimize or eliminate disagreement among the officials.

When proper mechanics are observed precisely, the game progresses without confusion or unnecessary delay. There is nothing complicated or magical about the officiating mechanics of any sport. Good mechanics are not difficult to develop *if* correct habits are established early in the official's career. Difficulty does occur when the new official unsuspectingly forms incorrect positioning, signals or teamwork habits. Mechanics, good or bad, are habitual actions. It is much easier to learn the correct habit than to unlearn an incorrect habit later.

Like playing rules, officiating mechanics are clearly specified and have evolved from the efforts of many people for many years and, therefore, should command the respect and acceptance of new officials. The first two obligations of a new official are to begin (1) to learn and understand the playing rules and (2) to develop the correct habits involved in officiating mechanics.

IV. Hustle

By the colloquial definition, "hustle" means to move or act with resolute energy. With the possible exception of good judgment, no quality commands more respect and approval than hustle. Hustle is highly valued on the athletic scene by all concerned, including fellow officials. It is the quality which improves athletes most, which coaches wish most to teach, and which is greatly admired and respected by spectators, coaches, and athletes alike.

Depending on the particular sport, hustle can be demonstrated in several different ways. It is broadly defined here to include such related attributes as alertness, physical effort, dedication and enthusiasm. Hustle—or the lack of it—*is apparent,* regardless of the sport you happen to be officiating. A hustling official will see more, display better mechanics, and enjoy the work more. The opposites are true of the official who is somewhat lazy or uninterested. As one dimension of the sports scene, the official is expected to demonstrate this valued attribute. But whether hustle is expected or not, the hustling official will certainly do a better job. Coaches continually rank hustle high on their list of positive officiating qualities.

V. Decisiveness

The decisive official converts a controversial or judgmental decision into an accepted decision through decisiveness. The usual result is a continuous contest apparently decided by the skills of the players, not an interrupted game "unfairly" affected by the "questionable" decisions of an official. The experienced, competent official realizes that judgment is not subject to formal protest in any case—that *unnecessary* and *hopeless* controversy can be avoided by ruling decisively on close decisions. *The closer the decision, the greater the decisiveness needed.* Compare these examples with your personal experience.

1. In football, when the ball carrier is struggling close to the goal line, the sideline official (head linesman or field judge) should (a) signal immediately whether or not a touchdown has been scored or (b) aggressively close in on the action if not yet certain. Either action conveys the impression of expert coverage decisively executed.
2. In basketball, when the period ends just before a "try" is in flight, the trailing official immediately and decisively should cancel the potential basket before the try reaches the basket.
3. In wrestling, a fall which is very close to being merely a near-fall should be accompanied by a much more decisive signal than the obvious fall.

When there is a hesitant, indecisive, delayed decision, one opponent or the other is sure to believe that the decision was incorrect. Since a decision must be made in any event, the competent official makes his or her decisions decisively.

VI. Poise

Athletic contests are exciting and, therefore, frequently arouse the emotions of the participants and spectators. Contests can get out of hand when emotions run high. Officials cannot control the emotions of others, but they are expected to control their own and to show poise, regardless of the circumstances.

Confidence and calmness are the basic components needed. Persons who lack personal confidence or who cannot control their emotions and excitement do not usually make good officials. Such persons add to existing tensions when they overreact in pressurized moments. On the other hand, the poised official contributes to a controlled atmosphere. During tense moments, gestures and movements become deliberate, almost slow, whenever possible. The greater the momentary tension the greater the need for calmness (e.g., removing the player from a contest for unsportsmanlike conduct). Obviously, to maintain poise under extreme tension is not easy. To do so under certain circumstances requires nearly superhuman personal control. Most outstanding officials have developed the habit, consciously or unconsciously, of *acting* calmly at a time when, in fact, they are very excited.

Athletic contest should be governed by the abilities of the players and the playing regulations, not by uncontrolled emotions. The sports official sometimes is the only person in the position and with the authority to return the game to the "healthy excitement" of properly supervised athletic competition.

VII. Consistency

If a count were taken of the officiating qualities most frequently criticized by and most upsetting to coaches and players, inconsistency would undoubtedly lead the list. Coaches and players expect the rules to apply equally to both teams. True consistency is open to misinterpretation by players, coaches, and spectators, and even by officials. True consistency results, not from attempting to even up both sides but, from applying the *correct rule interpretation* to each separate competitive act. The underlying truth is that *no two competitive situations are exactly alike.* If an official applies accurate judgment according to the letter and meaning of the rules to each separate decision, the decision will be consistent—because the *correct rule interpretation is unchanging.* Proper judgment and interpretation are the sources of consistency.

VIII. Courage

This quality is related to integrity and objectivity. Nevertheless, no list of necessary officiating qualities could be complete without emphasizing that personal courage is necessary for effective sports officiating.

It takes a degree of courage merely to don the black and white striped shirt and report to the contest. Unfortunately, sports officials in the United States traditionally do not arouse immediate feelings of congeniality and comradeship from players, coaches, spectators, and other officials. Unknown officials have to prove themselves, and everyone is aware of this.

Crucial and difficult rulings may be needed at any moment, and these are made by courageous officials just as accurately and unhesitatingly as routine decisions. Courage is a personal quality, but it also is largely based on the officials ability and willingness to understand and accept officiating responsibilities. Competitive rules empower and obligate the official *in behalf of athletes and coaches* to make the indicated rulings, including the tougher decisions, to the best of his or her albility. The responsible official is well aware that two of the *most unfavorable* things that can be done are to (1) *avoid* a decision where a decision is required, or (2) to *make* a decision merely because the players, coaches and/or spectators demand it.

IX. Rapport

References regarding rapport have already been made in the section dealing with sound relationships. Rapport refers to the quality of relating effectively to others. Good rapport with others is a desirable quality in any line of human endeavor; its importance in sports officiating is crucial.

While conscientiously meeting the many requirements of the job, the official must not neglect human relationships. The experienced official can show a humane and friendly nature without compromising performance; he or she knows that there are enough problems without creating additional difficulties in human relationships. Each official will discover individual methods of establishing rapport with fellow officials, players, coaches, and spectators. Your individual methods should reflect your individual personality.

Regardless of the individual personality, rapport will usually become evident if you:

1. Demonstrate courtesy and respect for coaches and players.
2. Show a sense of humor at appropriate moments.
3. Are approachable and receptive to questions.

X. Objectivity

As human beings, officials, like others, *can* be influenced by various pressures. But unlike many others, the official is *not supposed to be* influenced by external pressures. Perhaps an official's pre-game preparation should include mentally pledging: "I solemnly swear to call what I see and only what I see and *not* to be swayed by how people react, by my previous calls, or by self-seeking motives (including my own motives)."

Most officials benefit from, first, consciously recognizing their own susceptibility to being influenced and, second, seriously attempting to improve their complete objectivity in each game. Otherwise, the temptations of a given moment in the competition can lead the normally well-meaning individual to make a *popular* decision rather than a *correct* decision.

Perhaps the plate umpire in baseball best personifies the need for objectivity. The effective plate umpire does not try to "even them up" when making close ball and strike decisions, even though he or she is in a perfect position to do so. Each pitch is a different pitch. Each pitch is a ball or a strike, regardless of which player or team is at bat, what the score or the count is, or what was called previously. The less-than-great umpire, without realizing it, is tempted to "help" a team or a player (or oneself), and the result is an inconsistency which seriously harms the game. Soon no one knows what to expect. The suggestion most commonly associated with sports officiating in the United States is, "Call them as you see them." The fact that this phrase is not yet trite, in spite of its continuous usage, demonstrates the importance of objectivity to sports officiating.

XI. Reaction Time

Assuming that judgment is correct, decisions which are made quickly have a greater chance of being accepted without question. An official with a slow reaction time is open to question. An official with fast reactions frequently can make the decision almost simultaneously with the moment of the action. Thus, a "subtle influence" on the game is quickly and firmly established. The slow-reacting official frequently compensates by developing the poor habit of "anticipating" impending infractions and, consequently, calling infractions that did not occur.

The extent to which reaction time can be "improved" is open to question. Experimental evidence appears to indicate (1) that different individuals have different but definite physiological limits in the speed of their reactions or reflexes, and (2) that the speed of executing any given act can, within the individual's limits, be quickened by practice. A beginning official can expect some early quickening and improved control of whistle and signals *while learning the particular reaction.* Following this initial learning period, the speed of reactions to various situations will become stabilized within individual limits. It is clear, in any case, that a person with severe limits upon basic reaction time will be wise not to become a sports official.

XII. Conditioning and Appearance

These two qualifications are related since both can be improved up to minimum levels. Also, they both are associated with the pride and dedication of the official.

Conditioning. In several sports the quality of officiating performance can be limited by the physical condition of the official. Such is certainly the case in basketball, football, baseball and wrestling. To put it simply, in most sports good conditioning is necessary *throughout the contest* to enable you to: (1) be where you should be; (2) maintain your alertness and good judgment; and (3) hold up your end of the teamwork with your fellow official. A tired official cannot meet all the requirements of good officiating. The primary components of good officiating condition appear to be good cardio-respiratory endurance and strong legs. Most outstanding officials, especially those holding sedentary full-time jobs, put themselves through a graduated conditioning program prior to the start of each season. By doing so they avoid early season injuries, especially torn muscles, and measure up to expectations at their first assignment of the year. A jogging/running program is strongly recommended.

Appearance. A certain razor company once increased its sales through the slogan: "Look sharp! Feel sharp! Be sharp!" This slogan presents excellent advice to sports officials. "Feel sharp" has implications for physical and mental preparation, especially for conditioning. "Be sharp" suggests that an official react quickly, hustle, display good judgment and mechanics. We are concerned here with "looking sharp."

Most officials' associations have minimum dress regulations which should be observed. An official who reports for duty in an unkempt, dirty uniform does not inspire the confidence of players and coaches. Such officials start the game at a disadvantage.

Adequate conditioning and appearance *can* be attained. It makes no sense, nor is it justifiable, for an official to report for a game in an unfit or sloppy condition.

A review of the qualities advocated indicates the impossibility of your becoming a *perfect* official. How many officials have you observed who consistently demonstrate all of these qualities to the maximum degree? The point to be made here, however, is that you or any other prospective official can improve each of the qualities. Both your performance and your enjoyment of officiating will depend greatly upon your efforts to improve continually.

As the action and tempo of a contest progress and change, the official must frequently assume several different roles, depending upon the particular circumstances. It may be necessary for the sports official to assume partially the role of educator, salesman, psychologist and or statesman. The competent official recognizes the particular need under the given circumstance and assumes the indicated role.

Officiating Roles

As an educator. The rich developmental and learning potentials of competitive sports can be understood and fostered. During competition an athlete is constantly responding, achieving or falling short and, as a result, changing behavior. The chief behavioral changes created through athletics are skill and knowledge related. They are also attitudinal, social and personal in nature, because athletes are usually strongly motivated and emotionally involved. The official inevitably serves as an integral part of these significant learning processes. A good example of courtesy, respect, and emotional stability and effort can be demonstrated. When needed, the rule and its proper interpretation can be briefly explained.

As a salesman. The official can influence athletes and coaches toward fair, clean and sportsmanlike conduct by exemplifying in her/his own behavior a combination of respect, empathy, firmness, subtle suggestion, and encouragement.

As a psychologist. The often strong and emotional feelings of players, coaches and spectators can be understood and, to a point, accepted. Through demonstrated understanding, respect is shown and respect gained. The "psychologist official" understands that excessive "all-win" approaches, although not purely justified, have become habitual in many people, and that habits and attitudes resist change. Such an official is ready to penalize unabusively those excesses contrary to the rules, but realizes that he or she may be able to influence but *cannot change* habitual approaches. Such an official recognizes that, like any human beings, players, coaches, or spectators become excited, elated, frustrated, embarrassed, infuriated, etc. Such an official is prepared to accept and deal with his or her own emotions in a mature fashion so as not to "add fuel to the fire."

As a statesman. Beyond knowing the rules, ruling accurately, and executing the mechanics—the official can and should maintain a grasp of overall responsibilities, capabilities and motivations related to a specific contest. Such a grasp will enable the official to respond and communicate clearly, logically, and wisely, and to deal with emergencies appropriately. All truly outstanding sports officials exemplify this role.

Summary

There is an urgent need for qualified sports officials, both men and women, to meet the demands of an expanding sports scene. Regardless of the level of competition, the benefits of athletic competition are greater when the contest is guided by capable sports officials. The results of competition should depend entirely on the preparation, ability, sportsmanship and effort of players and coaches, on game strategy, and on luck. By applying the rules consistently and with good judgment, by setting an example of and encouraging good sportsmanship, by dealing with emergencies objectively and humanely—the official can exert a tremendous positive influence on the game.

Sports officials should be guided by an overall purpose of enabling the contest to progress smoothly, with as little interference as possible. The essential ingredients of effective sports officiating are (1) intelligent rule enforcement, (2) absolute integrity, (3) sound human relationships, and (4) a focus upon the protection of the individual athlete.

Competent sports officials continuously strive to improve themselves, and they measure their performance against standards such as the "qualities of a competent official" described in this book. They also are prepared to assume several different roles, according to the demands of the particular situation.

Sports officiating is a difficult but rewarding avocation. The primary rewards will relate more to personal development and satisfaction than to financial gain. When sports officials are well trained, highly dedicated and fully aware of the total requirements of their responsibilities, athletic competition will benefit.

2

Getting Off to a Good Start

The first few games you work can be of particular importance to your future as an official. A general pattern of relative success, adequacy, or failure becomes evident to you—and to the players and coaches for whom you work. (Obviously, the quality and direction of your work can change in either direction after these initial assignments.) Early success will encourage and motivate you to further improve your knowledge, judgment, mechanics and mannerisms. Early failure or mediocrity can hamper your development as a sports official. Premature discouragement undoubtedly is the greatest cause of a high "drop-out" rate during the first year of officiating. Much of this discouragement can be *avoided* through intelligent preparation and a more complete understanding of certain pitfalls which threaten the potentially successful career of the inexperienced official.

Our purpose is to provide you with practical suggestions which will help you to achieve success during your early officiating assignments. *Anyone* can follow these suggestions. The only requirements are effort and interest.

Preliminary Preparation

If you follow the suggestions of this section, you will be prepared in a general sense for the mental, physical and emotional realities of your first assignment.

Photo by Bob Coyle

1. **Watch as many games as you can, not as a spectator but as an official.** Whether you are watching the game in person or on television, imagine yourself as being one of that game's officials. Live the game with them. Make decisions with them (or criticize their decisions). Imagine yourself blowing the whistle, signaling, talking with the team captains, dealing with the emergencies that are a part of that game, and so forth.

   It is beneficial to watch any game at any level—professional, college, high school or recreational—but the benefits are greater if you can arrange to see contests at the same level as that of your first expected assignments. The requirements at each level are somewhat different.

   Try to arrive at the game in time to observe the officials during the pre-game activity. Bring a notebook and plan your analysis of the officials in an organized fashion. Know in advance what you are looking for. You might organize your notes under some of the following categories.

   a. What were the strengths and weaknesses of each official?
   b. What happened in the game that (1) created problems or (2) caused the game to progress well from the officials' points of view?
   c. Were there any particularly good or particularly poor decisions or mechanics? What were they and how much did they affect the game?
   d. Specifically, how well did the officials communicate, maintain good position, react decisively, know their rules and mechanics, and show good judgment?
   e. If you had the opportunity, how would you advise each official regarding individual improvement? (Refer to the twelve qualities discussed in Chapter 1)

   In officiating basketball and football, perhaps the most common and the most difficult fault for the inexperienced official to correct is that of habitually focusing complete attention on the ball, to the exclusion of action away from the ball. This habit can and must be broken. It can be corrected to a considerable degree before your first assignment if you actively avoid over-attention on the ball while watching other officials work. When you watch any game, *watch it as an official.*

2. **Participate actively in officials' meetings.** Unfortunately, many sports officials, especially the experienced officials, approach training meetings of the local officials' association with a degree of apathy.

Such an approach can "rub off" onto the young, prospective official, and will hamper development. Regardless of the attitudes of other officials, these meetings *can be* great learning experiences if they are approached in a positive and active manner. There is a wealth of knowledge and experience available to you at these meetings. You can find the answer to almost any officiating question that you have. You can gain the acquaintanceship of locally outstanding officials. Strong sports officials take pride in their work and are pleased to assist the less experienced official.

3. **Secure adequate officiating equipment.** Until you earn a reputation as a qualified sports official, you must at least *look* the part. Avoid the undesirable shortcuts of wrong colored shoes, socks, belts and jackets. Don't use a cheap whistle. Such compromises almost certainly will return to plague you. Until you demonstrate your skill, you are only an image, an impression. You might as well present a favorable professional image. Your first few assignments will be challenging enough in themselves without adding to the burden by *appearing to be unprepared.*

4. **Be sure that you are in good physical condition.** You will be surprised at how physically tiring your first games will be. The inexperienced official is tense and feels a need to overhustle. An inexperienced official runs farther than is necessary and does not know how or when to conserve energy.

5. **Volunteer your services at preseason scrimmages.** There is no substitute for direct experience. All coaches who plan preseason competitive experiences for their teams would like some of these to be officiated. The preseason scrimmage presents an opportunity for the official, as well as for players and coaches, to tune up, to identify and correct weaknesses in advance. An added benefit is the appreciation and good will of coaches which you gain by volunteering to help. Many new officials have found that their willingness to donate services before the season has resulted in more assignments later.

6. **Concentrate on the basics first.** You cannot "learn it all" before the first assignment. In fact, you will *never* learn it all. Too much concern over minor details early in your career bogs you down and is confusing to the learning process. For example, a new basketball official should not expect to know and demonstrate every hand signal at his first game. The "basics" for your early attention are:

a. A knowledge of the common rules and penalties.
b. An understanding of the fundamentals of positioning mechanics.
c. The ability to use routine signals properly.
d. A determination to employ the fundamental aspects of teamwork with fellow officials.

Pregame Preparation

This section is meant to help you feel prepared *specifically* for each of your first officiating assignments.

1. **If possible, know the teams and the playing areas.** The veteran official sometimes has an added advantage over the neophyte because of the former's advance knowledge about the opposing teams, their coaches and the playing site. Such an official is better prepared mentally for the job because he or she knows the playing styles, the coaches mannerisms, the number and emotional involvement of spectators, and characteristics of the playing area, such as space, obstacles, surface, timing device and special ground rules.

    The new official cannot possibly gather and digest all this information before his or her assignment, but by means of advance preparation, can learn some of it. Local newspapers can be checked, other officials can be asked, games or practice sessions may be observed prior to the assignment.

2. **If possible, plan to travel to the game with a fellow official.** A phone call or two a few days in advance of the contest can help to produce a better officiated game. There is no end to the number of points that can be discussed by officials working together in any sport. Mutual respect and confidence can grow during the trip. A good relationship with a fellow official is especially rewarding for the inexperienced official.

3. **Plan to be at the game early.** Do not accept an assignment if you cannot be there, dressed and ready, approximately one-half hour before the game's scheduled time. Estimate your travel time conservatively to avoid being late. The hurried official who runs onto the court two minutes before the center jump is asking for trouble and is creating a very bad initial impression.

4. **Be well rested and sharp.** Occasionally the official will experience a game in which one near-impossible situation after another will occur. If tired and dull-witted, these "near-impossible" situations *become impossible.* Be sure that you get a good night's sleep before each assignment. Avoid large meals immediately before the game.

5. **Never anticipate an easy game.** Fortunately, you will have easy games from time to time, but you will enjoy these more and *get more of them* if they come as pleasant surprises. It is not suggested that you should be worried or fearful, but that you approach each assignment with the same kind of respect and seriousness as that of a former nonswimmer approaching deep water. Your chances of meeting the challenge of a really tough game will be better.

At the Game

Each individual official soon develops an individual officiating personality and habit pattern. Until these become apparent and are further implemented and improved, the inexperienced official needs guidelines which will help to avoid trouble. Here are some suggestions.

1. **Don't try to oversell yourself.** Most new officials understandably want to prove immediately to players, coaches, and spectators alike that they are not only capable but friendly and personable; such an impression, however, will develop only as a result of the job you do. You want such an impression to prevail after the game more than before the game. A coach who does not know an official may distrust one whose approach is overly cordial or personal. You must be approachable, but as an "official" in every sense of the word, you are expected to maintain *distance* from players, coaches, and spectators.

    To summarize this important but rather subtle point it is suggested that you let good, positive relationships grow naturally and without force, based mostly on the skill that you demonstrate and partly on your willingness to cooperate and be approachable.

2. **Actively try to avoid the common mistakes frequently made by inexperienced officials.** Awareness of these common mistakes can help you to avoid them and will also reassure you that most inexperienced officials do make them. Following are some of the most mistakes commonly made, with suggestions on how to avoid them:

    a. *Over-anticipating.* Nothing can be called until it *happens.* It is better to be a split-second late in your decision than to rule incorrectly, or to rule on something that simply did not happen or that had no effect on the competition.

    b. *Rushing your signals.* The cause of this is the same as for over-anticipation, that is, over-anxiousness. Tell yourself: "Don't rush, let it happen"; be deliberate, then signal in a decisive manner when you know it happened. Many rushed signals are not even seen; thus the effect of a given decision is diminished or lost.

c. *Not enforcing the rules.* As an inexperienced official, you will probably approach your early assignments cautiously. Occasionally, this caution can result in overlooking rule infractions which, you might rationalize "really didn't affect the game that much," or which "the other official was in a better position to call." If you experience this type of difficulty, it is sometimes helpful to remind yourself that both teams and both coaches depend on you for a fair outcome of the game. You must try to enforce the rules.

d. *Being out of position.* The veteran official maintains good position habitually; the new official must compensate for lack of habits by mentally anticipating the flow of action. It is helpful to remind yourself constantly, during "dead spots" of the game, about the basic positioning mechanics found in any sport. Just before the jump ball in basketball, for example, the outside man can anticipate two or three possible movements depending upon the outcome of the jump.

e. *Overreacting to complaints.* Remind yourself that no matter how hard you work, or even how competently you perform, complaints will come to all officials in all sports. Your reaction to "beefs" early in your career will be of great importance to your development. Even when you *know* your decision was correct, react to the complaints with calmness and firmness. If the complaint concerns your judgment, nothing can be done about it. If, on the other hand, a rule interpretation is involved and you are not certain about the rule, you might wish to confer quickly with a fellow official. Incorrect rule interpretations can and should be reversed immediately.

Perhaps the most difficult circumstance for a new official is a confrontation with a coach who habitually baits officials. If such a coach decides that you have "rabbit ears," you will soon be in serious trouble. Under such circumstances, try to think of the game and the players—not of the coach or of yourself. Disregard the first taunts. If they continue, approach the coach *inconspicuously* and *positively, but not in anger.* You will be helping the game, the players and yourself (not to mention the coach) if you can regain control and settle the coach.

f. *Showing your nervousness.* Experience is the best cure for nervousness, but even the totally inexperienced official can use human traits to combat undesirable nervousness. Constantly talk yourself into being *deliberate,* not rushing. Be an actor. Even though you may be quite unsure of yourself, you don't have to *show* your lack of confidence. Actively *simulate* a confident manner. Play the role of the most poised official that you have ever seen. If you really throw yourself into this type of role-playing you will be amazed at the results.

After the Game

Certain procedures following each early assignment can guarantee improvement. These procedures are commonly overlooked by new officials. The idea is simple: "Be sure that you complete the learning process of each early assignment."

1. **After the game discuss it with fellow officials.** The other officials have seen you in action, they know what kind of a game it was, and they know something about officiating. Ask them for suggestions. Preferably, take notes on what they tell you.
2. **Keep your own "book" on your personal improvement.** As soon as possible after each early assignment, write down every significant fact that you can remember. Evaluate not only your own performance but that of the other officials. You can learn from their strengths and weaknesses as well as from your own. Your book might include some of the following sections:

   a. New rule interpretations that you learned.
   b. New mechanics or techniques that you observed in the other officials.
   c. Your identifiable weaknesses (rules, mechanics, judgment and relationships) in this particular game.
   d. Questions to ask at the next officials' meeting.
   e. Specific goals for improving at the next assigned game.

   Many of the best and most experienced professional and college sports officials keep such a notebook because they know that there is always room for improvement. Certainly the values accruing to an inexperienced official are greater.

   Hard work and intelligent preparation guarantee relative success for every athlete. The same is true for sports officials. Just as a college freshman basketball player would, you also should set high standards regarding preparation for your first sports officiating season.
   Good Luck!

3

Baseball and Softball

The Game

Baseball, "The Great American Pastime" remains today a significant part of this country's sport scene, having become the nation's first great spectator sport during the nineteenth century. More and more players have joined and strengthened this tradition as softball, Little League Baseball and slo-pitch were created and flourished. Today, thirty years after his death, Babe Ruth may still be the most familiar name in American sports. The umpire, although sometimes maligned, has always been an integral part of this heritage.

In baseball and softball umpires as well as players face stern *individual tests* within a *team setting.* The major challenges for the umpire involve (1) gaining the near-perfect position necessary to rule on close calls in a "game of inches;" (2) matching split-second action with split-second decisions; and (3) teaming with fellow umpires to cover the "anything can happen" situations that arise.

In the first few games, the beginning baseball or softball official will learn that this is a unique game which imposes unique demands on its officials. First, the umpire, especially the plate umpire, is more completely alone than officials in most other sports. This means that an umpire must possess a high level of personal confidence in his or her ability as an umpire. The umpire makes the decision, an isolated decision, and must live with it and make it stand, with little or no backing from anyone else, including fellow umpires.

Second, the beginning umpire will learn that to argue with a baseball or softball official is commonplace and traditional—far more so

Photo by UPI

than in other sports. Despite efforts to restrict complaints and histrionics, they remain a "part of the game," a reality that each official must learn to tolerate to a degree, *yet permit only so far and no farther.* This means that the umpire must show patience and must understand the game, its players and coaches. Under no circumstances, however, should the umpire tolerate ridicule, continuous badgering, profanity, or other gross demonstrations of disrespect.

The third challenge involves the extensive and precise rules of baseball and softball and the need for continuous study. To an amazing degree, almost every freak play that ever has happened or could happen is covered in the rules. There is no substitute for knowing the rules.

Fourth, almost every game produces several very close ball-or-strike and safe-or-out decisions. The umpire must possess *finely tuned eyesight* and *fast reactions* in order to rule correctly, immediately, and decisively.

Fifth, the umpire, as well as the spectator, will often find the pace of a baseball game to be hypnotically repetitive. The effect of such a pace, especially on the base umpire, can lull one to sleep. *Steady concentration* is a must. The better umpires frequently ask themselves during a game, "What could happen next?"—in order to maintain their alertness. Also, due to the pace of the game, both *physical* and *mental endurance* is required. The umpire is expected to rule just as effectively in the seventh or twelfth inning as in the first inning.

Finally, baseball and softball are games that do not progress according to a time schedule. It is a seven, nine or extra inning game which could last an hour and a half or *four* hours and a half.

Many umpires work both baseball and softball games, since the requirements, basic skills and equipment are very similar for each sport. Since softball field distances are shorter than baseball, the game seems faster. The emphasis in umpiring as well as in playing softball is on *quickness* and *anticipation.* The differences in umpiring baseball and softball will be emphasized in each applicable section of this chapter. A special section on slow pitch softball appears in the "miscellaneous considerations" section.

Officials and Their Responsibilities

The officials include the umpires and the scorer. From one to six umpires may officiate baseball, and from one to four in softball games, depending on the level of play. The vast majority of games, however, are officiated by just two umpires: the *plate umpire* (or the umpire-in-chief) and the *base umpire* (or field umpire). The major emphasis in this chapter is on the two umpire system.

Officials Uniforms and Equipment
The baseball or softball umpire wears a clean, pressed dark blue or black uniform, a light blue shirt, an umpire's cap, black polished shoes, dark blue or black socks and a trouser belt of dark leather. Black ties are optional. Umpires working a given game should be dressed alike, other than differences specified for the plate umpire. The plate umpire's cap is short visored. The shoes are metal reinforced for safety. Shin guards, inside or outside chest protector, a sturdy mask and a protective supporter and cup should be worn. The plate umpire also needs an accurate watch, a small whisk broom easily containable in a rear pant pocket, and a navy blue or black ball bag attached to the belt at the hip. All umpires in a crew, particularly the plate umpire, should have a ball and strike indicator. The base umpire should never be without a cap (which is longer visored than the plate umpire's).

Plate Umpire
The umpire-in-chief takes a position behind the catcher. He or she renders decisions on balls and strikes and almost all fair and fouled batted balls. The plate umpire has general responsibility for the conduct of the game, establishes, as is necessary, special "ground" rules or other regulations, informs the official scorer of changes in the lineups, and has the sole authority to forfeit the game. The plate umpire is constantly making decisions involving, among others an approximate 200 pitches per game. The plate umpire runs the game and sets the tempo. In almost all cases, the plate umpire is paid more than the base umpire—and for good reason.

Base Umpire
The base umpire varies field position according to the game situation and makes almost all of the decisions at the three bases and in the outfield. The field umpire has equal responsibility with the plate umpire for all rulings, including discipline and control, with the exception of those specified for the plate umpire. The base umpire covers a large territory, while the decisions rendered are fewer and more irregular. This official tends to be in the background far more than the plate umpire.

Umpires
Each umpire may rule on any matter not specifically covered in the rules. Each may disqualify any coach, player or substitute, and banish any other person from the playing field. One umpire may seek the assistance of another umpire on any decision, but *under no circumstances may any umpire seek to reverse the decision of a fellow umpire.* Umpires are encouraged to work both as plate and base umpires to enhance their opportunity for advancement. A degree of personal flexibility is necessary to adapt to either position, since the responsibilities of each are so different.

Official Scorer
Because of the complexities of baseball and softball statistics, the official scorer has a demanding job. One of ten baseball rules (Rule 9) and one of twelve softball rules (Rule 12) deal solely with scoring. The official scorer, therefore, should be a conscientious, meticulous and dedicated person who is avidly interested in baseball or softball.

The official scorer operates semi-independent of the umpires. Normally, the only contact with them occurs when there are lineup changes or questions concerning the scoring of a run or the number of outs. In certain lower levels of baseball, the scorer is required to report immediately to the plate umpire a player batting out of turn, in order to alleviate technicality rulings.

Basic Penalties and Rulings

The intent here, as in other chapters, is to emphasize the essentials and to present a logical framework for better understanding of the rulebook itself. There is no substitute for concentrated study of baseball rules.

The Four Cornerstone Rulings of Baseball and Softball
There are four routine decisions in baseball and softball: ruling whether each pitch is a *strike* or *ball;* whether each batted ball is *fair* or *foul;* whether each baserunner is *safe* or *out;* and whether or not a batter is out because a fly ball has been *caught.* At least ninety percent of all umpiring decisions involve these four decisions. The last of the four is usually a clear-cut, uncomplicated ruling: If any batted ball, fair or foul, is caught by a defensive player before the ball touches the ground or other fixed object, the batter is out.

The plate umpire shall call a pitch a "strike" if (1) the batter swings and misses or (2) if the batter does not swing and *any part of the ball passes over any part of home plate between the batter's armpits and top of the knees.* Thus, strikes may be categorized as "swinging" or "called." The softball strike zone is wider than the baseball strike zone because the ball is larger (softball cf.: 12″—baseball cf.: 9″). The difference is even greater in 16″ slow pitch. A strike is also ruled when there is (1) a foul ball with less than two strikes on the batter; (2) a "foul tip" (even on the third strike); or (3) a fouled bunt attempt with two

Fig. 3.1 Baseball field layout. (By courtesy of N.F.S.H.S.A.)

OFFICIAL DIMENSIONS
FOR SOFTBALL DIAMONDS

Prepared by The A.S.A. Playing Rules Committee

DISTANCE TABLE

ADULT

GAME	DIVISION	BASES	PITCHING	FENCES
Fast Pitch	Female	60' (18.29m)	40' (12.19m)	200' (60.96m)
	Male	60' (18.29m)	46' (14.02m)	225' (68.58m)
Modified	Female	60' (18.29m)	40' (12.19m)	200' (60.96m)
	Male	60' (18.29m)	46' (14.02m)	265' (80.80m)
Slow Pitch	Female	60' (18.29m)	46' (14.02m)	250' (76.20m)
	Male	65' (19.81m)	46' (14.02m)	275' (83.82m)
	Co-Ed	65' (19.81m)	46' (14.02m)	275' (83.82m)
	Super	65' (19.81m)	46' (14.02m)	300' (91.44m)
16 Inch	Female	55' (16.76m)	38' (11.58m)	200' (60.96m)
Slow Pitch	Male	55' (16.76m)	38' (11.58m)	250' (76.20m)

YOUTH

GAME	DIVISION	BASES	PITCHING	FENCES Minimum	FENCES Maximum
Slow	Girls 12-under	60' (18.29m)	35' (10.67m)	175' (53.34m)	200' (60.96m)
Pitch	Boys 12-under	60' (18.29m)	40' (12.19m)	175' (53.34m)	200' (60.96m)
	Girls 15-under	60' (18.29m)	40' (12.19m)	175' (53.34m)	200' (60.96m)
	Boys 15-under	60' (18.29m)	46' (14.02m)	225' (68.58m)	250' (76.20m)
	Girls 18-under	60' (18.29m)	46' (14.02m)	200' (60.96m)	225' (68.58m)
	Boys 18-under	60' (18.29m)	46' (14.02m)	250' (76.20m)	275' (83.82m)
Fast	Girls 12-under	60' (18.29m)	35' (10.67m)	175' (53.34m)	200' (60.96m)
Pitch	Boys 12-under	60' (18.29m)	40' (12.19m)	175' (53.34m)	200' (60.96m)
	Girls 15-under	60' (18.29m)	40' (12.19m)	175' (53.34m)	200' (60.96m)
	Boys 15-under	60' (18.29m)	46' (14.02m)	175' (53.34m)	200' (60.96m)
	Girls 18-under	60' (18.29m)	40' (12.19m)	200' (60.96m)	225' (68.58m)
	Boys 18-under	60' (18.29m)	46' (14.02m)	200' (60.96m)	225' (68.58m)

Fig. 3.2 Softball field layout. (By courtesy of Amateur Softball Association of America.)

PITCHER'S PLATE

6"
(15.24cm)

24"(60.96cm)

ON DECK CIRCLE

2'6"
(0.76m)

6"
(15.24cm)

17"
(43.18cm)

6"
(15.24cm)

4'
(1.22m)

7'(2.13m)

HP

3'
(0.91m)

3'
(0.91m)

10'(3.05m)

**BATTER'S
BOX**

**HOME PLATE
DETAILS
AND
CATCHER'S
BOX**

3'
(0.91m)

2'5"
(0.74m)

3'
(0.91m)

17"
(43.18cm)

8½"(21.59cm)

HOME PLATE

12"
(30.48cm)

15"(38.10cm)

15"(38.10cm)

5"(12.70cm)

BASE

FENCE

Refer to Distance Table

3

2

65' (19.81m)

60' (18.29m)

55' (16.76m)

HP

1

Skinned infields:
A 55' (16.76m) and 60' (18.29m)
radius may be used with the front
center of the 46" (14.02m) pitcher's
plate as the center point of the arc.
The 60' (18.29m) is recommended for 60' bases.
For 65' bases, a 65' (19.81m) radius is
recommended.

Backstop should be a minimum of 25' (7.62m)
or a maximum of 30' (9.14m) from home plate.

Fig. 3.2 Softball field layout (cont.)

strikes on the batter. All other pitches which are not batted are ruled "balls" by the plate umpire. Three strikes constitutes a "strike-out", or four balls results in a "base on balls" being awarded to the batter.

Each batted ball is ruled to be a "fair" or a "foul" ball. A batted ball is foul when it is *first touched, contacts any unnatural object, or leaves the park outside the foul lines,*—that is, to the right of the first base line or to the left of the third base line. All other batted balls are ruled to be fair balls. The baselines and all the bases, including home plate, are in fair territory. A ground ball bouncing directly over first or third base is a fair ball, even if the first bounce beyond the base is outside the base line. When a batted ball is touched near the first or third base line, the *position of the ball,* not the position of the player, is the deciding factor.

Only when a play is made on the runners is it necessary to signal a decision that the baserunner is "safe" or "out." The common reasons for ruling a baserunner "out" are either when the runner is tagged by a defensive player while the runner is not in contact with a base, or when the runner is "forced" out. In force play situations, it is necessary merely for the defensive player to have the ball and be in contact with the given base. A force out situation is created when the batter batting a ground ball (or a fly ball which is not caught) and becoming a baserunner "forces" runners to advance to the next base. Plays made on the batter-runner attempting to reach first base are always force plays. No baserunner except the batter-runner is forced if first base is not occupied. If all bases are occupied, a ground ball creates a force play at all three bases and home plate. If a *succeeding* runner is forced out, the "force" is removed for the *preceding* runners and preceding runners must be tagged.

Rule Differences: Baseball and Softball
The basic rule differences are:

1. Baserunning. In baseball, baserunners may "lead off" bases before a pitch. In softball, baserunners must maintain contact with their bases until the pitch is released. The softball umpire should rule a baserunner out if (1) the runner(s) leaves the base before a pitch is released; or (2) the runner(s), following a pitch or a play, fails to return to the base or advance to the next base, once the pitcher has the ball within an 8 foot radius of the pitcher's plate.

The technical nature of the above rules, and the "close calls" they produce, impose added demands on softball officials. Baseball and softball baserunning rules are the same regarding tag-outs, force-outs, interference, obstruction, appeal plays etc.

2. Pitching. One pitching delivery is specified in softball rules and two, "windup" and "set", in baseball rules. The set position is used for the purpose of holding runners close to their bases before the pitch. A violation of the pitching rules results in an "illegal pitch" in both softball and baseball. In baseball, an illegal pitch with one or more runners on base becomes a "balk." The penalty for an illegal pitch is to call a "ball" on the batter and rule the ball dead. When a balk is called each baserunner is advanced one base and the ball is ruled dead, but a ball is not called on the batter. These penalties are not enforced and the ball remains alive if action resulting from an illegal pitch causes the batter to advance at least one base and, in the case of a balk, causes all baserunners to advance at least one base. (The intent of the rules is to avoid interruption of game action if the offensive team gains the same or greater advantage without the penalty.) The plate umpire and / or base umpire should immediately and loudly call "ILLEGAL PITCH" or "BALK," but *withhold* any "dead ball" and enforcement rulings until after any extra action following the pitch, such as a batted ball or wild pitch.

Listed below are selected pitching rule interpretations for baseball and softball. Violations of these should be ruled *illegal pitches* or, when in baseball there are runners on base, *balks.* From the baseball *windup position,* the pitcher may not:

1. execute more than two pumps.
2. stop or alter his or her windup motion, once started, or
3. lift the pivot foot clearly off the pitcher's plate.

When executing the baseball *set position,* the pitcher must:

1. come to a complete stop before pitching;
2. not separate the hands without immediately delivering a pitch or throwing to an occupied base;
3. step towards home plate on a pitch or towards the particular base when attempting a "pick-off";
4. deliver the ball once committed to home plate or first base by any habitual movement; and
5. not assume a pitching position without the ball, or drop the ball, or feint toward the batter or runner at first base.

The softball pitcher must:

1. start the delivery with both feet in contact with the pitcher's plate;
2. come to a complete stop for at least two seconds before pitching;
3. step toward the batter;
4. take no more than one revolution in a "windmill" motion;
5. pitch underhanded, the wrist being below the hip and the wrist not farther from the body than the elbow.

Obviously, pitching rules are complicated. Considerable observation and experience as well as a thorough knowledge of the rules are required before an umpire can rule accurately and consistently.

Other than the above differences, plus differences in field dimensions and equipment regulations, the rules of baseball and softball are almost identical. Most successful baseball umpires can adjust to softball umpiring, and vice versa.

Mechanics

Mechanics are defined as the standard operating procedures for officials working a game. The focus here is on the two umpire system.

In baseball and softball umpiring mechanics, voice and hand signals make a considerable impression on the spectator but are comparatively uncomplicated and few in number. The major attention must be devoted to *positioning* mechanics, especially by the base umpire, and to *teamwork* mechanics. Positioning and teamwork are of great importance in umpiring because of the problems imposed in combination by *speed of action* and *distance.* The two umpires are responsible for covering action at all four bases and occasionally in the outfield and foul territory. The normally high velocity of batted or thrown balls creates problems for an umpire who started in or moved towards the wrong position or who was unaware of teamwork coverage guidelines, which specify which umpire is responsible for which decision and for which playing area.

Plate Umpire Positioning
Plate umpire positioning mechanics are the same in baseball and softball. The major differences between the two sports in calling balls and strikes concern the respective ball sizes and the respective time elements and movements of the pitches. These differences do not create major problems for an umpire with good eyesight and quick reactions. Because of the shorter pitching distance, the typical softball pitch reaches home plate more quickly and breaks less than the baseball pitch. The softball pitch is more easily seen because the ball is larger.

The difference between a called ball and a called strike can be as slight as you wish to imagine: an inch, a quarter of an inch or a sixteenth of an inch. In order to reduce the margin of error, it is necessary for the *plate umpire* to secure and maintain a low position close to the catcher. Most important, the view of the pitch must remain unobstructed by the catcher and the batter. The plate umpire should learn to glide slightly with each pitch but should *stay with* the pitch and avoid the natural tendency to "back off" or to "raise up" as the pitch arrives. A natural tendency to "blink", especially when the batter swings, can be reduced through practice.

Generally, there are two recommended plate umpire positions: the National League (inside corner) position and the American League (over the top) position. The inside corner position is recommended for softball plate umpires. The inexperienced baseball umpire should experiment with each before making a personal selection, and then should strive for improvement in technique relative to different types of pitches, catchers, and hitters. The beginning umpire will find that it is easier to umpire from the inside corner (that side edge of the plate closest to the hitter) with an inside chest protector than with a "balloon" type protector, and she or he will find that the inside corner position permits a closer view of the total strike zone and of the inside corner and low pitches. The over-the-top position permits more flexibility in moving with the pitch as it approaches the strike zone and more accuracy in calling the "high strike" and the outside corner.

Base Umpire Starting Positions

It should be emphasized from the outset that base umpire starting positions can be varied somewhat according to the particular situation and the preferences of individual umpires. Before each pitch the base umpire should find a position which promotes a feeling of readiness and confidence and does not obstruct the vision or movements of any defensive player or baserunner.

With no runners on base, the starting positions are approximately the same in baseball and softball in the two umpire system, although in softball the umpire is closer to first base. With runners on base, baseball base umpires position themselves inside the baselines, while softball field umpires stay behind the infielders. The behind-the-infielders position enables the softball field umpire to determine whether baserunners leave too soon and also reduces congestion in the smaller infield area.

Figures 3.3 and 3.4 show the basic starting positions for the umpire system in baseball and softball.

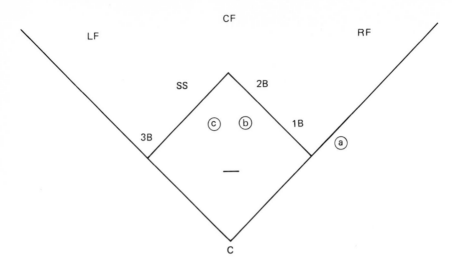

Fig. 3.3 Baseball base umpire starting positions in the two-umpire system (before the pitch). a—No baserunners; b—Runner on first; c—Runner on second, third, first and second, first and third, or base loaded.

Base Umpire Positioning on Specific Plays

Base hits to the outfield. On any base hit to the outfield, the field umpire wants to be inside the base lines as quickly as possible. This will shorten the distance to be run and allow a view of both the ball and the runner. The base umpire should attempt to maintain a slight lead on the batter-runner in order to provide sufficient time to get set for a ruling at second or third base without "racing" the batter-runner.

Putout at first base. The mechanics here are far more complicated than one would think. The principles are (1) to move as far as possible in the direction of the pitcher's mound to a position about ten to fifteen feet from first base *without obstructing the throw* and (2) to *get set* before making a decision. The base umpire moves farther toward the pitcher's mound when the throw is from the third baseman than would be the case on a throw from the second baseman or the shortstop. A position closer than ten feet restricts the umpire's perspective. The umpire should watch the ball as he or she moves into position, and continue to watch the ball as it is thrown. *Just before the throw arrives* at first base, the umpire should quickly transfer vision to the first baseman's base-tagging

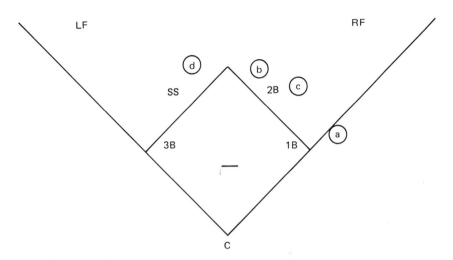

Fig. 3.4 Fast pitch and slow pitch
base umpire starting positions. a—No
baserunners; b—Runner on first; c—
(fast pitch only) Optional position,
runner on first; d—(fast pitch only)
Runner on second, first and second, or
bases loaded.

foot to be certain that it is in contact with the base. The basis for the
decision is then largely *auditory:* which sound occurred first?—the ball
striking the glove or the batter-runner's foot touching the base? Just at
the moment of ball impact, the umpire should quickly glance from the
tagging foot to the glove to assure that the throw has been held by the
first baseman. In some cases, when the ball is "in the dirt," a slight
hesitation is necessary before making the decision.

Force double plays and sacrifice bunts. Considerable experience is
required to enable the base umpire always to move in the correct
direction on second-to-first double plays and sacrifice bunt plays. The
underlying principle is to move toward the base where the play will be
the closest. On double plays, the base umpire must not over-anticipate
and turn the head too quickly toward first base after the first play at
second base. Look first for interference by the baserunner near second
base.

Attempts to steal second base. This is a much easier call in softball than in baseball, because the entire play is in front of the softball base umpire. All you need to do is (1) check for the runner leaving too early and (2) adjust your position to a point where the tag can be viewed— about ten feet from second base towards first base and to the outfield side, but not behind the runner. Since most slides on steal attempts are executed to the outfield side of the base, your angle should favor the outfield side of the base in order to avoid being screened out by the runner's slide.

In baseball, the umpire is positioned inside the baselines. The umpire must first concentrate on the possibility of a balk and then use anticipation and peripheral vision to detect the steal attempt. As the play develops, the umpire moves towards second base parallel to the base line while watching the catcher's throw. *The first time that the umpire should see the runner is when the ball arrives at second base.* Inexperienced umpires have a tendency to take their eyes off the catcher's throw in order to glance at the runner- or even turn toward first base rather than toward second base as the play develops. There is no advantage whatsoever for the umpire to observe the runner. On this play, as in most baseball plays, *nothing can happen without the ball.* As the tag is being attempted, the umpire should get set on both feet and avoid signaling any decision on the run. If there is considerable impact at the moment of the tag and the runner appears to be out, the umpire should delay the signal momentarily in order to be certain that the fielder has held the ball.

Signals
There are no differences between the basic baseball and softball signals, which are shown in Figure 3.5.

Umpires coordinate voice signals with hand signals. The principle is to use greater voice volume and greater hand signal decisiveness for close decisions than for obvious decisions. By withholding emphatic voice and gestures for close decisions, the umpire "tunes in" to the pace of the game and reduces the chance of arguments on close decisions. It is suggested that the umpire *never* use voice signals to call fair balls but only to call foul balls. This practice helps to prevent confusion.

Giving the count. The plate umpire should routinely communicate the count on the batter (number of balls and number of strikes) whenever there may be doubt about the count. The lower the level of play, the more often the count should be given. The count is signaled by steadily

Umpire Signal Chart

GAME SIGNALS

Safe: Extend arms, palms down. Make verbal call.

Out: Hold right fist above head. If plate umpire, hold mask in left hand. Make verbal call.

Strike: Raise right hand up and then extend to side indicating the number of strikes with the fingers. Make verbal call.

Fair Ball: Make a pumping motion toward the infield. *No verbal call.* Keep mask in opposite hand.

Foul Ball: Point away from the playing field with both arms. Make verbal call.

Time Out: Extend both arms above the head. Make verbal call.

Play Ball: Motion pitcher to deliver ball. Make verbal call.

Play Ball: Motion to pitcher in 8-foot radius for an appeal play. Make verbal call.

Delayed Dead Ball: Extend left arm horizontally.

Trapped Ball: Extend both arms horizontally, similar to the safe signal.

Foul Tip: Touch fingers of both hands together to indicate that the bat tipped the ball.

Count: Use the left hand for "Balls" and the right hand for "Strikes," using the fingers to indicate the number.

Infield Fly: Extend right hand above the head. Make verbal call. If near foul line, call "Infield Fly" if fair.

Fig. 3.5 (By courtesy of the Amateur Softball Association of America.)

holding up both hands, the fingers of the left hand indicating the number of balls and right hand, the strikes. Both fists closed indicate a "full" or three-and-two count. One fist shows either no balls or no strikes. When three fingers are shown, the middle, ring and little finger should be used.

Umpire Signal Chart

Double: Raise one arm above the head indicating with two fingers the number of bases awarded Make verbal call

Home Run: Raise one arm above the head with a closed fist and make a clockwise circling motion

No Pitch: Raise one hand with the palm facing the pitcher No verbal call necessary unless the pitcher pitches while signal is given

a.

Plate Umpire: Request help on a half or check swing by removing mask and pointing to field umpire

CREW SIGNALS

Ask	Return
a	b-c
f	g
h	i

b.

Field Umpire: Indicate yes it is a strike by giving a definite strike signal

c.

Field Umpire: Indicate no the batter did not swing by giving a safe signal

d.

Umpires: Indicate an infield fly situation by crossing right hand over left chest

e.

Umpires: Indicate an infield fly situation is now off by brushing left arm downward with right hand

f.

Umpires: Request the number of outs in the inning by clenching right fist and tapping on the right thigh

g.

Umpires: Indicate the number of outs by giving count on fingers on right thigh

h.

Umpires: Request the ball and strike count by holding open hands on the chest

i.

Umpires: Use the left hand for "Balls" and the right hand for "Strikes" using the fingers to indicate the number

ART WORK BY: Concepts Illustration Team, Campbell, CA

Fig. 3.5 cont.

Usually, the count is called as well as shown. The number of balls is called first, followed by the number of strikes. The best moment to give the count is immediately after the catcher has returned the ball to the pitcher; this is a good moment for attention. The voice should be loud enough to be heard and the signal steady and deliberate.

Teamwork

Umpires must constantly be ready to assist each other, in addition to carrying out their individual responsibilities. Following are the primary situations where the base umpire assist the plate umpire or vice versa. These situations apply to baseball and softball alike.

1. *Did the batter swing?* Since the plate umpire must concentrate attention on the pitched ball, there are times when he or she is not able to rule accurately on whether or not the batter completed the swing. The batter must do two things to swing—cause the end of the bat to pass over home plate *and* clearly "break" the wrists. Frequently, the base umpire has a clearer view. The plate umpire should step out in the direction of the base umpire to clearly indicate that assistance is needed on the call. The base umpire should immediately respond by giving the "strike" signal or the "safe" signal.—vice versa to indicate a ball.

2. *Was the force or tag really made?* Either umpire can assist the other at any base on tag or force plays. A common example occurs when the plate umpire assists the base umpire on a tag play down the first base line when the throw pulls the first baseman off the base. The plate umpire usually has a better angle to see whether or not such a tag was actually made.

3. *Fly ball putouts.* In a two umpire game, one official must watch the catch, and the other umpire the batter-runner tag the base. There must be agreement in advance as to who does what. The advice here is that the base umpire always watch the catch (except on foul flies near the plate umpire) and the plate umpire the tag. This will provide a consistent coverage procedure.

4. *Plate umpire calls at third base.* Routine mechanics call for the plate umpire to make all decisions at third base when, with first base occupied, there is a base hit to the outfield. This arrangement provides for accurate initial coverage at first and second base (field umpire) and third base and home plate (plate umpire). If there is a decision made at third base by the plate umpire, the *base umpire* must be prepared to rule on any subsequent play at home plate! The plate umpire should move about half way down the third base line as the play develops and prepare to make the initial decision at either third base or home plate. The base umpire is ready to make any decisions at either first or second base, and possibly to assist the plate umpire by making any secondary calls at third base or home plate. If there is a play to call at third base, the plate umpire must clearly commit to that play in order to establish which umpire is responsible for subsequent action, as well as to provide good coverage at third base.

There are two other situations when the plate umpire assumes responsibility for rulings at third base.

1. With a runner on second base or runners on first and second, a ground ball is hit to the infield and the first play is to first base.— Plate umpire takes a subsequent play at third.
2. With a runner on first base, a bunt is fielded by the third baseman who throws to first.—Plate umpire takes subsequent play at third. (The movement of a "heads-up" catcher to cover third can help to remind the plate umpire of this responsibility—but the plate umpire must be "heads up" regardless of the catcher.)

Problem Calls

Baseball and softball problem calls can be placed in two general categories: (1) calls where the complexity of the rule creates difficulty; and (2) calls where the complexity of mechanics creates difficulty.

Problem Rules

In addition to the four cornerstone rulings discussed in a previous section, five other rule categories frequently create problems for the umpire. Rule book coverage of these rules is difficult for the inexperienced umpire to comprehend, let alone to master to the point where she or he can rule without undue hesitation in a game situation. One of these five categories, *pitching rules,* has been discussed earlier.

The purpose of what follows is to introduce these difficult rulings to the prospective umpire. This must be supplemented by study of the rules and by observation and discussion. The four additional rules categories are:

1. Interference and obstruction
2. Appeal plays
3. "Book rules" for the awarding of bases
4. Infield fly rule

It is interesting to note that, while the four cornerstone rule areas dominate the umpire's attention during a game, very few of the baseball and softball rules refer to them. The bulk of the written rules refer to pitching rules and the four rule categories listed above.

Interference and obstruction. For the most part, baseball and softball are non-contact sports. Inevitably, however, physical contact betwen opposing players, a player and an umpire or a player and a spectator will occur. As in basketball, these cases of physical contact, whether intended or unintended, will frequently result in one team gaining an unfair advantage. On such occasions, a ruling is called for by the umpire in order to nullify the unfair advantage. For example, a catcher may contact the batter's swing, a base runner or base umpire may contact a batted ball before an infielder can make a play, the plate umpire may collide with the catcher who is attempting to make a play on the base runner, etc. Such situations can be complicated or simple, obvious or very negligible. While they occur rarely, especially where highly skilled players are involved, they *do occur* from time to time. The suggestions for the umpires are that they:

1. Know what is interference and what is not.
2. Try to anticipate interference situations.
3. Know the rule and the penalty.
4. Rule firmly and without undue hesitation.

A delayed or weak interference decision almost inevitably will lead to an argument.

For the purpose of definition, *obstruction* refers to when a defensive player *who is not making a play contacts a baserunner.* For example, a fielder who does not have the ball and is not playing the ball "impedes the progress" of the baserunner. All other examples of illegal contact are commonly called *interference.* In all interference situations, regardless of who is involved, there are four basic questions to be answered by the umpire:

1. Who interfered with whom?
2. What is the penalty?
3. Is the ball dead?
4. Where are the other runners placed after the interference is ruled?

The following guidelines should be considered in making the call. The baserunner has a "right of way" on the baseline in all cases *except* when a fielder is making a play on a *batted* ball, in which case, the fielder is "boss" and all others must give ground. In almost all cases, there must be some form of *physical contact* before interference may be ruled; person to person, ball to person, equipment to ball, etc. Any umpire who detects interference or obstruction should call it, regardless of that umpire's position relative to the play.

Appeal plays. In appeal play situations, the umpire(s) is *required not to rule unless the offended team appeals for a ruling.* Among the possible situations are: the batter bats out of order, the baserunner fails to touch a base or home plate, and a baserunner fails to "tag up" on a fly out. (Batting out of order is not officially designated as an "appeal play" by the rules, but meets all the criteria of this section.)

Appeal plays need not be a cause for particular concern if the umpire will pay heed to three principles which are always in effect during such situations:

1. The umpire must say or do nothing before the appeal to indicate to the offended team or anyone else that a successful appeal might be made.
2. No appeal may be granted *after the next pitch or after an intervening play* following the rule violation.
3. No appeal may be granted *if time is out* (for example: following a home run out of the park or a player's requested time out).

The ball must be in play at the time of the appeal.

"Book rules." These refer to the number of bases awarded to baserunners when a live ball goes out of play. The most important facet of the "book rule" is the overthrow. The award of bases is always two bases from *where the runners were when the throw was released.* For example, if a baserunner was just past second base and the batter-runner was not quite to first base when an overthrow from the outfield was released, a run would score and the batter-runner would be entitled to second base. In order to rule accurately, the umpire should "take a picture" of where the runners were when the throw was released. Whenever a live ball goes out of play, the umpires should immediately call "time" and award the bases as indicated. The "book rules" should not be confused with special ground rules which relate to the peculiarities of a given ball park, which are established before each game by the umpires and coaches.

Infield fly rule. When all the requirements of an infield fly are met, any umpire should immediately shout, "infield fly rule; if fair; the batter is out." If this is called, the batter *is* out, and the runners are not forced to advance, whether the fly ball is caught or not—but may advance at their own risk. All of the following requirements must exist before this rule can be enforced:

1. First and second or first, second and third must be occupied.
2. There must be less than two outs.
3. A batted ball must be high in the air and, in the judgment of the umpire, it must be "easily handled" by an infielder.
4. It must be a ball that was batted, not bunted.

The only reason for this rule is to prevent the defensive team from converting this given situation into a force double or triple play by intentionally failing to catch an infield fly. Fellow umpires should remind themselves about the rule whenever first and second are occupied or the bases are loaded and there are less than two outs. (See the Umpire Signal Chart Fig. 3.5.)

Problem Mechanics

Rundown plays. When a base runner is trapped between two bases by the defensive team, each umpire should take responsibility for one "end" of the play. The danger any time two umpires are involved in the same play is that one will rule "safe" and the other "out." This danger is usually eliminated if the decision is made only by that umpire who is located at the end of the rundown where the tag is made. The other umpire *must not* make the decision unless asked to do so by the umpire responsible for the tag.

Multiple baserunners touching the bases. The golden rule of umpiring is to "watch the ball." Umpires also must strive to see whether or not the baserunners tag each base in the event that there is an appeal. On extra base hits with two or more baserunners, it is difficult to watch both the ball and the baserunners. Generally, the plate umpire observes home and third, the base umpire first and second. Basic vision remains on the ball until a runner nears a base, when the umpire glances quickly to determine whether or not the base was tagged and then once again watches the ball. When a base is missed, the umpire should mentally note which runner was involved, because a possible appeal may not be granted unless the runner, as well as the base, is identified by the appealing team.

Tag plays. The most difficult problem in a tag play is attaining an adequate angle of vision so that neither the baserunner nor the defensive player screens the umpire's vision of the tag. No matter how close the umpire is to the play, he or she cannot see the tag if directly behind either player. The ideal angle would be between the runner and the fielder, somewhat more behind the runner than the fielder. The angle is even better if the umpire is *away* from the direction of the baserunner's slide. Otherwise, the slide can screen the umpire's vision at the last moment. A brief delay on the decision is advised when the runner appears to have been tagged out; then the umpire doesn't have to change a decision if the ball subsequently is dislodged from the fielder. There is an explosive quality to a tag play, especially when it occurs at home plate. This tends to add to the importance of a correct decision. A runner should be declared out, and possibly disqualified, if he or she deliberately crashes with great force into a defensive player, including the catcher, who is holding the ball and attempting to tag the runner.

Miscellaneous Considerations

One Umpire Games

Many lower classified scholastic and community leagues cannot afford more than one umpire. In addition, there are times when one umpire is not able to work an assigned game, leaving the other official to work the game alone. Most experts agree that the best place for one umpire is behind the plate, although some baseball umpires prefer to move behind the pitcher when there is a runner on first. The deciding argument is that the most crucial influences of an umpire are *calling balls and strikes and fair and foul balls.* Therefore, one umpire should sacrifice accuracy on a few decisions on the bases to maintain consistency and control of the strike zone and fair and foul territory.

Opinions vary regarding the advisability of using a volunteer base umpire. Many umpires and coaches prefer one umpire rather than taking a chance on an untrained person. The suggestion here is to avoid the use of a volunteer unless both coaches want a volunteer. Do not confuse a volunteer umpire with excessive instructions. Try to get the volunteer into the correct starting position before each pitch and provide encouragement and simple suggestions between innings.

An adequate job cannot be done by one umpire. Imagine yourself, when a runner from first base is attempting to steal second, trying to rule on a close tag at second base. Imagine the softball plate umpire, with a left handed batter at the plate, trying to decide *while the pitch is on the way* whether or not the runner on first base left too soon. Fortunately, one umpire games have been greatly reduced or eliminated in most areas of the country.

The Artistry in Plate Umpiring

There is much that plate umpires can do to promote their own cause and the cause of a smooth-running and enjoyable game. Plate umpiring can either be a very lonely and thankless job or a cooperative and rewarding one, depending somewhat on the artfulness employed. Here are some suggestions:

1. Do not assert yourself any more than is necessary to keep the game going and under control.
2. Save your decisiveness in signals and voice for the close and crucial calls.
3. Take advantage of every possibility to promote good will and positive relationships without compromising your authority.

The plate umpire can build sound relationships with key players, the pitcher and the catcher—especially the catcher. The plate umpire should communicate often with the catcher without being overly friendly and without interfering with the tempo of the game—should encourage the catcher to "stay down" on low pitches. In a friendly but firm manner, the umpire specifies to the catcher such routine matters as the number of warm-up pitches between innings and acceptable methods of getting a new ball into play. The pitcher's good will is almost as important as the catcher's, though more difficult to affect. Nevertheless, a feeling of near-comradeship frequently develops between a good plate umpire and the pitcher. Both are on their own, both have difficult jobs, and both know that they depend somewhat on mutual goodwill.

Umpire Safety
Table 3.1   Umpire Equipment—Proper Use

A. Plate Umpire
   1. Inside Chest Protector
      a. Should be adjusted so it fits snug and will not slip up or down.
      b. Always wear an undershirt, to prevent direct contact with the skin. Failure to do so may cause rashes.
      c. Be certain collar bones are protected.
      d. Be sure bicep and elbow guards are worn.
      e. The inside chest protector, when properly adjusted, should be slightly overlapped when mask is in place.
      f. When crouching into position, be sure back of hands are facing away from you, so if they are hit your wrists act as hinges and allow the hands to pivot.
      g. Do not place hands on knees.
   2. Outside Chest Protector
      a. Left hand should be holding strap so protector can be lifted snugly under chin, behind the mask, to protect the throat.
      b. Keep *both elbows* behind edges of protector.
      c. Protector should be square with Pitchers Rubber.
      d. Do not place hands under bottom of protector.
      e. Keep hands off knees.

Umpire Safety
On injuries occurring to fellow umpires, exercise extreme caution in the following situations:

1. Plate umpire struck in throat or adam's apple area.
   a. Check for swallowed tongue if unconscious, and know what Red Cross First Aid Manual advises. Time is of the essence to prevent choking.
2. Dislocated Jaw
   a. Check with Red Cross First Aid Manual and know what to do. This is a very painful injury and victim cannot communicate with you.

(By courtesy of the N.F.S.H.S.A.)

Slow Pitch Softball Umpiring
Many baseball and softball umpires enjoy the relative informality of umpiring slow pitch softball. The general differences between umpiring softball and 12 inch slow pitch are summarized below. (There are slight differences between 12 inch and 16 inch slowpitch rules.)

The batter. A batter is declared out who bunts or chops (strikes downward) a pitch. It is possible in slow pitch for the batter to hit a "foul tip" that does not rise above the batter's head and that can be fielded by the catcher. This is a *strike;* the batter should not be ruled out.

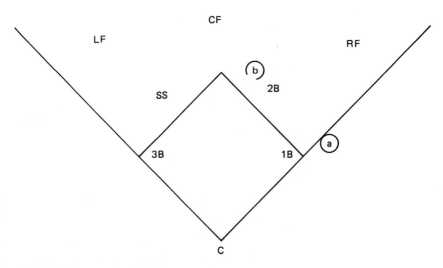

Fig. 3.6 Base umpire starting positions for slow pitch. a—No runners or runner on third base only; b—All other combinations of runners.

Baserunning. Base-stealing is not permitted (with the pitch or following the pitch). Baserunners may leave their bases only when a pitch is hit or the pitch reaches home plate.

Pitching. A pitch is in the strike zone if any part of the ball passes over any part of home plate between the batter's highest shoulder and knees.* The pitch must have an arc of at least six feet, but not go higher than twelve feet above the ground. Pitchers are not required to step towards home plate when delivering a pitch, but must pause for at least one second before the delivery.

Mechanics. The plate umpire is responsible for decisions at third base as well as home-plate. The only time the base umpire would rule at third base would be following a play at home plate which involved the plate umpire. As is shown in Figure 3.6 the base umpire takes only two different starting positions before a pitch.

Officiating Evaluated By Coaches
What qualities do you appreciate in a baseball official?

1. Clear and confident
2. Firm and friendly
3. Consistent
4. Dependable
5. Hustles
6. Good position
7. Knowledge of the rules
8. Appearance
9. Dedication to the game

Miscellaneous Comments
1. Quality officials feel each game they work is important.
2. The preferred official has the ability to command respect and get along with people without having to flaunt authority.

Officiating Evaluated by Officials
What is the most difficult play to call in baseball?

1. The steal of home
2. The half swing

*More and more slow pitch leagues are turning to the "strike zone mat" as a helpful tool for calling strikes and balls. A pitched ball which lands on home plate or the mat is automatically called a strike by the plate umpire. The mat is placed behind home plate.

3. The pulled foot of the first baseman when the official is on the infield
4. Calling the overhand curve

What is the most difficult phase of mechanics in officiating baseball?

1. General field coverage with only two officials
2. Pick-offs at first and third
3. The plate umpire attempting to cover the tag-up at third base on a sacrifice fly to right field

Miscellaneous Comments

1. It is necessary to "think ahead" to assure the best possible position to cover the play in a two umpire system.
2. An instinctive approach to the game, acquired through experience, is of utmost importance.

Play Rulings (2)

Situation: B1 hits ground ball which rolls along 3rd baseline and touches both outside and inside the line. Ball bounces directly over 3rd or touches 3rd. It alights on foul or fair ground. *Ruling:* Fair ball. (2-8-1)

Situation: With R1 on 1st, B2 hits foul which goes directly to the catcher and: (a) is caught by him or her; or (b) is dropped by him or her. In either case, R1 advances to 2nd. *Ruling:* In (a), it is a foul tip and is treated the same as any other strike, hence R1 has stolen 2nd. In (b) R1 must return to 1st. (2-8-2)

Situation: With R1 on 3rd base, R2 on 2nd base and R1 on 1st base and one out, B4 hits safely to right field. R1 scores, R2 misses 3rd base (witnessed by umpire) and scores and R1 is thrown out at 3rd base. Team B appeals at third base on R2 and umpire declares R2 out. How many runs score? *Ruling:* No runs score since the putout of R2 at 3rd base was in reality a force out and also was the third out of the inning. (2-12-4)

Situation: In a high school game of 7 innings, how many innings constitute a regulation game if the game is called? *Ruling:* At least 4½ innings. (4-2-4)

Situation: With R1 on 1st, B2 steps out of batter's box and then: (a) strikes at a pitch but misses; or (b) hits a foul or a fair ball. *Ruling:* No infraction in (a), unless B2 interferes with a throw by F2. In (b), B2 is out as in 7-3-1 and R1 returns to 1st. (5-1-1-b)

Situation: B1 goes to 1st because: (a) he or she is hit by pitched ball; or (b) or 4th ball; or (c) he or she hits single to the outfield. After B1 has touched 1st, F3 tags him or her off 1st by use of "hidden ball" trick. *Ruling:* In (a), runner is safe. Ball remains dead until held by pitcher on his or her plate and umpire calls "Play ball." In (b) and (c) B1 is out. (5-1-4)

Situation: Pitched ball strikes ground in front of home base and then strikes B1. *Ruling:* B1 is entitled to 1st base unless he or she made no effort to avoid being hit. (8-1-1-d)

Situation: B1 hits fair line drive over head of F5, who jumps high attempting to field ball. As he or she jumps upward, the glove accidentally dislodges from his or her hand and touches ball. *Ruling:* If umpire decides detached glove was not thrown nor tossed at contacted ball, there is no penalty. If umpire should decide the act was deliberate, he or she will advance B1 to 3rd. (8-3-3-b)

Situation: R1, R2, and R3 are on 3rd, 2nd and 1st bases, respectively, when B4 hits an infield fly ball which the umpire calls out. R3 thinking the ball will not be caught advances past R2 just beyond 2nd. The fly ball strikes R2 while he or she is off 2nd base. *Ruling:* Ball became dead when it struck R2. The play results in a triple out play. B4 is out by the infield fly rule. R3 is out for passing a preceding runner, and R2 is out for being hit by a batted fair ball. (8-4-2-f and h;7-4-f) (2)

BIBLIOGRAPHY

1. Amateur Softball Association of America, 1983 Rule Book. Oklahoma City, Oklahoma, 1983
2. National Federation of State High School Associations, *1978 Baseball Case Book.* Elgin, Illinois, 1978.
3. National Federation of State High School Associations, *1978 Baseball Rule Book.* Elgin, Illinois, 1978.
4. National Federation of State High School Associations, *1976-77 and 1977-78 Baseball Umpires Manual.* Elgin, Illinois, 1977.

4

Basketball

The Game

For good reason, athletic experts commonly believe basketball to be the most difficult and demanding sport to officiate. It is also a game in which opportunities for advancement of well-qualified officials are virtually unlimited. This great team game, invented and developed in the United States, combines the elements of fast and abruptly changing action, excitement and strong emotions, imprecise limits on the physical contact of players in a limited playing area, frequent penalties for rule violations, and close proximity of loyal, if not biased, coaches, reserves, and spectators. Each of these elements has important implications for basketball officials.

Basketball officiating requires a thorough knowledge of intricate mechanics and complex and changeable rules, sound judgment based on an understanding of the game, fast reactions and good physical condition, personal confidence and courage, and a considerate yet firm court personality. It has been said with considerable truth that basketball is a great game for players and spectators, and a tough one for coaches and officials.

There is a continual need for well-qualified basketball officials. More high school and college basketball games are played each year in this country than in any other sport. In addition, the demands and difficulties of basketball officiating cause attrition among officials. The recent tremendous growth in girls basketball has created an even greater shortage of qualified basketball officials. The reasonable

Photo by Bob Coyle

practice of a man-and-woman team or a two-woman team working a high school basketball game is with us and can be expected to spread. The presence of the female official has been accepted, and initial success is triggering a greater interest by prospective female officials.

From the official's viewpoint, basketball is a game of judgments— judgments which are constantly scrutinized by players, coaches, and spectators. Physical contact among opponents is inevitable. Much of this contact is incidental to the progress of the game and should not be penalized. The basketball official is constantly analyzing player contact and action preceding the contact, applying the Tower philosophy (see pp 4-5) and judging—(1) Was the contact technically illegal?—(2) If illegal, did it place an opponent in a disadvantageous position?— (3) Who was responsible for creating the disadvantageous situation?— (4) Should penalty be applied?—and finally, (5) What is the appropriate penalty (to be enforced without undue hesitation)? A given contact situation can be as borderline as imaginable. Fortunately, both high school and college basketball rules include rather extensive "comments on the rules" which deal with judgment of physical contact. The learning official should read and re-read these comments until they become a part of oneself, because decisions must be based on the rules and made instantaneously as well as accurately.

Because of the exciting and sometimes emotional nature of the game and because of the frequent penalties and closeness to the action of biased viewers—*good mechanics* are of super importance to a well officiated basketball game. In no other sport are the demands of positioning, signaling and teamwork more continuous and crucial. Because of the rapid pace of the game, all phases of mechanics must become habitual. Otherwise, the official will "pay the price" for being a step late, out of position, hesitant and apparently indecisive. The many routine movements and procedures prescribed for basketball officials must be converted into reflex reactions and habits—which can be accomplished only through extensive study, experience and discussion with fellow officials.

A particular mechanics problem constantly challenging any basketball official is that of maintaining a position on the floor where he or she is able to see all relevant action. Good positioning in basketball officiating is made difficult by the rapidity of action and the constant possibility of players obstructing play. The official should attempt to be close to the action, but not too close (almost never closer than five or six feet during live ball action). The basketball official should constantly move, anticipating ball and player movement in order to obtain an angle of vision through the action.

Basketball officiating is hard physical work. It demands *good physical condition,* especially cardio-respiratory fitness. In an average high school game, the official will walk quickly, skip, trot, run and sprint two to three miles. When both teams fast break and press defensively, this per-game distance may be doubled—at a faster rate of speed. The obvious solution is to *train* prior to and during the season—work out regularly, get adequate rest and observe a common sense diet, especially immediately before and after games. The official who is physically drained near the end of a game is more likely to lose control and "blow" a crucial, game-deciding decision.

The *psychological demands* of basketball officiating can be and frequently are excessive—especially when a game has drawn a large excited crowd, the stakes are high, the score is close, and/or unsportsmanlike acts occur. The officials have a profound influence on the trend and outcome of such games. Their decisions, mannerisms and relationships with others are in the spotlight. Only human beings themselves, the officials must "reach back" to master their own emotions and set examples of poise, courtesy and courage.

Basketball rule changes during the past two decades have decreased the relative number of free throws attempted and have reduced interruptions of game action. Nevertheless, the rules provide more opportunities than in any other sport for unimpeded scoring (free throws) as a means of penalizing rule infractions. This important aspect of the game underscores the extensive (some say "excessive") influence of basketball officials on this great game.

Officials and Their Responsibilities

The two floor officials are the referee and the umpire. They are assisted by one or two scorers and one or two timers seated at one side of the court. An "official scorer" and an "official timer" are designated before the start of the game. Current rules permit three floor officials, a referee and two umpires, when both teams agree. While most college conferences have gone to three officials, the likelihood of three in high school is doubtful because of the cost factor.

Officials Uniforms and Equipment
The floor officials' uniforms are entirely black and white—standard black and white vertically striped, short sleeved knit shirt and *black* pants, belt, socks, shoes and shoe laces. Each official should have available

two high quality whistles with cords and rubber caps over the whistle stem. A navy blue jacket is recommended for half-time and before the game. (2:8)

Referee

The referee is responsible for the following important areas:

1. Prior to the game, designate the official scorer and the official timer.
2. Decide if a goal shall count if there is disagreement.
3. Rule on any matters of disagreement between the scorers and timers.
4. Approve the score at the end of each half. (Approval at the end of the game terminates the jurisdiction of the officials.)
5. Forfeit a game.
6. Make decisions on points not covered in the rules.

The referee tosses the ball at center to start each period. Designated pregame responsibilities of the referee include (1) inspecting and approving all equipment (ball, baskets, backboards, court, timing devices, etc.), and (2) prohibiting dangerous player equipment as described in the rules. The referee is also responsible for having each team captain notified three minutes before each half is to begin.

Fig. 4.1 Players may not wear jewelry. This rule is for player safety. It is to protect the wearer and the opponents. The rule that permits dunking creates hazards for anyone wearing jewelry. (By courtesty of the N.F.S.H.S.A.)

Floor Officials

No specification of *umpire* responsibilities appear in the rules. Other than the specific responsibilities outlined for the referee, the floor officials work the game as equals. Neither the referee or the umpire has the authority to set aside or question decisions made by the other official. Their jurisdiction over the game begins at least fifteen minutes before the scheduled starting time and continues until approval of the final score by the referee.

Scorers

The scorers record field goals made, free throws made and missed and a running summary of points scored by each team. They also record personal and technical fouls and timeouts, and notify the nearest floor official when the limits of each has been reached. The official scorer sounds a horn or buzzer when it is necessary to gain the attention of the floor officials—for such matters as entering substitutes, reaching the limits above, correctable errors, etc. The signalling device may be used immediately if (or as soon as) the ball is dead, and, in the case of a correctable error, the ball is in control of the offending team. It is strongly preferred that the device not be sounded for an entering substitute after a floor official has handed the ball to a player for a throw-in or free throw. In case of a mistaken horn when the ball is alive, the horn should be disregarded. The sound of the official scorer's signalling device should be different from that of the timer.

The running summary of team points scored is particularly important. In case of discrepancies which cannot otherwise be resolved, the referee must accept the team scoring totals recorded in the running summary of the official scorebook. The home team's scorebook is the official scorebook unless previously ruled otherwise by the referee.

Timers

The official timer is responsible for starting and stopping the game clock and for regulating the duration of timeouts and intermissions between periods. The timer should have a stop watch or table clock available as a backup for a faulty scoreboard clock. The operating panel of electric scoreboard clocks normally contains a manual timer suitable for regulating team timeouts and intermissions after the first and third quarters. The duration of half-times is normally shown for all to see on the game clock. The timer sounds his or her horn or buzzer *fifteen seconds* before the termination of a timeout or intermission as a warning to coaches and players that play is about to be resumed.

The timer may be called on to help determine whether a try for a field goal was in flight before time expired at the end of a period. The scoreboard clock should be *started* when (1) on a jump, the ball is legally touched by one of the jumpers; (2) on a throw-in, the ball touches or is touched by a player inbounds; and (3) on a missed free throw attempt, the ball touches or is touched by a player inbounds. The clock should be *stopped* whenever a floor official's whistle sounds (for fouls, violations, held balls or time-outs) and a floor official signals by vertically extending his or her right arm. (Mechanics call for the whistle and signal to be executed simultaneously.) Usually, the whistle is the best cue, but when the crowd is noisy the timer may need to rely almost entirely on signals. The clock is not stopped, nor a floor official's whistle sounded following a field goal. The scorer and timer should recognize that they are important game officials.

A considerable amount of teamwork—between floor officials and timers and scorers, and between the timers and scorers themselves—is needed in order to provide a smoothly administered basketball game. Scorers and timers need to read thoroughly all applicable rules before the season, and review them briefly before each game. Well before the

BASKETBALL COURT DIAGRAM

Fig. 4.2 (By courtesy of the N.F.S.H.S.A.)

start of a game, the referee should set the stage for good teamwork by discussing proper procedures and responsibilities with the scorer and the timer.

Basic Penalties and Rulings

Floor officials call two broad types of infractions, *fouls* and *violations.* The penalties for fouls are greater than for violations:

1. Free throws may be awarded; and
2. Offenders are disqualified when a foul is "flagrant," or when a fifth personal foul is called on a player, or a third technical foul is called on a player, coach or follower. On a flagrant foul or a third technical foul the player must leave the vicinity of the bench. The disqualified coach or bench personnel must go to the team's locker room or leave the building.

Fouls fall into two categories, personal or technical. Personal fouls can only take place during live ball action. (Exception: The ball is "dead" during throw-ins until touched inbounds, but basketball rules permit personal fouls to be called for illegal contact during the time span when a player out of bounds has the ball ready for a throw-in.) Technical fouls may be called when the ball is alive or dead, but most often they are called during a dead ball period.

The list below shows all basketball rulings and, where applicable, their penalties.

Personal Fouls
The intent of penalizing personal fouls is to provide freedom of player movement by penalizing illegal contact. *Actual physical contact* between opponents must take place for a personal foul to be ruled. The contact must affect play. "Incidental" contact which places neither opponent at a disadvantage should be ignored. Illegal contact includes holding, pushing, charging, tripping, rough tactics, and impeding progress illegally.

Table 4.1   Comprehensive List of Basketball Penalties and Rulings

Rulings	Penalties
Fouls	
Personal Fouls	
Act of shooting	
—if shot is made	One free throw
—if shot is missed	Two free throws
Player control	Possession to offended team
Intentional	Two free throws
Flagrant	Two free throws and offending player disqualified plus possession to offended team at division line
Double	Jump at center circle by any two opponents
False double	Penalize each foul and enforce in order of occurrence
Multiple	One free throw for each foul
False multiple	Penalize each foul
All other personal fouls (common fouls)	Before bonus-penalty takes effect—possession to offended team
	After bonus-penalty takes effect—one free throw; bonus free throw if first successful
Technical Fouls (Non-flagrant)	One free throw to any offended player (including sub) plus possession at division line
Flagrant Technical foul for bench conduct	Two free throws to any offended player (including sub) plus possession at division line. Charge technical to both head coach and offender if the offender is known. If not known, charge coach.
Violations	
Basket interference or goal tending at opponent's goal	If on free throw, one point If on field goal, two points
All other violations	Possession to offended team at nearest out of bounds point
Other Rulings	
Jump Ball	
Call or grant team's request for time out	

Fig. 4.3 "One and One"—The bonus
penalty is in effect. (By courtesy of the
N.F.S.H.S.A.)

With the exception of certain personal fouls, discussed later in this
section, the penalties for personal fouls is as follows:

Number of Team Fouls Each Half	*Penalty*
Prior to the *fifth* team foul each half in high school games and the *seventh* in college games	Award possession of the ball to the offended team at the out-of-bounds spot nearest to the point of the foul.
Beginning with the *fifth* team foul each half in high school games and the seventh in college games.	Award a free throw to the player fouled; award a *bonus* free throw if the first is successful.

The "bonus rule" demonstrates the intent to increase penalties against
teams which commit more personal fouls.

Personal fouls in the act of shooting. The intent of basketball rules is to
impose a greater penalty when a personal foul is committed against a
shooter. The penalty varies according to whether or not the field goal try
is successful. If successful, the goal counts and the offended shooter is
awarded one free throw. If unsuccessful, two free throws are awarded.
The official's major problem regarding act-of-shooting fouls, as
distinguished from "common fouls," lies in deciding whether the illegal
contact occurred before, during or after the shot. If clearly before or
after the shot, the penalty is the same as if no shot had been
attempted. The penalty for an act-of-shooting foul should be invoked
when illegal contact occurs after a player "begins the motion which

habitually precedes the release of the ball" and until "the ball is clearly in flight." When an offensive player is driving to the basket for a shot, the official should penalize for an act-of-shooting foul if the illegal contact clearly took place after the offensive player picks up his or her dribble in preparation for the shot. Illegal contact against a player attempting a tip-in is not an act-of-shooting foul because the player is not in control of the ball, which makes such illegal contact a common foul.

Player control personal fouls. When illegal contact occurs while the offending player is holding or dribbling the ball, a player control foul is called. The offended team is awarded possession of the ball at the out-of-bounds spot closest to the infraction, regardless of the number of personal fouls previously charged to the offending team. The intent of this penalty is to impose an equitable penalty and to avoid an unnecessary delay in game action. The most common example of a player control foul is when a player with the ball charges into a defensive player. When a player control foul is called on a player who was in the act of shooting, an apparent *field goal cannot count.* (The ball became "dead" when the illegal contact occurred.)

Effective in the 1983–84 season a significant expansion of the high school player control foul rule was made. The definition of "player control" now includes the "airborne shooter". Thus player control continues, in the case of an offensive player attempting a shot while driving to or jumping towards the basket, until the airborne shooter returns to the floor. This change makes it impossible for a basket to count if the responsibility for contact is the shooter's. Furthermore, if the *defensive player* is responsible for the contact or such a play, an *intentional foul* penalty (two free throws) is to be enforced. This rule change should prove to be successful in reducing dangerous body contact situations and in simplifying the judgments of floor officials.

Intentional personal fouls. A floor official should call an intentional foul whenever an illegal contact was deliberate, designed or premeditated. The degree of roughness is irrelevent to calling an intentional foul. Two free throws are awarded to the offended player. Since judging a person's intentions can be risky, officials should call intentional fouls with discretion. Most, but not all, intentional fouls are committed by trailing teams on defense near the end of the game. The intent of this rule is to discourage the gaining of an unfair advantage and to maintain the integrity of the game.

Flagrant personal fouls. Physical contact which is unsportsmanlike and violent or savage results in a severe penalty—the offender is disqualified, two free throws are awarded to the offended player and the ball is awarded to the offended team at the division line. Examples of flagrant fouls are viciously kicking, kneeing, or striking an opponent with the fist or elbow, and running under an opponent who is in the air.

Judgment and courage are needed to make this call. When ruling a flagrant foul, the official should strive to regain a controlled emotional atmosphere by demonstrating poise and courtesy. Showing anger or disgust will not help. The intent of this penalty is to prevent injuries and to maintain control and enforce sportsmanship in physical contact situations.

Other types of personal fouls are *double, multiple, false double* and *false multiple fouls.* A double foul occurs when two opponents commit personal fouls against *each other* at approximately the same time. A personal foul is charged to each player, and the ball is put in play with a center jump involving any two opponents. A multiple foul should be called when two or more *teammates* commit personal fouls against a *single opponent* at approximately the same time. Both teammates are charged with a personal foul, and *one free throw for each foul* is

Fig. 4.4a Number 4 rises vertically from the floor on a try. His or her opponent is in a legal guarding position. Fig. 4.4b Flagrant foul—Number 5 moves under the shooter before the ball is in flight as a result of the try. Two free throws and disqualify number 5. **(By courtesy of the N.F.S.H.S.A.)**

awarded to the offended player, with no bonus free throws. Double and multiple fouls are rarely called, but should not be overlooked. The first illegal contact taking place causes the ball to be dead. Subsequent contact is considered incidental unless flagrant.

False double and false multiple fouls should be ruled when an additional foul occurs *while the clock is stopped* after a previously ruled foul. The second foul would be by the *same team* that committed the previous foul in a *false multiple* foul situation—and by the *other team* in order to create a *false double* foul situation. In the false double foul situation the penalty for each foul is enforced in the order of occurrence and as if the other had not occurred.

Technical Fouls

Unlike personal fouls, technical fouls may be charged against coaches and team followers as well as players. In addition, technical fouls may be charged against a team or against individuals, while personal fouls may be charged only to individual players.

Six team technical foul infractions and twenty-five individual technical foul infractions are specified in high school basketball rules. (3) Examples of team fouls are stalling tactics, exceeding the allotted number of timeouts, and having more than five players on the court. Unsportsmanlike conduct is the most common cause of individual technicals fouls—conduct by players, coaches or followers, such as baiting an opponent, speaking or gesturing disrespectfully to an official, and inciting undesirable crowd reactions. Grasping the ring, interfering with the ball after a goal, and failing immediately to pass the ball to the nearer floor official are also specified as causes for technical fouls.

Penalties for technical fouls are more severe than for personal fouls. When a non-flagrant and non-intentional technical foul is called on a player, the foul is charged to the offender; *any* player on the offended team is awarded one free throw; and the offended team gets ball possession for a throw-in at midcourt. The penalty against a player for a flagrant or intentional technical foul is the same, except that the offender is disqualified and the offended team is awarded two free throws. Good judgment is needed in calling flagrant technical fouls. The official must attempt to show poise and a degree of courtesy, especially when a coach is involved. Any technical foul called on a coach, team attendant, or follower results in two free throws and possession of the ball for a throw-in.

The purpose of technicals fouls are—from the pregame warmup period until the final score is approved by the referee—(1) to enforce technical requirements specified in the rules, such as team rosters, substitution procedures, number of players on the court, proper uniforms, (2) to enforce minimal respect, courtesy and sportsmanship, and (3) to control physical contact between opponents during dead ball periods.

Violations
Violations penalize illegal player movement and ball handling, and also discrepancies in specified restrictions regarding the basket and its upward cylinder, certain court areas and certain time durations. The purpose of violation rules is to penalize unskilled or uncontrolled play which otherwise might result in (a) sloppy, uncontinuous, disrupted or congested action and/or (b) placing one or the other team at an unfair disadvantage. Like personal fouls, violations may be called *only when the ball is alive* or is at the disposal of an out-of-bounds player for a throw-in. Unlike personal fouls, violations *never involve physical contact* between opposing players.

Major violations categories include (1) causing the ball to go out-of-bounds, (2) traveling, (3) illegal dribbles, (4) intentionally kicking the ball, (5) violating the free throw, jump ball or throw-in provisions, (6) basket interference, or goal tending, (7) returning the ball to back court and (8) three second (in the "key") or ten second (in back court) violations. Over thirty violations are specified in high school rules. (3:27–30) Considerable study and experience is necessary to learn and understand all of these rules.

The penalties for violations are relatively uncomplicated. For all violations except basket interference or goal tending at the opposing team's basket, the offended team is awarded the ball for a throw-in at the out-of-bounds spot nearest to the point of the violation. When there is basket interference, or goal tending at the opponents' basket, one point is awarded by the floor official on a free throw and two points on a field goal attempt.

Jump Balls
Each period of play, including extra periods, begins with a jump ball tossed by the referee. Jump balls may also result from decisions by the floor officials during game action, such as, (1) held balls, (2) double free throw violations, (3) a ball lodged in a basket support (4) double foul, and (5) a *ball out-of-bounds*—(a) when caused by a simultaneous touch by two opponents, (b) when the officials are in doubt as to who last touched the ball, or (c) when the officials disagree.

When jump balls are called the officials must know in which of the three circles the jump will be conducted. When the jump starts a period or is the result of a double foul, the toss must always be at the center circle. All other jumps are conducted at the *nearest circle,* including the center circle.

The officials must also know and follow the rules regarding which opponents shall be designated as the jumpers. Any two opponents may jump in all but two cases. The *two involved opponents must be designated when* (1) a held ball is called or (2) the jump results from the ball going out-of-bounds, as in (5) (a), (b) and (c) above. Accurately designating the two involved opponents can be an important and surprisingly difficult task, especially in the case of a ball out-of-bounds. Teams have been known to try to take advantage of this situation by inserting an uninvolved, taller player for the jump. This problem can be forestalled if the official (a) concentrates on the two opponents more than the flight and retrieval of the ball and (b) immediately indicates the two correct jumpers.

Jump balls are being phased out of the college game. Alternating possessions have become the enforcement result for most circumstances which previously called for a jump ball in college basketball. The future of the jump ball at the high school level is under consideration by the rules committee.

Summary
Complete mastery of basketball rules is problematic at best. First, there are countless infractions and definitions to learn. Second, some of the more important rules have been deliberately written in general terms rather than with precision, in order to leave room for a judgment of each separate circumstance by the official. Finally, different basketball rules overlap more than do the rules of other sports. Officials attempting to find answers in the rule book are constantly required to cross-reference from rule to rule and from page to page. The official who knows the rules and the reasons for the rules is going to find his assignment an easier one.

Mechanics

When a basketball game is officiated by floor officials who know their mechanics and execute them without hesitation, the game runs its course like a well tuned and lubricated engine. The officials are more likely to have the confidence of players, coaches and spectators. Attention is directed to the players and the action, not to the officials.

Positioning

Basketball officials must move constantly in order to observe the action from the most advantageous position. Stationary officials inevitably will find their vision screened by player movement. Playing experience helps an official to anticipate, then to move quickly and appropriately as play develops. The best position is where the official can *look through the action,* having the ball and adjacent opponents in view.

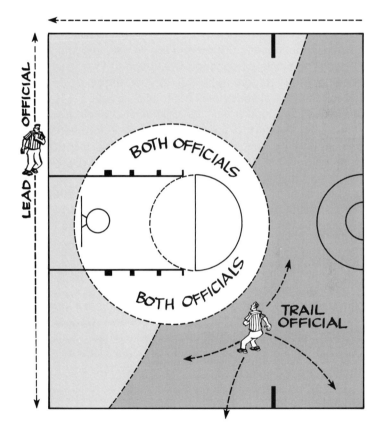

In the front court the trail official is responsible for the in-bounds area which is dotted and the clear white circle area. The lead official is responsible for the shaded area and the clear white circle area. This gives double coverage in the critical area which is the clear circle. However, in spite of the fact each official has primary responsibility for a definite area, it must be crystal clear that each official will call any infraction which he detects.

Figure 4.5 Responsibilities for front court coverage (By courtesy of the N.F.S.H.S.A.)

Basketball mechanics designate a *lead* and a *trail* floor official. During court action near either basket the lead official is positioned out-of-bounds adjacent to the end line. The trail official is positioned in-bounds in the mid-court area closer to the side line to his or her left. The *primary* responsibility of each official is divided semi-diagonally across the court. Responsibility is shared in the center of the front court. Regardless of these guidelines, both officials are directed to *call every infraction they detect.*

When team possession changes and action moves to the other end of the court, the previous lead official automatically becomes the trail official, and vice versa. At all times when the ball is in play in-bounds, both officials are responsible for the *end line to the right and the side line to the left.* The subtle but fundamental notion of "end line right—side line left" or "lead to your right, trail to your left" must be drummed into the official's consciousness until it becomes a reflex.

When "leading" a fast break, the official must avoid a natural tendency, while running at top speed, to take his or her eyes off the action. Seeing the play is more important than beating the players to the other end of the court. In many "controlled" fast break situations the lead official can "back-pedal" most or all of the distance. Be sure to stay wide, near the side line, in order to avoid obstructing play.

After any foul is called, the officials switch their respective end line and side line responsibilities, or "change sides," before the ball is again put into play. This procedure balances area responsibilities throughout the game. Otherwise, (1) each official would be continuously under the same basket, and (2) thanklessly, one official would continuously be adjacent to the players' benches.

Basketball is a difficult game to officiate. It becomes virtually impossible for the official who is often out of position. Coaches and players know when an official is not in position to make a call. *Move. Never take your eyes off the action. Be at the right place at the right time. Look through the action. End line right—side line left.*

Putting the Ball in Play
In basketball, the ball is put into play by three, and only three procedures—a jump ball, a throw-in or a free throw. Both floor officials must follow the correct mechanics for each procedure in order to provide a smooth and efficient game.

Jump balls. The official conducting the toss always faces the scorer's table sideline. The referee conducts the toss at the start of each period. For subsequent jumps, the toss is conducted by the official who is opposite the scorer's table. The officials do not change sides before a jump ball.

The *free official* takes a position opposite the tosser six to eight feet in-bounds from the scorer's table side line. If the jump is at either free throw circle, the free official should favor the "long end" of the court by three or four feet—in order to be ready for a fast break.

The toss must be vertical and should be thrown to a height slightly higher than the jumping ability of either player. The tosser should split his or her stance with the forward foot firmly planted. One or two hands may be used. Greater accuracy and consistency will usually result if the toss is started no lower than chest level, preferably at eye level. This is a skill that must be practiced. To avoid dental injuries, the whistle should not be in the mouth. The official must avoid a natural tendency to back off immediately after tossing for the jump. He or she should remain stationary until the players have made their moves following the jump.

During the jump, the tosser is responsible for illegal action by the jumpers. The free official is responsible for the eight non-jumpers. Either official may order a re-jump if the toss is inaccurate; the free official can usually order a re-jump more quickly and should not hesitate to do so.

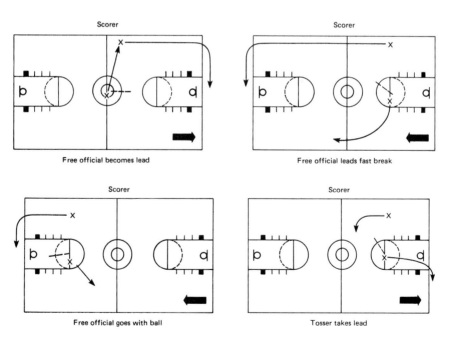

Fig. 4.6 Positioning before and after jump balls.

Following the jump, the *free official goes with the ball and almost always takes the lead position* in either direction, especially on a fast break from the jump. The tosser accordingly fills in as trail official. Since quick changes in possession can occur at any time, the free official is the key to maintaining adequate coverage following a jump, because the administering official is momentarily "locked in" by player congestion. There are rare occasions when the official administering the jump may take the lead position—for example, when the jump is at the free throw circle adjacent to the tosser's end line and the tap is away from the near basket into possession of the team going for the near basket. (See last diagram of figure 4.6.) In this case, the free official should react in the direction of the tap and can easily assume the trail position. On the other hand, it would be awkward for the tosser to fight through traffic to the trail position. One of the characteristics of a strong basketball official is a capability to be aware of the predicaments facing the other official and to adjust accordingly.

Throw-ins. The throw-in is the most frequent method of putting the ball in play. It follows timeouts, all successful field goals and free throws, all violations, and those common personal fouls prior to the bonus penalty. When the ball goes out of bounds, it is essential that the officials make it very clear which team will take possession. The throw-in shall be made from where a ball went out of bounds or at the nearest out of bounds spot to the point of an infraction. (Exception: The designated throw-in spot along an end line shall never be within the free throw lanes extended.) The throw-in is administered by the official responsible for the given side line or end line.

The mechanics for administering a throw-in are fairly routine and, following a violation, proceed in this order:

1. Stop the clock when the violation occurs, by sounding the whistle while vertically extending your right arm and hand.
2. Signal the type of violation (no signal for ball out of bounds).
3. Loudly call the jersey color and point the direction of the team gaining possession.
4. Using a sweeping arm gesture, point to the out-of-bounds spot of the throw-in.
5. Designate a player for the throw-in if none is immediately available.
6. Be sure that your fellow official is in position for the throw-in and that there are no substitutes waiting to enter the game; if waiting, wave them in.
7. Take the proper "boxing-in" position (see below) and hand, do not toss, the ball to the player who will make the throw-in.

8. Start the silent, visible five second count, using right hand chopping action at waist level.
9. Hold your position until the ball is in-bounded or five seconds expires.

The procedure for a throw-in *following a personal foul* is basically the same as above. After step 2 above, however, the official calling the foul reports it to the scorer, and the officials switch their end line / side line responsibilities. The throw-in should be administered (starting with step 3 above) by whichever official subsequently gains responsibility for the boundary line of the throw-in.

The position of the ball when a *time-out* is granted dictates the throw-in spot following the time-out. During the time-out period, the

The trail official administers the throw-in on sideline in front court to his left. The officials are using the "boxing-in" method. One official is on each side of the thrower-in and they have both sidelines, end line and division line covered.

The lead official administers the throw in on the side line to his or her left and he or she stands on the left of the thrower in. The official administering the throw-in is now the trail official. The trail official moves to the base line and becomes the lead official. The officials are using the "boxing-in" method.

The lead official administers the throw in on the end line and she or he stands on the left of thrower in. After handing the ball to the player making the throw in, the official will back up along the end line to get in proper coverage position.

Fig. 4.7 The "Boxing-in" method for throw-ins. (By courtesy of the N.F.S.H.S.A.)

The lead official administers the throw-in on the end line and he or she stands on the left of thrower-in. After handing the ball to the player making the throw-in, the official will back up along the end line to get in proper coverage position.

Fig. 4.8 Crossovers following throw-ins.

official responsible for that throw-in boundary spot holds the ball there, and the other official takes a position near the scorer's table.

Following a successful field goal or free throw, the team scored on proceeds with the throw-in without the official and without a designated spot *for the throw-in.* (A violation would be called against a player with the ball who moves from a *designated* throw-in spot.)

The idea of the "boxing-in" principle for throw-ins is to place the floor officials in advantageous starting positions. The floor officials should be positioned on each side of the action and each side of the player making the throw-in, "surrounding" the action.

Application of the "boxing-in" principle occasionally requires an official to "cross over" from one side line to another following a throw-in. Crossing over is necessary only when the throw-in is made by a team from the *right side line,* with reference to the team's direction. When made from the right side line in either the back court or front court, the administering official becomes the trail official and the other official becomes the lead official following the throw-in. See figure 4.8. The two officials should time their "cross-over" movements according to the developing play so that, as much as possible, both lines will remain covered. Many officiating teams agree before the game not to cross over when the throw-in is from the right front court side line between the free throw line extended and the corner. From this particular area, either method is problematic and somewhat awkward.

In summary, the most important considerations in conducting a throw-in are to (1) apply the "boxing-in" principle, and (2) make definite and deliberate signals prior to the throw-in to clearly emphasize possession and direction. In their pre-game conference, the officials should agree on the procedures they will follow on throw-ins from any position on the court.

Fouls/Free throws. Basically, when a foul is called, the official making the decision designates the offender and reports the foul to the scorer. The other official "freezes" *while observing all players,* thinks out his or her next position, and secures the ball when convenient. The officials will switch positions, or "change sides," regardless of the type of foul called or its location on the court. In order to demonstrate smooth mechanics, both officials must anticipate their subsequent switched position after a foul has been called.

The procedure of the official calling a personal foul is, first, to stop the clock by sounding the whistle while vertically extending the right fist and pointing an extended left arm, palm down, at the offending player's hip. The official should "close-in" on the offender while signalling, stop, and verbally inform the player of the call by stating the player's number and jersey color. The designated foul signal, e.g. "charging," "blocking," "holding," "technical foul," etc. may then be executed and the foul reported to the official scorer. If it is a free throw shooting situation, the ruling official should advise his/her partner of the number of the shooter before the foul is reported to the scorer. In reporting the offender to the scorer, the official may use fingers (one hand only) corresponding to the player's jersey number, but must be certain that the correct information has been communicated and understood.

If the foul results in a *throw-in,* the procedures specified in the previous section should be followed. Sufficient time should be allowed the official not administering the throw-in to secure the correct "boxing-in" position before the ball is handed to a player for the throw-in.

If a *technical foul* has been ruled, the official who made the call administers the free throw(s) independently. The other official waits at the intersection of the division line and either side line and, following the free throw(s), administers a throw-in to the offended team from that spot and becomes trail official.

When a *false double* foul occurs, either official first administers the free throw(s) for the first foul called. The other official waits at the other free throw line with the second offended player, who will subsequently shoot there. After the second offended player shoots her/his free throw, the game progresses as if the first foul had not occurred.

Technical and false double foul free throws occur infrequently. For the bulk of all free throws attempted, the officials work as a team. The official who did not call the foul begins the teamwork by waiting with the ball within the free throw lanes of the *correct basket.* Both officials anticipate their new, switched positions.

The new *lead official* holds the ball under the basket while the administering *trail official* enters the lane from the left of the free thrower

Fig. 4.9 Procedure during free throws.
(By courtesy of the N.F.S.H.S.A.) The
above diagram illustrates the primary
responsibilities of each official in the
administration of the free throw.

and takes charge—sees that the lane spaces are filled correctly and
informs the players of the number of free throws. The lead official tosses
the ball to the trail official and takes a position slightly out-of-bounds
outside the lane extended and opposite the trail official. Before handing
the ball to the shooter, the trail official checks the scorers table for
possible substitutes, waving them in if ready. After handing the ball to
the shooter, he or she starts a silent, visible ten second count and
backs off to a position slightly behind and to the left of the free thrower,
well out of the free throw circle. While backing off, the trail official
signals the number of free throws awarded.

    During a free throw, the lead official has one responsibility and the
trail official several. The lead official watches for rebounding fouls and
lane violations or fouls by players along the lane nearest the lead official
(to the shooter's right). The trail official continues the ten second count
and watches for (1) lane violations or fouls along the lane to the left of
the shooter, (2) a free throw line violation by the shooter, and (3) basket
interference or goal tending by either team.

    If the shooter is entitled to additional free throws, the lead official
quickly retrieves the ball after the first attempt and tosses it to the trail
official, who again takes charge for the next attempt. If a free throw
attempt is to be "in play if missed," the lead official may move forward
along the end line after the attempted throw is in the air in order to gain
a better view.

Well administered free throws can do much to build communication and confidence between officials and players. The players can and should be cautioned to avoid needless lane violations. If the players of either or both teams are upset, the official can help by demonstrating calmness and by providing a little extra time for a "cooling off period." Generally, the actions and communications of the officials during free throws should be definite, brisk and direct, featuring compatible mannerisms and good eye contact.

Signals

Twenty-three different officials' signals are specified and illustrated by the National Federation. With conscientious effort, the new official can master these signals during his or her first season of officiating. During the first game or two of that "rookie" season the official should be intelligently selective about which signals to learn and which can be executed. In the first game or scrimmage, the new official should be able to execute the following signals:

Blowing the whistle with authority.

Stopping the clock for a foul, violation, or jump ball.

Calling the jersey color and signalling the direction for a throw-in.

Signaling the number of free throws awarded.

Signaling whether an apparent free throw or field goal counts or is cancelled.

Signaling a player control foul.

Players and other officials need the above signals in order to continue the game without interruption or confusion. In subsequent assignments the official can progressively add new signals.

As in football, the basketball official must occasionally execute several signals following one decision. For example, when a player with the ball charges into a defensive player, the following signals would be given: (1) stop the clock for foul, point at offender, (2) player control foul; and (3) direction of offended team. If the offending player "scored" an apparent field goal on the play, the official would also signal "no score." In such a circumstance, the official should be deliberate in executing each separate signal. Otherwise, confusion will result.

Fig. 4.10 Official basketball signals
(By courtesy of the N.F.S.H.S.A.)

Here are some suggestions:

1. Strong whistles only.
2. Be decisive and definite, but avoid "show-boating."
3. Don't rush the signals; the idea is to *communicate*.
4. Adjust your signaling mannerisms to the tempo and emotional level of the particular game; force yourself to act calmly and deliberately when the game's pace is hectic and/or one or both teams are upset.
5. When a field goal or free throw is scored, the trail official should immediately signal the number of points scored (one or two fingers) and the lead official then points down court, in the direction of the team gaining possession.
6. Immediately "back-up" your partner's signal to *stop the clock* by executing the same vertical right hand or fist signal. Backing up other signals should be avoided unless (a) you are *certain* of the call and (b) a back up signal will help reduce confusion.
7. Practice the signals and common signal sequences.

Teamwork

Floor officials rely on each other for a smooth, well-officiated game. They must be on the same wave length regarding all phases of mechanics. They must be receptive to and cooperative with each other. To a large degree, the floor officials will succeed or fail together.

Who calls what? Floor officials generally should call everything they see. Certain rulings however, are more clearly the responsibility of the trail official. The *trail official only* is responsible for back court and free throw ten second violations, mid-court five second jump balls, and lack of sufficient action. The *trail official also has primary responsibility* for basket interference and ruling whether a field goal counts at the end of a period. Each official, lead and trail, is primarily responsible for ruling on possession when the ball goes out-of-bounds at his or her end or side lines of responsibility. When a jump ball is tapped directly out-of-bounds without being touched by a non-jumper, the official who tossed for the jump has primary responsibility for awarding possession to the correct team, or ordering a re-jump.

Either official may and should call three second (in the key) violations. Either official may and should call *any foul anywhere on the court,* including fast break fouls when the lead official is obviously closer to the play but is screened out. (A better angle of vision is more reliable than proximity to the play.) Players and coaches may not understand or appreciate infractions called from a distance, but the officials' first obligation is to the game and to call every definite infraction of the rules.

Assisting each other on rulings. The most common situation where assistance is needed occurs when the ball goes out-of-bounds. If the official responsible for the given boundary line is in doubt or simply did not see who caused the ball to go out-of-bounds—he or she should stop the clock and quickly look to the other official. The other official should immediately signal the proper direction or, if also in doubt, immediately signal a jump ball. A brief delay is more fair to both teams than is a guess.

Another situation where help is needed occurs when the *lead official calls a foul during a try for a field goal.* The trail official has primary responsibility for counting or cancelling field goals, but the lead official knows or should know whether the foul occurred before, during or after the try. If the lead official knows the foul occurred *during the try,* he or she should ask the trail official if the try was successful and, if successful, immediately signal that the "basket counts." *If before or after the try,* the lead official can and should immediately cancel the "goal" without help and without even knowing whether the attempt went in the basket.

Mechanics for Three Floor Officials

A third floor official significantly increases officiating coverage of a basketball game. A referee and two umpires make up the team. These officials are designated as "center," "lead" and "trail" during game action, and prescribed mechanics are based upon these designations. A given official will rotate, as prescribed, from one designation to another throughout the game. The officials attempt to maintain triangular coverage, surrounding the action.

While play is in progress at either front court—(1) the *lead* official is at the end line; (2) the *trail* official is always on the scorer's table side

Fig. 4.11 Front court coverage and movement by three floor officials.
Key: L—lead official
       T—trail official
       C—center official
(By courtesy of the N.F.S.H.S.A.)

of the court at a distance similar to the trail official in two officials mechanics; (3) the *center* official is adjacent to the side line away from the table, closer to the end line than the trail official. When possession changes and the ball moves to the other end of the court, the lead official becomes the trail official and the trail the lead; the center official remains center official at the other end of the court, away from the table.

Throw-ins are simplified by three officials mechanics, because it is almost always obvious which official is responsible for a given boundary line. The center official always has the side line opposite the table. The lead or trail official will take the other side line, depending on the ball's location. The remaining official will take the "relevant" end line. Crossing over is eliminated.

Jump ball mechanics are somewhat more complicated but, with experience, becomes more simple than in two officials mechanics. The *center official always makes the toss, facing the scorer's table. The free*

Fig. 4.12 Jump ball coverage by three officials
Key: R—referee
     U—umpire
     L—lead official
     T—trail official
     C—center official
(By courtesy of the N.F.S.H.S.A.)

Fig. 4.13 Free throw coverage by
three officials. (By courtesy of the
N.F.S.H.S.A.)

*officials take positions adjacent to the two side lines, each of them
favoring the end line to his or her right* by six to ten feet. The free
officials must be ready to react quickly to the direction following the
jump. There is no immediate rush for the official making the toss.

When the direction of possession is known following the jump, the
free officials know immediately which of them has become lead official.
The other free official will become trail or center official, depending on
the direction of the team gaining possession. If the direction is to the
right of the tosser, the tosser remains center official and the other free
official becomes the trail official. If to the *left,* the tosser moves towards
the scorers bench and becomes trail official; the other free official is in
good position to become the center official, since he or she was already
away from the scorer's table.

When there is a foul, the official calling the foul becomes (or
remains) the center official and administers the free throws, if any by the
offended player. The other two officials rotate positions. Only the center
and the lead officials are involved in supervising free throws. In three
officials free throw situations the positioning and orientation of the two
officials supervising the free throws are the same as in two officials
games at one end of the court—and *exactly the opposite at the other
end.*

Problem Calls

Discussion of selected basketball problem calls in this book will provide
a starting point and an analysis of components. There is no substitute,
however, for individual study of basketball rules, comments on the rules
and the "Basketball Case Book"—supplemented by game experience
and discussion.

Rebounding

Many coaches have said that "Games are won or lost on the boards." No one can dispute the fact that the dominant rebounding team will get more shots and thereby have a greater chance of winning. The official must prevent players of either team from gaining an unfair rebounding advantage through illegal contact. An added obligation is imposed by the potential for serious injuries from illegal rebounding contact. The word "rebounding"—legal or illegal—is meant here to include (1) player attempts to "block out" their opponents in securing an advantageous position from which to gain possession, and (2) actually leaping for the ball.

Both lead and trail officials are responsible for calling rebounding fouls. Both are or should be in proper position to call illegal rebounding contact. The trail official's added responsibilites for the flight of the ball and basket interference need divert only momentarily his or her concentration on rebounding fouls. The lead official usually will disregard the flight of the ball.

The most common rebounding fouls involve illegal *blocking* during the shot, and an outside player "coming over the top" of (*charging*) the inside player. Comments in the "charging-blocking" and "screens" problem calls section also relate to rebounding fouls.

The basic principles of legal and illegal contact apply. Incidental contact will occur on almost every rebound and *should be disregarded.* Contact which affects the play *must be called.* A player may not interfere with an opponent's rebound opportunity by muscling that opponent from a legally earned position, pushing from the side, charging from behind or impeding movement through holding or an unnaturally extended body position.

Here are some suggestions:

1. Be sure to call rebounding fouls early in the game. If players sense "loose" rebounding officiating, rougher play will surely follow.
2. The lead official will gain a better rebounding perspective if *not too close* to the action. Back off slightly on an outside shot.
3. Unnatural movements or positions in the air are usually the result of holding, pushing or charging. Do not call a foul, however, unless *you know who caused illegal contact.* It might have been a teammate of the "offended" player.
4. To promote game continuity, do not call a foul on an outside man when the inside rebounder gains possession of the ball unless the contact is obvious or severe.

Charging or Blocking?

For decades basketball officials have been coping with this difficult, debatable contact situation. Charging/blocking decisions continue to cause problems despite gradual clarifications in official rule interpretations. When opponents run into each other, "charging" refers to illegal contact by the *offensive* player, and "blocking" to illegal contact by the *defensive* player.

One of the most common charging or blocking situations involves contact between a defensive player and an offensive player driving for the basket. If the defensive player has both feet down and takes a normal and stationary position in front of and facing the dribbler, *charging* should be called when significant contact occurs. If, on the other hand the defensive player moves laterally into the path of the dribbler, especially after the dribble has advanced his or her head and shoulders beyond the defensive player, *blocking* would be the correct ruling. Unfortunately, game situations are not always this clear cut, and the official is left with the question: "Who had the greater responsibility for the contact?" If the dribbler and the defender are shoulder to shoulder, they must continue to move in a straight line. Any pressure contact exerted to crowd the dribbler to the outside should result in a blocking foul.

Fig. 4.14 The dribbler must not charge into the guard. A guard may move into the path of a dribbler at any time providing she or he is able to establish a guarding position legally. To establish this position, she or he must be facing the dribbler with her or his feet on the floor. Subsequently, he may turn, crouch or retreat in order to avoid injury if he or she is charged by the dribbler. (By courtesy of the N.F.S.H.S.A.)

Another common and difficult charging/blocking situation occurs in pivot play. An offensive player with the ball and his or her back to the basket will turn or drive for the basket. In this situation, contact will often take place on the first move for the basket by the player with the ball. The player with the ball is responsible for illegal contact if he or she turns or backs into a defensive player who is in a normal and stationary defensive stance. The defensive player is responsible if contact occurs after the offensive player has taken the first step past the defensive player and is then pressured from the side by the defensive player. The legalization of dunking increases the responsibilities of officials to penalize unfair advantages gained by illegal physical contact. Charging should be called if a player attempting a dunk "muscles" *through* a defensive player who has attained a legal position between the offensive player and the basket.

The practice of defensive players "acting as if charged" is widespread and is having adverse effects on basketball. Coaches should discourage such histrionics, and officials should ignore them, attempting to rule only on the actual contact as it occurred. If a player persists in acting as if charged and the official believes the game is being harmed, a technical foul for unsportsmanlike conduct may be called after first warning the player.

The reader is referred to the section on rebounding and screening problem calls for other examples of charging and blocking fouls.

Fig. 4.15 The defensive player is entitled to an upright position. Here the foul is on the offensive player. (By courtesy of the N.F.S.H.S.A.)

Contact with the Shooter

The importance of thorough and consistent calls is obvious when contact involves a player trying for a field goal. Slight, almost invisible contact can significantly affect a shot. The same degree of contact on a non-shooter might be disregarded.

A flesh-striking-flesh slap sound may or may not involve illegal contact. A shooter's hand (not wrist) in contact with the ball is considered to be *a part of the ball.* To ignore a slap sound heard by everyone will surely cause criticism, especially by uninformed observers; nevertheless, the correct and fair ruling must be made.

Criticism will also occur when a foul is called on a defender who executes a "beautiful block" of a shot attempt but, in the process, charges or pushes the shooter. Body contact is illegal if it affects play and gives the defensive player an unfair advantage over the shooter.

Physical contact with the shooter occurring after a score should be disregarded unless flagrant. On the other hand, a foul should be called if the defender takes a position on the floor while the shooter is in the air in order to cause contact-and, in so doing, places the shooter at a disadvantage. This circumstance may occur on jump shots, hook shots or shots off a drive for the basket and should be ruled an intentional foul, with two free throws awarded to the offended player.

Fig. 4.16 The guard used the left hand and arm to push the shooter off balance. When the officials take good position and the proper angle they can vividly see this type of contact. (By courtesy of the N.F.S.H.S.A.)

Fig. 4.17 When number 22, after
jumping from the floor, drops the ball
to the floor to avoid having the try
blocked and then recovers or dribbles
the ball, it is a traveling violation. (By
courtesy of the N.F.S.H.S.A.)

Traveling

This call should not be difficult for the official who is willing to study the
rules thoroughly. The key is to be able to *identify the pivot foot* of the
player with the ball. Some of the most common examples of traveling
are:

1. When a player starting a dribble moves the pivot foot before
   dribbling.
2. When attempting to stop, a player is unable to establish the pivot
   foot and drags it or takes an extra step.
3. When a player attempting a jump shot, slides both feet together just
   before the jump.

    Each of the above must be called closely.

    A missed or "broken" dribble is not illegal. By definition, a player
cannot be called for traveling while dribbling. It may not be traveling
when a player fakes the defender, takes a long step with the non-pivot
foot and then leaps ten to fifteen feet before shooting or passing.

Legal and Illegal Screens

A screen can be defined as the act of taking a position to impede the
movement of the opponent. Judging whether a screen is legal or illegal
is complicated by the number of variables involved. The variables are
(1) whether the screen is stationary or moving; (2) the distance from the
player screened; (3) the screener's body position; and (4) whether or

not the player screened can see the screen. As in all personal fouls, contact must take place for illegal contact to be ruled. Screening principles apply to offensive and defensive (e.g. rebound positioning) players alike, and to players with or without the ball.

A *stationary* screen is legal at any distance if the player screened can see it. A screen set behind an opponent, out of vision, must be set *one step* away from the opponent. A distance of one to two strides is required if the opponent is moving; judgment of the official should vary according to the opponent's speed and vision of the screen in this circumstance. A screener may face in any direction, but may not assume an unusual stance which extends a knee, hip, shoulder or arm into an opponent's path.

The above guidelines assign responsibility for significant contact to the screener or to the player screened. A foul should be charged to the responsible player if significant contact occurs. In the case of a legal "blind" screen, however, no foul should be charged if the player screened stops on contact and proceeds around the screen. When two opponents are moving in the same direction along the same route, the player behind, as in the case of motor vehicles, is responsible for contact.

4.18 The player wearing the black uniform is fouling number 12 when he or she illegally contacts him or her with his or her arms in an effort to obstruct his or her movement. (By courtesy of the N.F.S.H.S.A.)

Fig. 4.19 Here is a typical example of the screen off the ball. Both the officials frequently watch the ball, allowing number 24 to establish a "perfect moving screen 'illegally' " and bump B out of the way so number 32 is now free for an unguarded try at the basket. The foul by number 24 should be called. One official must be looking away from the ball at all times. (By courtesy of the N.F.S.H.S.A.)

Considerable alertness and judgment are needed to rule on legal and illegal screens. Guidelines help, but the official must "put it all together" and attempt to come up with the right answer. The popularity of offenses featuring screens away from the ball does not make the official's job any easier.

Pressing Defenses

Pressing defenses apply pressure on the official, as well as on the team with the ball. Personal fouls and back court, traveling and illegal dribble violations are more likely to occur. Opposing coaches and followers want their teams, respectively, to be "protected" or "unhampered" by the officials. Pressing defenses may be categorized as full court, ¾ court or half court; the primary emphasis here is upon full court and ¾ court pressing defenses.

The lead, as well as the trail official must take responsibility. Only the trail official calls a ten seconds violation; otherwise, the load should be shared equally. Figure 4.20 shows the positioning of lead and trail officials in the back court in a typical zone press situation. The lead

Key: L—lead official
      T—trail official
      Ⓧ—offensive player with ball
      O—defensive players

Fig. 4.20 Back court coverage of
pressing defense.

official's quandary is obvious. He or she must help in the mid-court area
and also be ready to sprint to the front court end line if the ball is
passed there.

The player with the ball in figure 4.20 has been "trapped" by two
defensive players. To be legal, a trap must conform to the guidelines for
legal screens. A "trapper" may establish and maintain a position *within
a step* of the player with the ball if the trapper can be seen by the
player with the ball. A defensive player approaching from a blind side
must initially provide a *full step*. If this defensive positioning conforms to
legal screening guidelines, responsibility for any significant contact is
with the player with the ball. Defensive players may not reach in from
behind and contact a player with the ball. The player with the ball may
pivot freely unless in so doing he or she significantly contacts a
defensive player who has established a legal position.

Recent interpretations stress that defensive and offensive players
should be penalized stringently for illegal use of the hands and arms. A
dribbler commits a personal foul when he or she pushes a defensive
player. A defensive player should be penalized who "hand checks" an
offensive player. A pressing defense will produce more illegal hand and
arm infractions than usual.

Lack-of-Sufficient-Action
Lack of sufficient action rules place responsibility on one team or the
other to "force action" and, thus, obviate gross stalling tactics. These
rules relate only to the mid-court areas of the floor. If the score is tied,
the *defensive team* is responsible; otherwise, the *team behind* is
responsible. The leading team is never responsible. The penalty is a
technical foul for each infraction—enforced by the trail official.
Continued violations can lead to a forfeit.

Fig. 4.21 A team's fore-court extends from the nearer edge of the mid-court area marker to the inside edge of the end boundary. (By courtesy of the N.F.S.H.S.A.)

Fig. 4.22a When the offense is behind they must move the ball out of the mid-court area in ten (10) seconds when the defense does not provide continuous and aggressive action. The official will move onto the court and point in the direction the offense must advance and call out, "Play ball." (By courtesy of the N.F.S.H.S.A.)

Lack of sufficient action may be penalized only after a *warning* by the trail official. When the responsible team, whether on offense or defense, allows a lack of action in a mid-court area for *ten seconds*—the trail official should move to an easily seen position and call "play

Fig. 4.22b When the defense is responsible for providing action, it will be warned by the official the first time the defense permitsTeam A to have the ball in A's mid-court for ten seconds without Team B being continuously aggressive in an attempt to gain control of the ball. In the above situation, B is warned by the official and two B players must immediately go into the midcourt of A to create and maintain continuously aggressive efforts to obtain control of the ball. (By courtesy of the N.F.S.H.S.A.)

ball.'' The lead official will also give the signal. After being warned, the responsible team has only five seconds in which to force action. Failure to comply results in a technical foul. Each team is entitled to one warning for each period of play, which means that the officials must remember or record which team has been warned in a given period.

Fortunately, the rule and its severe penalty have largely eliminated lack of sufficient action infractions. Nevertheless, officials should occasionally review this rule and its rather complicated enforcement procedures.

Basket Interference
Dunking has been legalized, but other basket interference restrictions remain. It is not basket interference if a ball, in downward flight with a chance to go in, is touched when it had been previously touched away from the basket by an intervening player. If a player ''pins'' a shot against the backboard, basket interference may or may not be ruled— depending on whether or not the ball was in its downward flight with a chance to go in.

A player may legally dunk and in so doing penetrate and touch the basket, but only after having gained control of the ball away from the

Number 3 is committing a violation when touching the field goal try after the ball has started its downward flight and is entirely above the basket ring level with the possibility of entering the basket. The offended team is awarded 2 points.

In (A) it is basket interference by the offense at its basket and is a violation. This is not dunking because the ball is being tipped into the basket rather than being forced in, thus it is not a technical foul. There is no goal, however, because the violation caused this ball to become dead and there can be no score with a dead ball. In (B) the action is legal.

Fig. 4.23 Basket interference and dunking. (By courtesy of the N.F.S.H.S.A.)

basket and its cylinder. Dunking before the game and during intermissions remains prohibited and should be penalized by the officials.

The trail official has primary responsibility for calling basket interference. The ball is awarded to the offended team for a throw-in at the free throw line extended and no points are scored, when the violation occurs at the *offending team's basket.* If at the *offended team's basket,* two points are awarded on a field goal attempt and one point on a free throw.

Back Court Violations

It is difficult for an inexperienced official to apply the language of National Federation rule 9, section 9 (3:29), to real action. The intent of the rules is to penalize a team in control of the ball if that team returns the ball from the front court to the back court. The division line is a part of the back court for the team in control. In most cases the back court violations are obvious: a player standing in the front court with the ball pivots and steps on or over the division line; a bad pass is thrown from the front court to the back court and is first touched there by a player of the team which had been in control in the front court; etc.

Following are two of the not-so-easy applications of the rule. It is a back court violation if a player on a team in control:

1. *When the ball is in the back court,* leaps from the front court, catches the ball in the air, and lands in the back court or on the division line; or
2. *When the ball is in the front court,* leaps from the back court, catches the ball in the air, and lands in the front court or on the division line.

If the ball is caused to go from the front court to the back court by (1) an uncontrolled rebound, (2) an uncontrolled jump ball tap, or (3) a deflection of the ball by a defensive player directly to the back court— there is no back court violation.

When an official understands the principles of (a) team control, and (b) player location when in the air—back court rules are not difficult to apply. A player in the air is "located" where he or she *last touched the floor.* The same principle is applied in determining whether a player is out-of-bounds when catching the ball in the air near a boundary line and landing in-bounds; it is a violation if the player jumped from an out-of-bounds spot.

In (A), player number 4 jumps from front court and while airborne catches the ball in flight which was passed from back court. The result of the play becomes a violation when No. 4 touches the floor in the back court. In (B) this is not a violation because the ball has not been in front court. Number 4 is in the back court before touching the ball.

In (A), player number 4 causes the ball to be in back court when he or she touches it before he or she touches the floor in front court. In (B) this ball has not been to back court since it has not touched the back court or anyone in it.

Fig. 4.24 (By courtesy of the N.F.S.H.S.A.)

Fig. 4.25 Number 10 does not get possession so this is not a violation when the ball goes to the back court following a jump at the free throw circle in front court. (By courtesy of the N.F.S.H.S.A.)

Miscellaneous Considerations

Pregame officials conference. A thorough pre-game conference is a must, especially if the officials have not worked together previously. The referee should take the lead, but the officials must treat each other as equals and speak candidly. Important topics should include pre-game responsibilities, switching, throw-in coverage, pressing defense coverage, and back up signals. The officials should clarify which decision may or may not be called by the trail and by the lead official. A procedure should be established for the "off" official to assist with a ruling when the responsible official is screened out or otherwise unable to make the call. Questionable rules and recent rule changes may need discussion.

Postgame procedure. Following the game, officials should refrain from conversation with either the winning or losing coach. The outcome of the game has been determined by numerous judgments. To defend any one call at this time would be neither feasible nor ethical. In the privacy of the dressing room, officials should take advantage of the opportunity to review specific game situations in an effort to become more proficient.

Officiating Evaluated by Coaches

What qualities do you appreciate in a basketball official?

1. Background
2. Knowledge of the rules
3. Humor
4. Confidence
5. Consistency
6. Hustle
7. Firmness
8. Conditioning
9. Receptiveness
10. Credibility under pressure
11. Courtesy
12. Dependability
13. Honesty
14. Judgment
15. Professional approach

Miscellaneous Comments

1. It is important that the official understands and appreciates the pressures of basketball on players and coaches in order to counteract occasional emotional outbursts.
2. The competent official fully understands the role of assuring that the game be conducted according to the rules.

Officiating Evaluated by Officials
What is the most difficult play to call in basketball?

1. Charging and blocking
2. Goal tending
3. Illegal screens
4. Double foul situations
5. A play away from the basket when a player is driving to the basket

What is the most difficult phase of mechanics in officiating basketball?

1. Getting back to cover the fast break.
2. Lead official's view of the lane is often blocked by large players.

Miscellaneous Comments

1. There is no substitute for experience.
2. The level of officiating performance is directly related to individual's dedication and enjoyment of the game.

Play Rulings (1)

Situation: What guidelines should be exercised by the officials when spectators' actions are such that they interfere with the administration of the game? *Ruling:* In response to the question "Who is responsible for the behavior of spectators" the rule book states "the official may call fouls on either team if its supporters act in such a way as to interfere with the proper conduct of the game." It is significant to note the word used is "may." This gives permission, but does not in any way imply that the officials must call fouls on team followers or supporters. The word "may" was selected with care. Thus, while officials do have the authority to penalize a team whose spectators interfere with the proper conduct of the game, this authority must be used with extreme caution and judiciousness. While the authority is there, an official will almost never use it, because experience has demonstrated that calling technical fouls on the crowd does not accomplish the purpose for which the call was intended. The spectators, already in an antagonistic mood, almost always react negatively when a technical foul is called on them. The calling of such a foul causes the followers of the penalized team to go to greater lengths to display their disapproval of the officiating, or the opponent. (10-3-9; 10-4; 2-6)

   Comment: In the final analysis the responsibility of the behavior of spectators is that of the game committee or management. This is specifically covered in the rule book which stipulates that insofar as the management can reasonably be expected to control the spectators, it is its responsibility to do so. First of all, the management has the responsibility of providing a site where the game can proceed in a sportsmanlike manner. The official is not responsible for this aspect of the contest or for assuming the duties of management. If the conduct of spectators or a spectator prohibits the orderly continuance of a game, the officials invariably use the very best judgment by having a representative of game management take whatever action is advisable and necessary. This may require the removal of a team follower(s), or the clearing of the court of coins, debris, ice, or paper before the contest is permitted to continue. If the disruption is not brought under control and the contest cannot safely continue, rather than assess technical fouls, the official is advised to suspend or forfeit the game. This action is taken only as a last resort.

Situation: A1 lobs the ball to A2 above the level of the ring and outside the cylinder. A2 catches the pass and while high in the air: (a) stuffs the ball through the basket; or (b) attempts to dunk but misses and the ball rebounds toward a sideline. In both cases, A2 fouls B1 before returning to the floor. *Ruling:* A player control foul is charged to A2 in both (a) and (b). In (a), the goal is cancelled even though the ball was through the basket before the illegal contact occurred. The ball is given to Team B for a throw-in at either side of the court at the free throw line extended. (4-7-1)

Situation: A1 drives to the basket and leaves the floor near the free throw line in an attempt to dunk the ball or get an easy lay-up. B1 comes into the area at an angle originally attempting to stop A1's drive. However, B1 gets there late and makes no attempt to block the shot but rather takes a position on the floor where A1 will land. B1 assumes this position after A1 has left the floor. A1 releases the ball and then collides with B1 in returning to the floor. The ball goes through the basket. *Ruling:* The goal counts and B1 is charged with an intentional foul. It should be clear that B1 took the position in hopes of drawing a player control foul on A1 or simply to intimidate by undercutting. If this type of moving under is not penalized with 2 shots, it will only encourage defenders to get into the airborne player's path. If the defender actually plays legitimate defense and tries to block the shot and does not simply stand flat-footed in A1's landing spot, it is not automatically an intentional foul. If the undercutting is of such nature that it is ruled flagrant, B1 must be disqualified. (4-7-1)

Situation: A1 is fouled by B1 during a field-goal attempt and the try is successful. A2 is erroneously awarded the free throw. While A2's successful attempt is in the air: (a) B1 fouls A3; or (b) B1 intentionally fouls A3. Prior to the ball becoming alive, the coach of Team B properly asks the referee to correct the error of awarding the free throw to the wrong player. *Ruling:* The free throw by A2 is cancelled and A1 will properly attempt the free throw which should have been given originally. The common foul by B1 in (a) is cancelled. The intentional foul in (b) cannot be cancelled. The error is corrected when A1 is given the free throw attempt, which A1 was entitled to as a result of the original foul. In (b), the game continues with the administration of the 2 free throws to A3 resulting from the intentional foul by B1. If the corrected error is a free throw by the wrong player or at the wrong basket, or the awarding of an unmerited free throw, the free throw and the activity during it other than unsportsmanlike, flagrant, intentional or technical fouls are cancelled. (2-10)

Situation: Substitute A6 comes into the game wearing the following items of headwear: (a) an elastic band; (b) a metal clasp; (c) a hard plastic barrette; (d) a ribbon; (e) a headband made of elastic material. *Ruling:* The items in (a) and (e) are legal. The items in (b), (c) and (d) are illegal whether they are used to control the hair or not. Long hair may be controlled by using either a headband or rubber (elastic) band. (3-1)

Comment: Squad members may not be allowed to become players if wearing illegal equipment. Compliance with the rules is required before participation. If a player is discovered to be wearing illegal equipment, he or she must immediately remove the equipment or leave the game and may not reenter until they have complied. A specific penalty is prescribed for wearing an illegal shirt.

Situation: While opponents are contesting for a rebound, B1, in attempting to secure control, taps the ball high into the air. B1 does not have control, but is able to tap it a second time after which: (a) B1 allows the ball to strike the floor to begin a dribble; or (b) B1 catches the ball and then pushes the ball to the floor to begin a dribble. *Ruling:* Legal in both (a) and (b). The dribble does not begin until B1 has established control. (4-10-1)

Situation: The official is in Team A's frontcourt when he or she runs into a pass thrown by A1 from Team A's backcourt. After touching the official, the ball: (a) goes out-of-bounds; or (b) rebounds to the backcourt where it is recovered by A2. *Ruling:* Touching the official is the same as touching the floor where the official is standing. In (a), the ball is awarded to B for a throw-in. In (b), the ball has been in the frontcourt and then has gone to the backcourt. Since A1 was the last player to touch it before it went to the backcourt, A1 caused it to go there. Consequently, this is a violation. (9-9; 4-21)

Situation: A1 catches the ball while both feet are off the floor, alights on one foot, jumps off that foot and comes to a stop with both feet hitting the floor simultaneously. A1 then lifts one foot and throws for a goal or passes. *Ruling:* Legal. A1 may lift either foot in passing or throwing for a goal in this situation. However, A1 may not pivot, that is, A1 may not lift one foot from the floor and then step with that foot before the ball has left the hand or hands. By rule, a pivot means a player "steps once or more than once with the same foot. . . ." (4-25)

Situation: A1 is at the free throw line to attempt a free throw. As A1 starts the motion to throw, B1, without disconcerting A1, steps through the plane of the lane line after which the foot of A1 breaks the plane of the free throw line. Both acts occur before the ball is released by A1.

Ruling: Double violation. The ball is put in play with a jump between any 2 opponents at the free throw circle where the violations occurred. If A1 rather than B1 is the first to violate, the ball would become dead immediately. The action by B1 would then have occurred during a dead ball. The violation by A1 would have caused the ball to become immediately dead. (9-1 Penalty) (6-3-3)

Situation: The ball is in flight during a try for field goal or a tap by A1 toward the tapper's basket when time for a period expires. As time expires, the ball is on the ring or in the basket or is touching the cylinder above the basket when it is touched by: (a) A2; or (b) B1. The ball then goes through the basket or does not go through. *Ruling:* In (a) or (b), the ball became dead when touched by anyone. In (a), no points can be scored because of the offensive basket interference by A2. However, in (b), since the touching is by B1, 2 points are awarded to A1. Whether or not the ball goes through the basket has no effect upon either ruling. (4-2; 6-7 Ques.; 9-12)

Situation: During a jump ball, or while the ball is in flight during an unsuccessful field-goal attempt, or while it is in flight from the batting of a rebound, the official sounds the whistle: (a) accidentally; or (b) because the ball has lodged on the basket flange; or (c) because a player has been seriously injured and the play is completed; or (d) to signify basket interference or goaltending. *Ruling:* Play is resumed in (a), (b), and (c) by a jump ball between any 2 opponents in the circle which is nearest to where the ball becomes dead. In (d), the penalty for the violation is administered followig the ball becoming dead. (6-3-4; 9-12; 6-7-5)

Situation: The official has designated a throw-in spot and hands the ball to thrower-in A1. A1 takes several steps laterally from the spot and then throws the ball to a teammate inbounds. *Ruling:* Violation. The thrower-in must keep one foot on or over the designated spot until the ball is released. The designated spot is interpreted to be 3 feet in width and is established when the spot is designated and the ball is given to the thrower-in. The thrower-in may legally step toward the left or to the right laterally as long as 1 foot remains on or over the original designated spot (3 feet across). The amount of legal lateral movement possible would depend on the length of the stride taken by the thrower-in while keeping 1 foot on or over the original designated spot. The thrower-in may legally move several steps directly backward to avoid the inbounds pressure by the defense. In this situation, the thrower-in is still considered to be on the designated spot (3 feet across). (7-5; 7-6; 9-3)

Situation: A1 steps on the free throw line before releasing the ball in an attempt, after which B1 disconcerts. *Ruling:* The ball became dead when A1 stepped on the line, therefore, the action of B1 is not penalized. The ball is awarded to Team B out-of-bounds at the free throw line extended. (9-1-5 Penalty)

Situation: A1 attempts a free throw, and momentarily before the ball is released, B1 commits a lane violation. The free throw try does not touch the basket ring nor is it successful. *Ruling:* This is a double violation, and the ball is put in play with a jump ball between any 2 opponents at that free throw circle where A1 attempted the free throw. (9-1 Penalty)

Situation: A technical foul is charged to: (a) a Team A substitute; or (b) Team B's manager; or (c) Team a's trainer; or (d) Team B's assistant coach. In all cases, the foul is charged because of uncomplimentary remarks addressed to an official. *Ruling:* All fouls charged to "bench personnel" will result in 2 free throws plus the ball for a throw-in. The individuals in (a), (b), (c) and (d) are well considered to be bench personnel and have violated the rules governing conduct while on the "bench." In addition, the head coach of that team is also charged with a technical foul in all 4 cases. (10-4-1)

Situation: A1 is running toward A's goal but is looking back to receive a fast break pass-out. B1 takes a position in the path of A1 while A1 is 10 feet away from B1. (a) A1 runs into B1 before receiving the ball; or (b) A1 receives the ball and before taking a step contacts B1. *Ruling:* In both (a) and (b), A1 is responsible for contact. In (a), B1's position is legal if A1 has been given 2 strides prior to contact. In (b), since the position of B1 is legal when A1 has the ball the contact is charging by A1. (10-6-2)

BIBLIOGRAPHY

1. National Federation of State High School Associations. *1983-84 Basektball Case Book.* Kansas City, Missouri, 1983.
2. National Federation of State High School Associations. *1983-84 and 1984-85 Basketball Officials Manual.* Kansas City, Missouri, 1983.
3. National Federation of State High School Associations. *1983-84 Rule Book.* Kansas City, Missouri, 1983.
4. National Federation of State High School Associations. *1977-78 Basketball Rules, Simplified and Illustrated.* Elgin, Illinois, 1977.

5

Football

The Game

Football is a physical semi-combative sport. Players collectively pit their physical attributes as well as skills against an opposing team. An emotional and uniquely intense atmosphere contributes to tremendous developmental benefits to players and strong spectator interest. Injuries, some of them very serious, are almost inevitable.

Football officials as well as coaches play an extremely important role in promoting maximum benefits and preventing unwanted harmful by-products. The officials are expected not only to assist in the orderly progress of the game but to keep it free from flagrant and uncontrolled violence. Injury prevention must be foremost in the minds of football officials.

The greatest difficulty in officiating football involves gaining and maintaining advantageous positioning without obstructing play. With twenty-two players in motion at the snap, officials are frequently screened out of the play. Consequently, they must be constantly moving and anticipating the movement of the ball and the players in order to establish or reestablish the best possible position to observe the action.

Despite the advent of instant replays the judgment and decisions of football officials are less subject to public scrutiny and criticism than in other sports. Football field and stadium dimensions place the action and the officials in positions more remote from the spectators. Player congestion at the scrimmage line obstructs vision from the bench areas

Photo by UPI

and grandstands. The football official is thereby placed (advantageously) in a more independent position from which to exercise control. Remoteness and scrimmage-line congestion, on the other hand, impose an extra obligation on football officials to meet their responsibilities with integrity and unbiased objectivity. For the best interests of the players and the game, fouls must be called, control maintained, and injuries prevented.

Football officiating is enjoyable as well as challenging. The atmosphere is exciting. With more officials on the crew, feelings of "team spirit", morale, cooperation and friendship are more likely to develop.

In the United States "football is king" in terms of community interest, media emphasis and economic factors. Football is as integral to the American culture as ham and eggs and hot dogs. Football officials can continue to make an important contribution toward maintaining and encouraging this great heritage.

Officials and Their Responsibilities

Depending upon the level of competition, the number of field officials varies from two to seven. The chart below shows a typical pattern for the number of officials assigned at different levels of competition in the United States:

Number in Crew	Designations	Common Level of Competition
Two*	Referee and Linesman	Grade school; high school frosh.
Three	Referee, Linesman and Umpire	High school Jv and frosh
Four	Referee, Linesman, Umpire and Line Judge	High school varsity
Five	Referee, Linesman, Umpire, Line Judge and Back Judge	High school varsity and playoffs, small college
Six	Referee, Linesman, Umpire, Line Judge, Back Judge and Side Judge	College
Seven	Referee, Linesman, Umpire, Line Judge, Back Judge, Side Judge and Field Judge	Professional

The emphasis in this book is on a crew of four field officials.

*Two official games should be avoided if at all possible. Most football officials associations urge their members to refuse assignments to games where only two officials are used.

Officials Uniforms and Equipment

High school football officials' uniforms and equipment are prescribed in detail. Shirts are to be black and white one-inch vertically striped. They may be long or short sleeved, but the same for all members of a given crew. All-white tapered knickers should be worn, with a short overlap below the knee. High school and NCAA officials now wear identical stockings with a modified northwestern striping ($\frac{1}{2}''$ white, $\frac{1}{2}''$ black, $1''$ white, $\frac{1}{2}''$ black, $\frac{1}{2}''$ white). The shoes should be shined before each game and are solid black with black laces. The belt should be black and not narrow. The cap, other than the referee's cap, is to be a black baseball type with white pipings. Referee caps must be white regardless of the number of officials in the crew. If worn during the game, jackets must be black and white vertically striped. (2:7)

Prescribed equipment includes a whistle (an extra whistle is recommended), a $15'' \times 15''$ light gold penalty marker, game card, pencil and two connected rubber bands with which to keep track of the correct down (one band around the wrist, tied to the second band which is stretched around one or more fingers, according to the down). (2:8) The referee needs a watch for regulating the twenty-five seconds before a down. It is recommended that the linesman use a harness snap with cloth to attach to the line-to-gain chain at the yardline nearest the rear stake. All officials should have a white colored bean bag with which to spot the point where a kick is first touched.

Pregame Responsibilities

Referee.

1. Visit team dressing rooms and provide each head coach with a list of the officials.
2. Conduct the pre-game officials conference.
3. Designate the clock operator and review timing procedures.
4. Approve game ball(s) and give to field judge.
5. Conduct pre-game toss and introduce team captains to each other and to the remainder of the crew.

Linesman.

1. Secure stakes, chain and down-marker.
2. With line-to-gain crew, review "do's" and don't's" of (a) moving the chains and down-marker and (b) acting in a partisan manner.

Fig. 5.1 Football field. (By courtesy of the N.F.S.H.S.A.)

Umpire. Before the pre-game conference the umpire should check player equipment in the team dressing rooms and, without exception, disapprove illegal equipment. This should be done well in advance of the warmup period so that necessary adjustments can be accomplished with little disruption.

Line Judge.

1. Check proper working order of watch.
2. Assist in starting the game on time.
3. If there will be more than one game ball, orientate the ball boy, who will be on your side of the field.

The game responsibilities of each official are covered in the "mechanics" section of this chapter. The referee has final authority for resolving disagreements among officials and for decisions not specifically delegated to another official.

Timer. The timer or electric game-clock operator, is not designated in high school football rules as a member of the officiating crew. Nevertheless, the timer is essential to an efficient and smooth running game, as in all sports. If possible, the timer should be present at the pre-game officials conference when procedures for starting and stopping the clock are reviewed. The clock operator should check the proper working order of the clock before the game.

The timer starts or stops the clock primarily as dictated by the signals of field officials. If the officials inadvertently fail to signal, or the timer does not see a signal—the timer should follow indicated timing procedures independently. No official's signal is given to start a stopped clock at the snap—the timer is responsible. Experienced timers respond semi-independently to obvious cues such as clearly incomplete passes. Nevertheless, timers should avoid a natural tendency to go on their own and neglect the signals of officials. Field officials have a far better position from which to rule on borderline timing-related decisions. Timing errors are correctable by the referee, but the process is judgmental and disruptive to game continuity.

Guidelines for starting and stopping the clock are described in the "Mechanics" section of this chapter.

Basic Penalties and Rulings

The objectives of a football team are to advance the ball to the opponent's goal line and score, and to prevent the opposing team from advancing and scoring. Scoring results from *touchdowns* (six points), successful *tries-for-points* following touchdowns (one point if by kick, two if by run or pass), *field goals* (three points) or *safeties* (two points.) Teams may advance the ball by kicking it (with the expectation of losing possession), running with it, or passing it. The ball may be passed forwards from behind the scrimmage line and backwards from any point on the field. The team in possession of the ball has a series of four plays or "downs" in which to score, advance the distance-to-gain (ten yards), or surrender possession to the other team. A first down in a new series is awarded when the offensive team makes the distance-to-gain in four downs or less.

Fouls and Penalties

Fouls may be called on teams, players, substitutes, coaches, or attendants—but not on followers—for acts which violate football rules. Penalties range from running off yardage to awarding scores or, ultimately, forfeiting the game. Players may be disqualified for flagrant personal fouls or flagrant unsportsmanlike conduct. Following "unfair acts" the referee may enforce any penalty he considers equitable, including yardage, awarding a score or, in the case of repeatedly delaying the game, forfeiting the game.

Almost all penalties are yardage penalties—15 yards for a "major penalty" and 5 yards for a "minor penalty." A down during which a penalty occurred is replayed if the offended team accepts the penalty. (Exception: forward pass fouls by the offense.) If a penalty is declined, the down counts. Illegal forward pass fouls by the offensive team call for an additional penalty of a "loss of down." These include purposely incompleted forward passes, forward passes thrown from beyond the neutral zone, and forward passes first touching ineligible receivers. Forward pass infractions by the defensive team result in an automatic first down.

Table 5.1   Summary of Penalties

Loss of 5 Yards

Rule
Section
Article

Signal

	Rule Section Article	Signal
1. Delay of game or illegal substitution	3-7-1, 3-6-2	5
2. Encroachment	6-1-3, 7-1-1	24-1
3. False start or any illegal act by the snapper	7-1-2, 3. or 7-2-6	2
4. Less than 7 players on A's line at snap	7-2-1	2
5. Illegal position at snap	7-2-2, 7-2-3	2
6. Player of A illegally in motion	7-2-4	3
7. Illegal shift	7-2-5	4

Table 5.1   *Continued.*

8. Illegally handling ball forward 7-3-1, 7-3-2	2
9. Illegal forward pass by A or B (if by A the down counts— give signals 12 and 27) 7-5-2	12
10. Crawling by the runner... 9-6-1	24-5
11. Substitute or coach needlessly walking along sideline 9-7-3	5

Loss of 15 Yards

1. Delaying start of either half... 9-4-1	9
2. Fair catch interference 6-5-5	13
3. Contact with fair catcher 6-5-2	6
4. Forward pass interference (also the down counts if by A— give signals 13 and 27; new series if by B)............................ 7-5-6	13
5. Ineligible receiver downfield 7-5-6	14
6. Illegal blocking.. 9-1-1	10
7. Illegal block below waist .... 9-1-3&4	29
8. Illegal use of hand 9-2	10
9. Clipping.. 9-3-2	7
10. Tripping; striking head or neck with heel, back or side of hand; charging into player obviously out of play 9-3-2	6
11. Grasping opponent's face protector (also disqualification if flagrant) 9-3-2	28
12. Invalid fair catch signal.. 9-3-2f	6
13. Roughing the kicker.. 9-3-4	8
14. Unsportsmanlike player conduct... 9-4-1	9
15. Illegal participation 9-5-1	9
16. Illegally kicking a ball 9-5-4	15
17. Illegal batting of: a kick; or a grounded backward pass or a fumble 9-5-5	15
18. Unsportsmanlike conduct by coach or attendant 9-7-1	9
19. Attendant illegally on the field 9-7-2	9
20. Failure to wear required equipment 9-3-2g	6-11
21. Helping the runner.. 9-2-2	17

Disqualification Associated with Certain 15-Yard Penalties

1. Striking, kicking, kneeing, spearing 9-3-1	6
2. Any act listed above if unduly rough or flagrant 9-3-2, 3	9

Forfeiture of Game is not a penalty but is an edict by the referee.
Failure to play within 2 minutes when ordered by the referee
(3-6-4) of repeatedly committing fouls to delay the game 9-8-2   9

Measurement Reduced to Half Distance to Goal Line
1. When measurement spot for a 15-yard or 5-yard penalty is
inside the offender's 30 to 10 yardlines, respectively........... 10-5-1

(By courtesy of the N.F.S.H.S.A.)

The yards penalized are *half-the-distance-to-the-goal-line* when (a) a "minor penalty" is measured from within the ten yardline of the offending team or (b) a major penalty is measured from within the thirty. For example, a minor penalty measured from the eight yardline would take the ball to the four; a major penalty measured from the twenty-six yardline would take the ball to the thirteen.

Penalty Enforcement

One of the important responsibilities of the referee is determining the spot on the field from which a yardage penalty should be measured. This spot is called the "basic spot." Depending on the foul, the basic spot may be the "previous spot" (where the ball had last been snapped or free kicked), the "succeeding spot" (where the ball will next be put in play by a snap or free kick), the end of the run, or the point of the foul.

The basic enforcement spot is easily determined when a foul occurs simultaneous with the snap or between downs. ("Between downs" refers to the time period after the whistle ended the previous down until the ball is snapped on the next down.) When the foul is

10-3-3 Any live ball foul (other than a foul by the defense during a successful try for point or during a down which results in a successful field goal or touchdown or a foul simultaneous with the snap) is penalized according to the all-but-one enforcement principle. All fouls are penalized from the basic spot, except the foul by the offense which occurs behind the spot. The penalty for this foul is administered from the spot of the foul.

Figure 5.2 "All but One" enforcement principle. (By courtesy of the N.F.S.H.S.A.)

simultaneous with the snap, as in illegal motion, an accepted penalty would be measured from the *previous* spot (or the line of scrimmage). When the foul is *between downs,* as in dead ball fouls, the penalty would be run off from the *succeeding spot.*

Determining the correct enforcement spot for a foul occurring *during a down* is more complicated. First, offficials must decide whether the foul occurred during a "loose ball play" or a "running play." A play must be categorized one way or the other whenever a foul occurs during a down.

The basic spot for a running-play foul is the *end of the run.* The basic spot for a loose-ball-play foul is the *previous* spot. For both types of play the penalty should be measured from the basic spot *unless* the foul was *by the offensive team behind the basic spot* ("all but one" enforcement principle). If by the offensive team behind the basic spot, an accepted penalty should be measured from the *spot of the foul.*

A down is categorized as a running-play down unless the down includes a forward pass, a scrimmage kick or a free kick, which are loose ball plays. A forward pass play becomes a "running play" after a player on either team legally catches the pass. A scrimmage kick or free kick down becomes a "running play" when the receiving team gains possession and returns the kick.

The correct enforcement spot for fouls during downs can usually be determined without difficulty if the officials carefully consider two types of questions:

1. Was the foul a loose ball foul or a running play foul?
2. Was the foul by the offense or the defense? If by the offense, was the foul behind the basic spot? ("all but one" enforcement principle)

Mechanics

During a play, or down, the four officials jockey for position, attempting together to surround the action and keep all twenty-two players in view. A proper distance and angle must be maintained. A too-distant position weakens "presence" and control. A too-close position may blur vision and/or obstruct play. When a whistle ends a down, the officials near the ball should quickly close in on the action and spot the ball for the next down. Decisive and efficient movements by the officials after a down help considerably to maintain a fast moving, organized and disciplined game.

Fig. 5.3 Running play from scrimmage.
(By courtesy of the N.F.S.H.S.A.)

Starting Positions on Scrimmage Plays
Figure 5.3 shows where the officials are when the ball is snapped and
basic coverage patterns following the snap.

The *referee* takes a position to one side and slightly behind the
offensive team's backfield. He is to the *"wide side"* of the field, or, if the
ball is in the middle of the field as in the diagram, *away from the
linesman.* The umpire is behind the interior of the defensive line clear of
the linebacker's initial movements.

The *linesman's* starting position is outside the widest defensive
and offensive players and *in the neutral zone.* (On a scrimmage play the
neutral zone is the space established by running imaginery lines from
the front and back tips of the ball directly to the side lines.) The
linesman, one of the two "flank" officials, is on the side of the field
opposite the press box. The other flank official, the *field judge,* is
opposite the linesman outside all offensive and defensive players to his
side of the field. The field judge may be positioned in the neutral zone
("on" mechanics) or five or more yards downfield ("off" mechanics).
The field judge's starting position is dictated by the play expected—
"on" if a running play is anticipated, and "off" for a pass or punt. On a
given play, the other officials check to see whether the field judge is
"on" or "off", because their own play coverage responsibilities are
affected.

Scrimmage Play Coverage
Comprehensive coverage of a scrimmage play comes from a blend of
fluctuating responsibilites and movement patterns as the play develops.
Each official must know and cover his own responsibilities and also help
with shared responsibilities.

Referee. The referee is responsibile for fouls committed by or against a passer and against a punter. To fully protect a passer or punter, the referee should not immediately follow the flight of a pass or punt but watch for illegal contact after the ball is in the air. The referee rules on illegal passes and watches for illegal blocks behind the scrimmage line. He shares responsibility for any illegal motion other than when an offensive back is in lateral motion, which is the responsibility of a flank official.

On a running play, the referee trails the ball carrier and frequently whistles the ball dead. Since the initial direction of offensive backs is sometimes deceptive, the referee should not immediately commit himself towards the scrimmage line, where he might hinder a reverse or screen pass. When the field judge has lined up *off* the scrimmage line the referee must cover that sideline if the field judge is downfield.

Following most downs either the referee or the umpire will spot the ball. The general guideline is for the referee to spot the ball when forward progress is behind or to the neutral zone, and for the umpire to do so if progress is beyond the neutral zone. Whoever spots the ball usually gets the correct forward progress from a blank official. After the ball is marked, the referee announces the coming down and distance-to-gain and checks the down marker from a position adjacent to the ball. He steps away from the ball and executes the "ready for play" signal— a short blast of the whistle accompanied by a downward pump of the right arm. The 25 second period between plays starts with the ready-for-play signal and is enforced by the referee.

Umpire. Fouls by interior linesmen are the chief responsibility of the umpire. Since it is impossible for him to see near-simultaneous contact involving nine or ten different players at the snap, the umpire should alternate his starting position from down to down, concentrating on different sets of opponents on each down. Even though he alternates his starting position and concentration, the umpire should be ready to call any foul he sees by any interior lineman on every down.

If the field judge is in an "off" position, the umpire should be positioned to that side of the field. The umpire shares responsibility for calling encroachment and false starts. The umpire rarely whistles a play dead—only if a fellow official is screened out or not in position. The umpire spots the ball more often than any other official.

On running plays to either side zone, the umpire should go with the play and look for fouls adjacent to the ball carrier. On pass plays, the umpire is primarily responsible for ineligible receivers and determining whether a forward pass goes beyond the scrimmage line. *Move to the neutral zone* when the offense appears committed to a pass play. Follow the flight of a pass and help to rule whether it is legally caught. Being in the center of the action, the umpire cannot afford to worry about what happens behind him.

The umpire's movements and location can be likened to a "bullfighter in no-man's-land." The umpire must utilize peripheral vision, experience and instincts in order to avoid the obstruction of linebackers, pass receivers, downfield blockers, and ball carriers.

Linesman. When the field judge lines up *off* the neutral zone, the linesman is chiefly responsible for encroachment by any player. In addition, he calls illegal use of the hands on his side and improper direction by a man in motion towards the opposite sideline. On each down, the linesman must check and remember which players on his side line up as eligible pass receivers. He should anticipate tackle-eligible pass plays.

On quick running plays up the middle, the linesman, as a flank official, is responsibile for determining the forward progress of the ball. When the ball is whistled dead, point one foot clearly in front of the other to show the forward-most progress to the official spotting the ball. If a running play comes to your side beyond the hash marks, take over as "referee" to cover the ball carrier and blow the ball dead. Get the sideline spot and stop the clock if the ball carrier goes out-of-bounds, watching for unsportsmanlike conduct out-of-bounds. If a running play comes right at the linesman, he must make his first move opposite the direction of the ball carrier in order to stay clear, and then follow the play along the sideline. *Never turn your back to the play.*

On pass plays the linesman move downfield and observes contact between pass receivers and defensive backs. The linesman should know whether a pass was in flight when a foul occurred, because penalties vary accordingly.

The linesman must maintain close communication with the line-to-gain crew, constantly reminding them not to move the down marker and chains or advance the down until instructed to do so by the referee or the linesman. When the equipment is incorrectly moved following a play in which a foul occurred, the officials may be faced with a problem, if the yards penalized should be from the previous line of scrimmage. The linesman, backed up by the referee, is responsible for having the correct down shown on the down marker.

Field judge. The responsibilities and general coverage of the field judge *when on the line of scrimmage are basically the same as those of the* *linesman.* The only differences are that the linesman is responsible for the line-to-gain crew, and the *field judge* has *primary responsibility for covering the goal line and end line.*

When the field judge lines up *off the line of scrimmage,* overall coverage is weakened regarding the neutral zone, fouls prior to or at the snap and illegal use of hands. Therefore, the field judge should line up *on* the line of scrimmage unless there is a strong possibility of a punt or pass play. When a punt is expected, the field judge should position himself about fifteen yards downfield. The "off" distance on a pass play should vary according to the passing patterns shown by the team on offense and the individual preference of the field judge.

All officials.

1. Fumbles can create problems for the officials. Most fumbles occur when the ball carrier is tackled, frequently quite near the time when the official would normally sound the whistle to end the play. Withhold the whistle if a fumble occurs before the ball carrier has been downed. Do not blow the whistle if away from the play. Remember that a fumble after the ball carrier has been downed is irrelevant.

2. When the team on offense is in a spread formation, all officials should widen their starting positions in order to gain a better view of all players.

3. *Hustle during and immediately after the down.* Active officials make their presence known to the players, which helps to reduce fouls.

Coverage of Special Plays

Approximately three out of four football plays are running or pass plays from scrimmage, to which the previous section applies. The football official must also be prepared to cover punts, plays near the goal line, tries-for-point and kick-offs.

Punts. When the offensive team lines up for a punt, or "scrimmage kick," the *referee* takes a position opposite the linesman, three or four yards in advance of and at least five yards to the side of the punter. This position will provide a good view of player contact with the punter. If it is possible that a rusher will contact the punter, do not initially watch the flight of the punt, but stay with the action near the punter. Be prepared to assist the umpire in ruling where and by whom the punt is first touched just *beyond the neutral zone.* A punt caught or recovered behind the neutral zone may be advanced by either team.

When a long punt goes out-of-bounds in flight, the referee should get a line on, hold his position and, through an arm signal, assist the linesman or field judge in locating the out of bounds spot. On short punts out of bounds, to his side, whether in flight or not, the referee should run immediately to the out-of-bounds spot.

When a punt may go out-of-bounds, the referee must quickly adjust his position in order to get an accurate line on the path of the ball. The adjustment is much greater when a punt goes out of bounds on the field judge's side of the field, as is shown in figure 5.4. Behind a punt inbounds the referee moves slowly down the field, watching for fouls and being ready to cover a long runback.

The *umpire* is primarily responsible for determining whether a punt is beyond the neutral zone when first touched, and who touched it. Before the snap the umpire should favor the field judge's side of the field. Following the snap, the umpire should watch for illegal contact in the line and *move to the neutral zone.* If the punt is blocked, assist the referee in determining possession. Otherwise, move slowly downfield, observing contact away from the ball. The umpire is in an excellent position to rule on clipping and illegal blocks below the waist.

The *linesman* has challenging responsibilities on punt plays. He watches for encroachment and motion at the snap. Following the snap, he sprints downfield and takes punt return coverage responsibilities on his side of the field, whistling the ball dead following the return or

Fig. 5.4 Scrimmage-Kick. (By courtesy of the N.F.S.H.S.A.)

Fig. 5.5 Goal line plays. (By courtesy
of the N.F.S.H.S.A.)

stopping the clock if the punt goes out-of-bounds. If a punt *bounces* out-
of-bounds downfield, the linesman holds the out-of-bounds spot or marks
it with a bean bag or his hat and retrieves the ball. If out-of-bounds *in
flight,* the linesman moves gradually along the sideline until the referee
signals the correct out-of-bounds spot. Before they play caution the line-
to-gain crew not to move until released by the referee.

On punt plays, the *field judge* takes a position about fifteen yards
beyond the neutral zone, adjusting his distance according to the ability
of the punter and the wind factor. The field judge enforces "fair catch"
restrictions or "referees" a punt return up the middle or to his side of
the field. His responsibilities are the same as the linesman's on punts
out of bounds to his side of the field. If a player on the kicking team first
touches the ball downfield, mark the yardline of the touch with a bean
bag or your cap, and stay with the play.

The field judge is responsible for calling touchbacks on punt plays.
The touchback signal should be executed immediately when an
untouched punt contacts anything on or beyond the goal line inbounds.
Be familiar with "force" principals in the rules as they apply to punts
touched or caught near the goal line.

Scrimmage plays near the goal line. The intensity frequently found in a
football goal line play is rarely, if ever, matched in other team sports.
Twenty-two players "psych" themselves toward extra efforts. Emotion
and violence levels are high. Fumbles and fouls of all kinds are more
likely, especially by inexperienced teams. Pileups surround the ball
carrier and obscure his penetration towards the goal line. Obviously, the
officials must be certain of their respective responsibilities on goal line

plays and carry them out without hesitation. Personal qualities such as poise, confidence, courage and integrity become more critically important near the goal line.

The official's starting positions and responsibilities are basically the same as for other scrimmage plays, but, because forward progress is more crucial, the field judge varies his mechanics slightly. When the ball is marked inside the two yard line, the field judge lines up straddling the goal line. When the ball is between the two and five yard lines, he should be on the scrimmage line at the snap and move to the goal line following the snap. On a running play close to the goal line, both flank officials should be at the goal line in order best to determine whether a *live ball in possession of the offensive team has penetrated the plane of the goal line.* Because of their poor visual angles, the referee and umpire should avoid ruling a touchdown unless certain of proper possession and penetration of the plane.

The touchdown signal should be given immediately by an official certain of a touchdown. If no fouls have been called, the referee then signals to verify the touchdown. No signal other than the "ball is dead" signal is given if there was no touchdown. When, because of a pileup, flank officials are uncertain of a touchdown, they should close in on the action decisively and, when certain, signal either a touchdown or a dead ball.

Correct positioning by flank officials can also be of critical importance on pass plays near the goal line. Passes thrown near the

Fig. 5.6 Penetrating the plane. Touchdown, ball has broken plane of the goal line. (By courtesy of the N.F.S.H.S.A.)

Fig. 5.7 Positions for Try-for-Point or
Field-Goal attempt. (By courtesy of
the N.F.S.H.S.A.)

intersection of a *boundary line* with (a) the goal line or (b) the end line
require expert positioning. In such circumstances, it is difficult, without
hindering players, to gain a good visual angle of both lines and the
players' feet. You must not be too close to this play. If possible, take a
position slightly out-of-bounds. The ruling is dictated by the feet of the
receiver or interceptor and the position of the ball in possession relative
to the plane of the goal line. The field judge has primary responsibility
for the end line.

Try-for-point plays. If the team attempting the try lines up for a run or
pass, the responsibilities of all officials are the same as for any goal line
play. If the team shows a kicking formation, the field judge immediately
runs to a position adjacent to the goal posts. The field judge signals
"thumbs up" if the kick is above the crossbar or "no score" if below the
crossbar. The referee then signals "touchdown" if the kick passed
between the vertical uprights or "no score" if wide to either side.

Before the snap the referee takes a position five to seven yards
behind the point where the holder will spot the ball and slightly to the
side away from the holder. After the snap the referee moves more
directly behind the kicker in order to secure a more accurate line on the
kick in flight. The linesman assumes his normal position, observes the
neutral zone and rules on roughing the kicker or holder after the kick is
in flight. The umpire watches for illegal use of the hands or roughness in
the line.

Kick-offs. Figure 5.8 shows the officials' starting positions and basic
movements on a kick-off. The referee and linesman are positioned on

Fig. 5.8 Kick-off. (By courtesy of the
N.F.S.H.S.A.)

opposite sides of the field near the five or ten yard line of the receiving
team, about ten yards inbounds. The linesman is opposite the press box
near the side line of the line-to-gain crew. The referee and linesman
check to be sure there are eleven players on the receiving team.

The umpire is on the same side of the field as the linesman, just
out-of-bounds between the receiving team's forty-five and fifty yard line.
Five receiving-team players must be between the 45 and 50 when the
ball is kicked. Be alert for an on-side kick.

The field judge hands the ball to the kicker and tells him to kick
when the referee signals. He then counts for eleven kicking team
players behind their 40 yard line. If either team has an incorrect number
of players on the field or has players out of position, the *official
responsible should call the error to the attention of a team captain so it
can be corrected before the kick-off* is signalled by the referee. The field
judge then runs to the intersection of the side line and the 40 yard line.
All officials raise their right arm to indicate readiness, and the referee
then drops his arm and sounds his whistle for the kick-off.

The umpire and field judge check for encroachment in their
respective zones before the ball is kicked. When the kick is first legally
touched inbounds, the nearest official signals to start the clock. All other
officials back up this signal. The clock is not started if kicked to the end
zone, out-of-bounds, short of the 50 or if a member of the kicking team
first touches the ball. Kick-off fouls are enforced by the field judge if
measured before a re-kick.

On runbacks to his side or up the middle, the referee stays with the ball carrier and the linesman moves upfield observing action away from the ball. If the runback is to the linesman's side of the field, these responsibilities are reversed. The umpire and field judge stay wide as they go with the kick-off, looking for fouls away from the ball and alert for a kick out-of-bounds or a player running out of bounds. On long, break-away returns, the field judge or umpire, respectively, will usually pick up coverage of the ball carrier from the referee or linesman, who then concentrate on action away from the ball.

Important Routine Procedures

The prescribed mechanics regarding starting and stopping the clock, measurements for first downs, relocating the ball and chains after the first and third periods and administering penalties should be followed closely. These situations occur regularly and are described below.

Starting and stopping the clock. Basically, the *clock starts* when:

1. A *free kick,* such as a kick-off is *legally touched* by a player.
2. The *ball is snapped,* except on a try-for-point; or
3. The referee signals to start the clock after *marking the ball ready for play.*

Football rules specify which of these three applies, *depending upon why the clock was stopped.* The list below shows the different circumstances which cause the clock to be stopped and, for each, the correct time to re-start the clock. The *clock is stopped* when there is:

1. An official's time-out (RFP), the three most common reasons being—a change in team possession, a first down, and measurement of a possible first down.
2. A *foul* (RFP)—but the clock should not be stopped during a down for a foul.
3. A granted *team time-out* (S).
4. A *ball out-of-bounds* (S).
5. An *incomplete pass* (S).
6. An *ended period* (S).
7. A *made fair catch* (S or FK); or
8. A *score* (FK).

Key: RFP   —clock should be started when the ball is marked *ready for play.*

S   —clock should be started on the *snap.*

FK   —clock should be started when a *free kick* is legally touched.

The word "O-F-F-I-C-E-R-S" can be used as a memory crutch for remembering the different occurrences that cause the clock to be stopped.

O   ut of bounds (S).
F   air catch (S).
F   oul (RFP).
I   ncomplete pass (S).
C   harged time-out (S).
E   nd of period (S).
R   eferee time-out (RFP)—includes changes in possession, first downs and measurements.
S   core (FK).

The referee and field judge have primary responsibility for being sure that the game clock starts and stops at the correct times. Nevertheless, all officials should back up another official's signal to start or stop the clock. The official closest to the play should signal first on a ball out-of-bounds, an incomplete pass, a made fair catch or a score. The official calling the foul is responsible to stop the clock when the ball becomes dead.

Measurements for first downs. Measurements should always be made where the ball became dead—at the out-of-bounds spot, in either side zone or between the side zones. The referee decides whether a measurement is required and if required beckons the linesman to bring in the chains. The linesman should see that the chain is tightened toward the backward stake. He should then grasp the chain at the center of the yardline nearest the rear stake, instructing the down-marker man to place the down marker at the point of the forward stake. The linesman and two stake men then run toward the position of the ball, and the linesman carefully places the chain in the center of the same yardline as close as possible to the position of the ball. The field judge should keep players from both teams back and away from the measurement. The umpire takes the forward stake and, when the linesman is ready, stretches the chain and places the stake near the ball.

The referee determines whether or not the first down has been made. Any part of the ball extending beyond or touching the inside surface of the stake indicates sufficient gain. The referee signals the first down or shows the distance needed with his hands.

If the first down was made, the linesman personally supervises the new positioning of the chain. If not made, the linesman *must retain his grasp* and relocate the chain by returning to the same sideline/chalkline

When a measurement is ordered by the referee, the head linesman will mark the intersection of the yardline and the chain nearest the rear stake. Then he and the line-to-gain crew will bring the chain onto the field for measurement.

The umpire will take the front stake to hold for the referee to determine whether the line-to-gain has been reached.

Fig. 5.9 Measurement for first down.
(By courtesy of the N.F.S.H.S.A.)

intersection. If the first down was not made and the measurement was taken at an out-of-bounds spot or in a side-zone—the referee grasps the chain at the forward point of the ball and, with the assistance of the linesman and the umpire, positions the ball at the inbounds line.

Most experienced linesmen make preparations in advance of measurements by securing a clip-with-cloth-attached to the chain where the sideline and chalkline nearest the rear stake intersect. This is done before the first down of each new series of downs. Use of a clip eliminates the danger of losing the grip on the chain and also speeds up the measurement procedure.

Relocating the ball and the chain at the ends of the first and third periods. The referee is responsible for relocating the ball when team directions change following the first and third quarters. Any penalty accepted from the previous down should be run off before the ball is relocated at the other end of the field. Both the referee and linesman should record the yardline position of the ball, the down and the distance-to-gain before moving to the other end of the field.

The referee measures the distance from the nearest yardline to the forward point of the ball, estimates the ball's distance, if any, from the inbounds line and runs *diagonally* to the corresponding position at the other end of the field—spotting the ball there.

The linesman grasps the chain at a convenient yardline, *noting which yardline it is,* and instructs the chain crew to *reverse their positions.* The linesman and chain crew then run to the corresponding yardline at the other end of the field. *After the referee has spotted the ball,* the stakes and chain are relocated and the down marker is placed opposite the forward point of the ball. When the first or third period ends with the forward point of the ball exactly on a yardline and the distance-to-gain is exactly ten yards, this entire chain-crew procedure is unnecessary.

Administering penalties. When a foul is detected *during a down,* note the spot of the foul and the number of the offending player, drop your penalty marker and *continue to officiate. Do not sound your whistle.* When the ball is dead, the time-out signal should be executed and *full information* given to the referee by each official who called a foul—the number of the offender, type of foul and team in possession when the foul occurred. If the foul occurred before or during a forward pass or kick was in flight, tell the referee it was a "loose ball foul." If the foul occurred after the ball had been whistled dead, it was a "dead ball foul." The umpire secures the ball.

Fig. 5.10 Explaining the options. (By
courtesy of the N.F.S.H.S.A.)

The referee gives the preliminary signal for the foul, facing the
offending team's goal line. He then goes to the enforcement spot to
present the options to the captain of the offended team. The options
should be precise. "Captain, if you accept the penalty, you will have the
ball second and six at the 15 yardline. If you decline, you will have the
ball third and two at the eleven." If the captain's choice is obvious,
quickly inform him what the obvious choice is, giving him a brief chance
to disagree. If he says nothing, proceed with the obvious choice.

If the penalty is accepted, visualize the distance, get the ball from
the umpire and *run it off.* Do not step off the yards unless the field is
poorly marked. Give the signal for the foul to both sidelines and check
the down and down marker. Check the readiness of both captains and
signal ready-for-play. If possible, give the offending player's number to
the offending team captain. When a player is disqualified, the official
calling the foul will report it to the referee and to the coach.

If the penalty is declined, the referee goes to the spot of the ball
and signals the foul followed by the declination signal to both sidelines.

If double fouls cancel each other, the referee properly spots the
ball, faces the proper directions while signalling each foul and then
gives the declination signal. When multiple fouls are called, run off the

distance penalties for each, placing the ball and signaling after each distance is run off.

All officials should check the correctness of the enforcement spot and the distance of all penalties. Too frequently, football officials who seldom referee do not wish to "get involved" and/or or do not know the correct enforcement spot.

Undoubtedly, more inadvertent mistakes are made by field officials when fouls are called and penalties administered than in any other phase of football officiating mechanics. Here is a list of some of the errors or omissions which can result in errors:

1. Sounding the whistle when the ball is in play.
2. Failing to note the spot of the foul, possession and the offending player's number.
3. Failing to follow the play to its conclusion after dropping the penalty marker.
4. Moving the down-marker and/or chains too soon.
5. Inadequate communication between the referee and the official(s) who called the foul.
6. Presenting inaccurate or unclear options; and
7. Penalizing from the wrong basic spot. (See "basic rules and penalties.")

Awareness of these common errors and omissions can help to prevent unnecessary and unwanted inequities.

Signals

Football officiating signals include the whistle, the penalty marker, and prescribed hand signals. The *whistle* is used for only three reasons: (1) to kill play and curtail further action when the ball becomes dead at the end of a play; (2) by the referee only, to call attention to the ready-for-play signal after a down or before a free kick; and (3) rarely, when necessary to gain the attention of another official. The whistle ending a down should always be blown with a sharp blast and only by the official or officials ruling that the ball became dead. Consecutive short blasts are occasionally needed when attention is not readily gained. *The whistle should not be blown* (1) when a foul is detected with the ball alive, (2) when a fumble has occurred with the ball alive, or (3) as a "back-up" whistle by an official away from the action. Many football officials prefer to carry the whistle in the hand rather than in the mouth in order to prevent inadvertent whistles. The umpire should hold the whistle in his hand.

When not in use, the *penalty marker* should be tucked into a hip pocket with a protruding corner providing an easy grasp. The spot of a foul can be better identified and retained if the marker is dropped or

Fig. 5.11 Officials' signals. (By courtesy of the N.F.S.H.S.A.)

OFFICIAL FOOTBALL SIGNALS
HIGH SCHOOL AND COLLEGE

27 Unsportsmanlike conduct Noncontact foul

28 Illegal participation

29 Sideline interference (NCAA only)

30 Roughing kicker or holder

31 Ball illegally kicked, batted or touched

32 Invalid fair catch signal Illegal fair catch signal

33 Forward pass interference Kick catching interference

34 Roughing passer

35 Illegal pass Illegal forward handing

36 Intentional grounding

37 Ineligible downfield on pass

38 Personal foul

39 Clipping

40 Blocking below waist Illegal block

41 Chop block

42 Holding or obstructing

43 Illegal use of hands or arms

44 Helping runner Interlocked interference

45 Grasping face mask or helmet opening

46 Tripping

47 Player disqualification

NOTE: Signals number 15, 16, 17, 24, 25 and 26 are for future expansion.

2-83

Fig. 5.11 cont.

thrown to a spot. Nevertheless, the responsibility is greater to continue to cover the action than to get the marker to the exact point of the foul. The penalty marker should be thrown high in the air or aggressively towards the spot of the foul when the official detecting the foul is a distance from the center of the action. The bean bag or your hat, *not the penalty marker,* should be used to mark out-of-bounds spots and first-touch-of-kick spots.

Only the referee gives *signals* which designate the type of foul. (Exception: when the *field judge* runs off a penalty before a repeated kickoff.) This is done twice for each foul—once just before presenting the options and again, to both sidelines, after the penalty has either been run off or declined. All officials may and should give signals regarding starting or stopping the clock, dead ball, incomplete pass, a score or a touchback. (Touchbacks are rarely, if ever, signalled by the umpire). Other signals given only by the referee are: first down, penalty declined, no score, ready-for-play and official's or team time-out.

Signals should be given authoritatively and decisively, but not for the purpose of showmanship. In stopping the clock, the arms should be crossed back and forth two to four times; *all officials repeat this signal.* An incomplete pass signal is always followed by the stop-the-clock signal. The incomplete pass signal should be given instantly with only *one distinct* sweep of the arms, executed in a semi-crouched position. This is immediately followed by the stop-the-clock signal executed two to four times in an *upright position.*

Teamwork

It is essential that the football officiating crew work closely together as a unit. Football officials have twenty-two players to supervise on a playing area of 57,000-plus square feet on which a very physical and emotional game is played, and in which there are many different responsibilities to fill and procedures to follow. A football down cannot be run without several types of officiating teamwork being noticeable.

Who calls what? As specified earlier, the referee protects the passer or punter and administers penalties; the umpire concentrates on interior linesmen; the linesman supervises the line-to-gain crew; the field judge is responsible for the end line and fair catches; and so forth. In other play situations responsibilities are shared by two or more different officials. For example, any or all of the four officials may call a false start or encroachment; both flank officials look for forward progress; the referee and umpire share responsibilities regarding first touches of punts just beyond the neutral zone and ruling on possession following blocked punts.

The following guidelines are suggested:

1. Do not make a call if you know that it is the responsibility of another official. You must assume that the other official knows it is his responsibility and has a reason for not calling it, or for delaying momentarily before calling it.

2. If you have total responsibility or a share in the responsibility for a call, rule on it without delay. If the responsibility is shared, do not wait for another official to do the job—he may not have seen the play or the foul, or he might even be waiting for you to rule on it.
3. Your main obligation is to the game. Therefore, *make your ruling without delay* if you are not certain who has responsibility but *know* that a foul has occurred, that the ball has become dead, etc.

Rotating coverage. At any given moment of live ball action one official will have responsibility for the ball carrier. As the play develops, this responsibility may rotate from one official to another. Such rotations almost always occur when a ball carrier breaks loose for a long gain. They are also common on scrimmage running plays to a side zone when responsibility shifts from the referee to one of the flank officials. The common sense guidelines for both officials involved are (1) to retain initial coverage responsibilities *until the rotation becomes obvious* and then (2) to accept the rotation as a fact and concentrate on the new responsibilities. *Observation of play away from the ball is important and should not be neglected.* When the ball is carried into a side zone and the flank official to that side had lined up on the scrimmage line before the play, the rotation usually occurs at the hash marks. Some officials use simple pointing signals to communicate the switch to the other official.

Communication. Football officials cannot afford to spend time in running conversations or "bull sessions" when on the field. They are officials with an important job to do. Neverthless, brief and to-the-point communication can improve efficiency and performance and also help to develop a sense of teamwork and *esprit de crops* during a game.

Certain verbal and visual reminders are commonly used by experienced officials. *After every down* the officials should repeat to each other and to the players the *down* and *distance-to-gain,* showing the down with fingers (one, two, three or a fist for fourth down). When the clock is started or stopped or the ball becomes dead, the officials can occasionally yell "wind it up," or "stop the clock" or "dead ball, dead ball." When a ball carrier is very close to a first down, flank officials can help the referee and umpire by yelling "close, close" as a reminder to spot the ball with care.

Relaying the ball. The officials *relay the ball* back to the proper inbounds spot when the ball is a distance from the spot following a down. This routine is common following incomplete passes, kicks or plays out-of-bounds and touchbacks. One, two or even three relays may be needed. Following a long incomplete pass the ball may be relayed from one flank official, to the other flank official, to the umpire and to the referee at the previous scrimmage line. While the ball is being retrieved, a chain should be formed and the ball relayed to the correct spot by short, underhand passes. Relay passes should be thrown no farther than ten to fifteen yards. If the distance is greater, the official should run the ball back before throwing it. The umpire is most frequently involved in relaying the ball, but all officials should be ready to help according to the particular circumstance. Accurate, hustling techniques in relaying the ball keep the game moving and show the officials in a good light.

Mechanics for Two Officials

Two officials cannot provide adequate coverage of any level of football competition, for several reasons: too many players, too large a field, wide variety of officiating responsibilities—and the potential for injuries and/or unsportsmanlike conduct.

The two officials are designated as referee and linesman. On scrimmage plays the referee lines up wide of and slightly behind the offensive backfield to the opposite side from the linesman. The linesman lines up in the neutral zone outside the widest offensive player.

On kickoffs the referee takes the same position as the umpire in four man mechanics, and the linesman takes the responsibilities of the field judge in four man mechanics.

On punts the linesman breaks downfield following the snap, taking his sideline and refereeing the ball carrier on punt returns. The referee is totally responsible for the other sideline, getting the out of bounds spot of the punt or the runback.

On scrimmage plays near the goal line, it is recommended that the referee line up in the neutral zone opposite the linesman in order to rule more effectively on forward progress to that side. If the offense were to show a pass play, the referee's tendency would be to the offensive backfield. On try-for-point plays involving an attempted kick, the linesman, following the snap, breaks toward the goal posts in order to rule whether or not the kick clears the crossbar. This leaves the referee to do the best he can to both protect the kicker and holder and to determine whether or not the kick passes between the uprights.

Scrimmage play responsibilities. The linesman calls encroachment, attempts to call all fouls in the neutral zone, becomes "referee" on runs into his side zone, marks forward progress, calls ineligibles downfield, and covers passes and punts downfield. The referee, in addition to four man mechanics responsibilities, covers runs to his side zone and spots the ball.

Alternate alignments. Although not recommended here, some officials prefer to divide two man scrimmage play responsibilities differently from what is described above. One method is to place the referee on the scrimmage line, from which he drifts to the offensive backfield at the snap—and to place the linesman adjacent to one of the deeper defensive backs, opposite the referee. This alignment somewhat strengthens coverage of interior line play, but greatly weakens (1) sideline coverage away from the referee and (2) accurate judgment of forward progress.

Another method places both officials in the neutral zone, from which the referee drifts to the offensive backfield.

Mechanics for Three Officials

The three officials are designated as referee, linesman and umpire. On scrimmage plays the referee lines up in a normal position to the side of and slightly behind the offensive backs and to the opposite side from the linesman. The linesman is in the neutral zone facing the press box outside the widest offensive player. The umpire normally takes a position three to five yards behind the defensive line somewhat to the referee's side of the field. On expected passes the umpire moves further to the referee's side.

Positions and responsibilities on kickoffs differs from four man in that the umpire takes the kicking team, and the linesman is responsible for the neutral zone of the receiving team.

On punts the positions and responsibilities of the linesman are the same as in four man mechanics. The umpire takes a position about twenty yards downfield outside the widest defensive back opposite the linesman and becomes responsible for that sideline.

Coverage of pass plays by three field officials is somewhat awkward. As in four man mechanics, the umpire moves to the neutral zone when the offense shows pass. This leaves the linesman with extensive responsibilities regarding illegal contact downfield. The referee must attempt to rule on such illegal contact in the side zone to his side of the field, but is hampered by his protect-the-passer/illegal passes responsibilities. The umpire can pick up some of the slack by (1) assuming primary responsibility for all illegal offensive or defensive contact during the pass rush and (2) when the pass is in flight, quickly shifting his vision in the direction of the pass downfield.

Fig. 5.12 Positions during scrimmage-
kick (three officials). (By courtesy of
the N.F.S.H.S.A.)

Coverage of scrimmage plays near the goalline is also awkward, in
that forward progress away from the linesman may be difficult to
determine.

On try-for-point plays when a kick is attempted, the umpire takes a
position near the endline outside of the goal posts opposite the
linesman, and rules whether or not the kick clears the crossbar.

Scrimmage play responsibilities. As in two man mechanics, the referee
must cover plays into his side zone. (Only on punts and kickoffs does
the umpire have sideline repsonsibilities in three officials games.) The
linesman marks all forward progress and the referee and umpire divide
spotting-the-ball responsibilities the same as in four man mechanics.

Problem Calls

Pass Interference
More judgment is needed for pass interference calls than for any other
football infraction. Furthermore, the judgments rendered are more
subject to criticism because:

1. Borderline pass interference decisions are fairly common.
2. The success or failure of pass plays is usually considered more
   critical than running plays.

3. Pass interference situations are more likely to take place "out in the open" where everyone can evaluate the decision.
4. Many spectators and players, and some coaches do not know the correct pass interference rule interpretations.

When a forward pass is in flight all defensive players and all eligible receivers have an *equal right to the ball.* The two key questions are:

1. Did a player interfere with an opponent's opportunity to play the ball?
2. Did either player play the man and not the ball?

A player of either team may not run through an opponent who has established an advantageous position before the ball arrives. By the same token, *no foul should be called* when opponents having an equally advantageous position contact each other while attempting to play the ball. Pass interference should be called *with or without contact* if a player "face guards" an opponent, or changes direction or stops with an obvious intention to impede his opponent. Under high school rules, pass interference can only occur on forward passes thrown *beyond the neutral zone.*

When two eligible pass receivers are making a simultaneous and bona fide attempt to catch or bat the ball, and there is unavoidable contact, there is no foul.

Fig. 5.13 Pass interference. (By courtesy of the N.F.S.H.S.A.)

It is illegal to "play through" a man in order to get to the ball during a forward pass. In this illustration, it will be interference if No. 20 contacts No. 85 before the ball reaches him.

Defensive pass interference. Here No. 18 has directed his attention to the vision of the receiver which indicates an intent to hinder the receiver rather than catch or bat the ball and it is, therefore, interference.

Fig. 5.14 Pass interference. (By courtesy of the N.F.S.H.S.A.)

Here are some interpretations:

1. When a potential receiver for either team is tripped, it is not pass interference if both players were playing the ball.
2. Offensive players downfield may not block or use their hands to push off from an opponent.
3. Defensive backs may legally block a potential pass receiver before the pass is in flight, but may not impede the potential receiver after he makes his cut.

Restrictions on the *defense* relate only to the period when a *forward pass is in flight.* On the other hand, *offensive players* are restricted *from the time of the snap until the flight ends.* Offensive pass interference, therefore, is especially difficult to enforce when the initial play action appears to show a running play but suddenly becomes a pass play.

Pass interference cannot be ruled until a forward pass is thrown. For example, when a defensive back following the snap impedes a potential receiver after the cut or an offensive player blocks or pushes off downfield, *the penalty flag must be withheld until the forward pass is thrown.* For this reason, flank officials must *mentally record what happened before the pass.* It helps to "think pass" if in doubt whether a play will become a run or a pass play.

Fig. 5.15 No Foul. When two players are running side by side and shoulder-to-shoulder, the contact as illustrated is incidental, unless there is intent by either player to push or trip his opponent. This is no foul. (By courtesy of the N.F.S.H.S.A.)

Fouls Regarding the Passer and Punter
These are the primary responsibility of the referee. Alertness and accurate judgment are needed.

Roughing the passer or punter. A defensive player may not charge into the passer or punter clearly after the ball is in flight. No foul should be called if the rusher clearly attempts to avoid illegal contact and the

It is roughing the kicker for a defensive player to charge into the kicker when contact is avoidable.

When contact is unavoidable because a defensive player blocks or partially blocks the kick near the kicker, contact does not constitute roughing the kicker.

Fig. 5.16 Roughing the kicker. (By courtesy of the N.F.S.H.S.A.)

contact is incidental. Roughing the passer should not be ruled if the defensive player is close to the passer and his momentum causes him to contact the passer just after the pass is in flight. Roughing the punter should not be called when contact seems unavoidable in these circumstances—(1) the punt is blocked and (2) the would-be-punter has momentarily fumbled and/or is running with the ball. Significant contact following an unblocked punt should always be called.

Fumble or incomplete pass? When an offensive player is tackled when attempting a forward pass and the ball comes loose, the referee must decide whether or not the passing arm had started its forward motion. If so, signal an incomplete pass. If not, the ball is alive until whistled dead with either team in possession. The referee must make a decisive decision on this play, but also be careful not to blow his whistle too soon.

Intentional grounding. This infraction is officially designated "pass purposely incompleted." (3:41) The passer's intent may be to prevent a loss of yardage by throwing the ball out of the reach of any player. This is strictly a judgment call. A foul should be called only if the "curcumstantial evidence" seems clear-cut, since judging a person's intentions is risky. Was the passer about to be tackled? Did the

Fig. 5.17 Intentional grounding. Purposely incompleting a forward pass is an illegal pass. Here the defense has gained an advantage and to overlook this foul nullifies good defensive play. (By courtesy of the N.F.S.H.S.A.)

passer's grip on the ball slip? Was he off-balance? What was the
intended direction of the throw?

Neutral Zone Fouls

A great number and variety of infractions may take place just before,
during and after the ball is snapped. All officials should be "super alert"
when the teams line up for a down.

Just before the snap all officials should look for encroachment,
false starts and illegal shifts or positions. Off-sides is no longer a part of
high school rules. Encroachment should be called when a *player of
either team* other than the center *enters the neutral zone before the
snap* and after the center has adjusted the ball. The first player who
encroaches is called. If an offensive player *false starts first,* no
encroachment would be called. A false start is any accidental or
intentional movement by any offensive player which is similar to a
starting movement. A personal foul may be called on a defensive player
if he deliberately charges into an offensive player after a false start. The
whistle should be *blown immediately* and the flag thrown when a player
encroaches, even if he encroaches just at the snap. False starts *clearly
before the snap* should also be whistled immediately.

At the moment of the snap, flank officials should look for illegal
lateral motion and all officials should be alert for illegal snaps. If there is
illegal lateral motion the penalty flag should be dropped, but the whistle

Fig. 5.18 Defensive encroachment
because #55 entered the neutral zone
following final adjustment by the
snapper. (By courtesy of the
N.F.S.H.S.A.)

Fig. 5.19 Offensive encroachment.
The first offender will be penalized and
unless the subsequent foul is
unsportsmanlike, it will be ignored. (By
courtesy of the N.F.S.H.S.A.)

Fig. 5.20 This simulates action at the
snap. False start. (By courtesy of the
N.F.S.H.S.A.)

should not be sounded; continue to officiate. In the case of an illegal
snap, sound the whistle immediately.

After the ball is snapped, the umpire, linesman and field judge
should concentrate on initial contact along the line within their
respective jurisdictions. Look for personal fouls such as striking an

Fig. 5.21 Illegal snaps. Each of these snap infractions causes the ball to remain dead and the down cannot be started. The penalty for snap infraction is 5 yards measured from the succeeding spot. (By courtesy of the N.F.S.H.S.A.)

opponent with a fist, illegal use of hands or arms and illegal "crackback" blocks. If any of these are detected, drop the flag and stay with the play.

In summary, the whistle should *always be sounded immediately* when there is:

1. Encroachment or
2. An illegal snap.

Sound the whistle immediately when a *false start* by an offensive player *occurs clearly before the snap.*

Throw the flag but withhold the whistle and continue to officiate when there is:

1. Illegal shift before the snap
2. Illegal motion at the snap
3. Illegal position at the snap
4. A false start just before the snap or
5. Any other foul after the snap

Thorough coverage of the neutral zone on every down is difficult but not impossible. Each official should be aware of his responsibilities and shift his concentration as the down progresses from illegal shifts, encroachment or false starts—to illegal motion, positions or snaps—to illegal blocks and personal fouls.

Butt-Blocking and Face-Tackling

The intent of butt-blocking and face-tackling rules is to prevent serious injuries. Prior to the inclusion of these rules, some players were being taught to aim their helmets or face masks directly at an opponent when forcefully blocking or tackling. The understandable results were head and neck injuries. Existing rules now require the blocker or tackler to shift his head to the side at the moment of contact in order to block or tackle with the shoulder rather than the head. *These rules must be strictly enforced.*

Grasping the Face Mask

This rule now applies to all helmet openings (i.e. under the helmet opening, front or back) as well as the protective bar(s) on the helmet. For the infraction to be ruled, the bar(s) or helmet opening must be securely grasped, the infraction must be signalled without hesitation.

Fig. 5.22 Butt-blocking. Butt-blocking is a personal foul and consists of driving the face mask, frontal area or top of the helmet directly into an opponent, as the primary point of contact, either in close line play or in the open field. (By courtesy of the N.F.S.H.S.A.)

Fig. 5.23 No foul. Legal—75 has not
grasped the mask. (By courtesy of the
N.F.S.H.S.A.)

Clipping

The incidence of clipping infractions has been reduced in recent years,
largely because of additions to football rules. Blocking below the waist
is now illegal on kick plays. "Crack-block" blocks below the waist are
also illegal. Nevertheless, clipping has not been eliminated and must be
called rigidly in order to prevent serious leg injuries.

A clipping infraction is defined as accidentally or intentionally
charging into a player other than a ball carrier from the rear—*above or
below the waist.* The classic clip occurs when a player throws himself
against the back of an opponent's knees. *Clipping is legal* (1) against a
ball carrier, and (2) within the "free-blocking zone," an imaginary eight
yards by six yards area for each separate down—four yards to each
side of the ball and three yards to each side of the scrimmage line.
Officials should not call clipping unless they see the initial contact.
Borderline clips should be judged according to whether or not the player
blocked was able to see and evade the blocker. Obviously,
considerable judgment may be required in order to rule accurately on
clipping.

Late Hitting

The officials' control of a football game can hinge largely on their ability
to enforce the rules regarding late hitting. Unnecessary injuries and
unwanted flareups may result from looseness or inconsistency in this
area. The most important requirements are to hustle and be on top of

When the player being blocked can see his opponent and initial contact is from the front, there is no clipping even though, at the completion of the action, the blocker may make contact with the back of his opponent. Because completion of this block may appear to be clipping, it is a clear example why officials should not call the foul unless they observe the block in its entirety.

It is legal to block from behind in free-blocking zone immediately after the snap provided the blocker was in this zone at the time of the snap.

Fig. 5.24 Clipping. (By courtesy of the N.F.S.H.S.A.)

the play—to whistle the play dead quickly and decisively—and then to close in on the action. Frequently, the officials can talk players out of late hitting—"GO EASY, THE BALL IS DEAD." "STAND UP, HE IS OUT-OF-BOUNDS."

Considerable alertness and judgment are needed. Players are expected to react to the whistle. A personal foul should be called when a player, clearly after the whistle, drives into or piles on an opponent. When such contact is flagrantly late and rough, the player should not only be penalized but warned or disqualified. If, on the other hand, the player clearly attempts to avoid and reduce the contact when he hears the whistle or sees the opponent out-of-bounds, no foul should be called. Officials away from the play occasionally have a better perspective for judging late hitting and should not hesitate to make the call.

Late hits out-of-bounds near a team bench can be particularly difficult. The flank official may be busy determining the out-of-bounds spot. Players and coaches create congestion and confusion. In this situation, all officials must make an extra effort to provide coverage. The flank official should immediately mark the out-of-bounds spot and concentrate fully on making his presence known.

Inadvertent Whistle

Despite their determination to avoid it, officials do occasionally sound their whistles when they shouldn't. To do this is embarassing as well as inevitably unfair to one or both teams. Converted basketball officials accustomed to sounding their whistles for every infraction must particularly take care to avoid inadvertent whistles. Football officials should consider carrying the whistle in the hand rather than in the mouth.

Inadvertent whistles most commonly occur in the following circumstances:

1. When a foul is detected, especially at or immediately after the snap; and
2. When a down is about to end, possibly just as a live ball is fumbled.

When an inadvertent whistle sounds, *it counts and should not be ignored.* The ball becomes dead. To ignore an inadvertent whistle would be unfair to those players who heard it and probably reacted to it.

The adjustment made depends on the location and possession of the ball when the inadvertent whistle sounded. The down may or may not count. The rules regarding correct adjustments are complicated and beyond the scope of this book. The complexity of these rules serves further to motivate officials to avoid inadvertent whistles.

Miscellaneous Considerations

Pregame Officials Conference
The conference should be held after the officials are dressed, approximately one hour before the game. Through advance planning the referee can zero in on important rule and mechanics matters and materially improve the officiating that day. The referee conducts the conference but should welcome the expression of suggestions, questions and concerns from the other field officials. Among the topics to be covered are:

1. Review coin-toss mechanics.
2. Discuss free-kicks reviewing positions and responsibilities.
3. Preview of coverage during scrimmage plays.
   a. Running plays positions and coverage
   b. Forward passes, eligibility of receivers and interference
   c. Illegal forward passes (from beyond line, purposeful incompletion, thrown to ineligible on or behind the line)
4. Positions and coverage during scrimmage-kicks.
   a. No blocking below waist during return
   b. First touching by K
   c. Fair catch situations
   d. Kicks out-of-bounds
   e. Interference
5. Goal line plays and tries-for-point.
   a. Variation of positions near goal line
6. Review of substitution rule.
7. Discuss stopping and starting the clock.
8. Review procedures during measurement for possible first down.
9. Duties during time-outs and the intermission between periods.
10. Penalizing personal and unsportsmanlike fouls.
11. Review penalty administration. (2–9)

Following the conference all of the officials should enter the playing area at least fifteen minutes before the kick-off in order to accomplish their several important on-the-field pregame responsibilities.

Officiating Evaluated by Coaches

What qualities do you appreciate in a football official?

1. Integrity
2. Control
3. In good condition

  4. Thorough knowledge of the rules
  5. Poise
  6. Willing to provide rule interpretations
  7. Competed in the sport
  8. Courage of convictions
  9. Friendly
10. Efficient

Miscellaneous Comments

  1. There is a definite need to provide more work for young officials to get the needed experience to move up the ladder.
  2. A team should not be penalized because they are superior.
  3. Complaints are more justified about what officials *do not call* than what they do call, especially when the call is obvious or a game is one-sided and the officials are in a hurry to end the game.
  4. Officiating is a state of mind. Top officials show a positive attitude toward the game.

Officiating Evaluated by Officials

What is the most difficult play to call in football?

  1. Pass interference
  2. Deliberate grounding of the pass
  3. Clipping—crackback blocking
  4. Quarterback being hit from the side and deciding whether the arm went forward for incomplete pass or if it was a fumble

What is the most difficult phase of mechanics in officiating football?

  1. Being in the right place at the right time
  2. Covering side zones and the deep pass play

Miscellaneous Comments

  1. A large number of officials work only subordinate responsibilities while being "carried" by the referee.
  2. Preventive officiating techniques must be learned quickly by the beginning official.
  3. To fellow officials, good mechanics are just as important as knowledge of the rules.
  4. The intent of each rule must be understood.
  5. All positions in the crew are as important as any other.
  6. To have played the game had have a desire to get back on the field is not enough. One must have a spirit for the work.

General Procedure for Becoming a Football Official

Interested individuals must first join their local officiating association. The Association will make available, as a part of the membership dues, a kit of instructional materials which will include a study guide, rule books, mechanics book and a case book. Association training programs feature required meetings, field work clinics, actual scrimmages, classification and other written examinations. Successful candidates are then classified. A qualified list is forwarded to the area commissioner whose office is responsible for making the actual game assignments.

Official Ratings

Officials are continually rated by coaches, senior fellow officials and Association instructors to determine their strengths and weaknesses. This procedure assists the commissioner's office in making future assignments. Capable, qualified and experienced officials are rewarded for their dedicated efforts by being assigned to important games and higher level competition.

A.I.A.   **RATING OF FOOTBALL OFFICIALS**   **A.I.A.**

HOME TEAM: _____ ⬜ VISITORS: _____ ⬜ DATE: _____
Score   Score

REFEREE	UMPIRE		LINESMAN		JUDGE

INSTRUCTIONS: Rate each official in each area on a 1 - 5 point basis as listed on bottom of form.	REFEREE	UMPIRE	LINESMAN	JUDGE
MECHANICS: Present Classification				
a. Hand Signals				
b. Sharp Whistle & Quick Positive Decisions				
c. Field Coverage & Positioning				
d. Pre-Game & Halftime Preparation				
e. Penalty Communication & Game Administration				
PERSONAL ATTRIBUTES:				
a. Hustle				
b. Appearance (uniform, grooming, & physical condition)				
c. Application of Rules				
d. Control of Game (Poise)				
e. Promptness				
f. Relationship with fellow officials, players and coaches				
g. °Judgment				
TOTAL: (Possible 60 Pts.)				
°(Below list comments on judgment or other needed area of improvement) (Circle One) ➔	(V-JV-FR)	(V-JV-FR)	(V-JV-FR)	(V-JV-FR)

_____
_____
_____
_____
_____

5 - Outstanding   4 - Good   3 - Average   **2 - Below Average   **1 - Unsatisfactory
**Requires written explanation.

Signed _____

NOTE: Referee must mail this report to the Regional Commissioner immediately following the contest.

By courtesy of the Arizona Interscholastic Association.)

Play Rulings (1)

Situation: Prior to the game, the head coach asks the umpire to examine some player equipment before he verifies that all players are legally equipped. The umpire discovers that 5 offensive linemen: (a) do not have legal hip pads; (b) have abrasive gloves; (c) have knee pads attached to the pants at the hips; or (d) are wearing a type of sliding pad. *Ruling:* In (a), legal hip pads must be secured. In (b), the gloves may not be worn. In (c) and (d), the umpire must determine whether the hip pads offer adequate player protection. (1-5-1)

Situation: Following a play during which A1 caught a pass, it is discovered: (a) A1's hands are coated with a sticky material; (b) A1 has a quantity of sticky material on his socks; or (c) A1 has smeared sticky material on the sleeves of his jersey. *Ruling:* Sticky substances are illegal in (a), (b) and (c). A 15-yard penalty is enforced from the succeeding spot. This is an unsportsmanlike foul charged to the coach of Team A since he verified that all players would be legally equipped. A1 may not participate until the sticky material has been removed. (1-5-3j; 9-7-1g)

Situation: From a 4-point stance on the offensive line, interior lineman A1: (a) contacts his opponent by driving his face mask directly into an opponent's numbers; or (b) contacts his opponent with his shoulder so his head is to the side of his opponent's body; or (c) attempts to block an opponent with a shoulder but because of a defensive slant, primary contact with the opponent is made with the helmet. *Ruling:* The block in (a) is illegal butt blocking. This is a personal foul. In (b), even though there was some contact with the helmet, the block is legal because the helmet or face mask was not used to deliver a blow. In (c) the covering official will have to read intent in judging the act. Because of defensive slants and stunts, there will probably be a number of instances in which the blocker attempts to make a legal shoulder block but unintentionally contacts his opponent with either the face mask or helmet. When this is the case, contact does not result in a direct blow and would probably not be illegal. Butt blocking is an intentional act which is dangerous to both the blocker and his opponent. (9-3-2k)

Situation: A pass from A1 is near the intersection of the sideline and the goal line. A2, running toward the goal line, leaps to gain possession of the pass at the 3-yard line and is forcibly: (a) blocked by B1 coming from the end zone so that A2 contacts the ground out-of-bounds opposite B's 4-yard line; or (b) contacted from the side by B2 and A2 first contacts the ground out-of-bounds opposite the 3-yard line; or

(c) tackled from behind by B3 so that first contact with the ground by A2 is out-of-bounds 1 yard beyond the goal line; or (d) tackled from behind by B4 so that A2 first contacts the ground in the end zone. *Ruling:* Completed pass in both (a) and (b). In (c), the pass is incomplete. It is a completed pass and a touchdown in (d). In (a) and (b), the contact by B1 and B2 changed the direction of A2, and he is given his farthest advance. In (c) and (d), the added force, in the general direction the player was moving, is not considered a factor affecting his spot of landing. Therefore, when A2 landed out-of-bounds in (c), the pass was incomplete. Landing in B's end zone in (d), resulted in a touchdown. (8-2-2)

Situation   A passed or fumbled ball is near a boundary. B1 gets the ball in his hands while his foot is on the line. *Ruling:* The ball becomes dead when touched. Since touching precedes player possession, there is no "catch" or "recovery." (2-3-1)

Situation: Airborne A1 and B1 gain joint possession of a legal forward pass near the goal line and return to the ground where: (a) they alight in the field of play inbounds; or (b) they alight in the end zone with the ball beyond the goal line; or (c) A1 lands in the end zone and B1 in the field of play inbounds; or (d) B1 comes down in the end zone and A1 lands in the field of play. *Ruling:* In (a), the ball is dead and belongs to A at the yard line through the foremost point of the ball when A1 and B1 contacted the ground inbounds. It is a touchdown in (b). In (c) and (d), the ball becomes dead and the pass is complete at the yard line through the foremost point of the ball when the players contacted the ground inbounds. If the ball has penetrated the plane of the goal line in either (c) or (d), it will result in a touchdown. (4-2-2c; 7-5-3; 8-2-2)

   Comment: In order for there to be a simultaneous catch, 2 requirements must be met. First, opposing players hold the ball and second, both must be in contact with the ground inbounds. The players' contact with ground need not necessarily be exactly simultaneous. If A1 and B1 were to jointly possess a pass while airborne and both land inbounds, it is a completed pass and the ball is dead at that point. If there was a simultaneous recovery of a fumble, the ball would be dead and belong to the team which last had sole possession. If there was simultaneous recovery of a kick, the ball is dead and belongs to the receiving team.

Situation: With the score B-7 and A-6, it is 2nd and goal from Team B's 9-yard line. The clock is stopped due to an incomplete pass and there are 5 seconds remaining in the game. A1 throws a legal forward pass into the end zone where B1 intercepts and advances to his 30-yard line where he is downed. Following the interception and during the run by B1, there is clipping in the end zone by B2. Time expired during the run back. *Ruling:* If the penalty for the foul by B2 is declined, the period is over. If the penalty is accepted, it results in a safety for A and the period will be extended by an untimed down. (3-3-3a; 10-5-3)

Situation: With 4th and goal on B's 4-yard line, A1 is hit and fumbles, and as the ball goes into the end zone, an inadvertent whistle is sounded. The fumble occurs: (a) at the 5-yard line; or (b) at the 3-yard line. *Ruling:* In (a), the down will be replayed. In (b), it will be 1st and 10 for B at the 3-yard line. (4-2-3)

Comment: Whenever an inadvertent whistle sounds while the ball is loose following a fumble, the ball is returned to the spot of the fumble, or spot of last possession. Theoretically, this is where the ball becomes dead. If the spot of fumble is behind the line, you replay the down unless there has been a change of possession prior to the fumble. If the spot of fumble is beyond the line, the down counts if an inadvertent whistle sounds during the down.

Situation: On 4th and goal from the 5-yard line, the ball is declared ready-for-play with the nose of the ball just touching the 5-yard line. Following A's incomplete pass, B takes over and the referee places the ball in line with the down box as it was prior to A's 4th down incomplete forward pass, i.e. with the foremost point (nose) of the ball on the 5-yard line. *Ruling:* This is incorrect. The ball should be spotted in the same position it was at the start of the down. When a team fails to reach its line-to-gain on a 4th down run, the foremost point of the ball at the time it became dead would become the rear point when direction of the offense is changed, and after a 4th down incomplete pass, the ball is placed "as it was at the start of the down" (or previous 4th down play). Unless the 4th down play resulted in a touchback or safety, or A reached its line-to-gain, Team B will gain approximately 11½ inches (the length of the football) in field position, and the down box will invariably have to be moved. Following a touchback or safety the ball is placed with its foremost point touching the 20-yard line. Many officials seem to find to convenient to merely reset the line-to-gain chains following an incomplete 4th down pass by using the previous line of scrimmage (down box) as the position for the rear stake when the direction is changed. This is not supported by the rules.

Situation: A1 and B1 simultaneously gain possession of a live ball which is a: (a) legal forward pass in the air and 1 player lands out-of-bounds; or (b) legal forward pass while both players are touching inbounds; or (c) scrimmage kick muffed by R beyond the neutral zone; or (d) fumble by A1 on a running play. *Ruling:* In (a), incomplete pass; (b) complete pass, down is ended, ball belongs to A at the spot of completion; (c) the down is ended, ball belongs to R at the spot of recovery; (d) the down is ended, the ball belongs to A at the spot of recovery.

Situation: Eligible receiver A1 blocks an opponent 10 yards downfield while the pass is in flight. The pass is completed to A2 who is: (a) beyond the line of scrimmage; or (b) behind the line of scrimmage when he catches the ball. When the covering official observes the block by eligible A1 during a forward pass, he immediately throws his flag to indicate an infraction. *Ruling:* It is a foul for pass interference in (a), and a legal block in (b). It was proper for the covering official to indicate an infraction because he had no way of knowing whether the pass did or did not cross the line of scrimmage. In (a), there is no problem because it was clearly offensive pass interference. In (b), it will be necessary for the official to recover his flag and explain to coach of Team B why there was no foul. The referee should use the signal which indicates disregard the flag. (7-5-6b)

Situation: R1 makes an over-the-shoulder catch of a scrimmage kick on the 2-yard line, running full speed in the direction of his own goal line. His momentum carries him into the end zone with the ball. *Ruling:* Since the momentum of R1 carried him into his own end zone, if the ball becomes dead in his possession in the end zone, it will be R's ball at the spot of the catch. This would also be true if the ball goes out-of-bounds behind the goal line after R1's momentum carried him there and he was last in possession of the ball. (8-5-2a Exception)

Situation: With 4th and 3 from his own 10-yard line, the scrimmage kick by K1 is blocked so it rebounds into the end zone and: (a) is muffed out-of-bounds in the end zone by either K or R; or (b) is simultaneously recovered in the end zone by K2 and R1. *Ruling:* In (a), it is a safety. R will be awarded 2 points and K will put the ball in play by a free kick from its 20-yard line. It is a touchdown for R in (b). (8-2-2; 8-5-2b)

Situation: Wide receiver A1 goes downfield 15 yards, cuts sharply to the outside and stops near the sideline. A pass from A2 is overthrown out-of-bounds as B1 moves up to cover and intentionally drives his helmet into A1 after the ball has gone out-of-bounds. *Ruling:* The use of the helmet to punish is spearing by B1. The penalty is 15 yards from the succeeding spot. If the spearing is flagrant, B1 must be disqualified. (2-29; 9-3-2k)

Comment: Face tackling and spearing are similar but distinctly different fouls. Both are illegal and penalized by 15 yards. The difference between the 2 fouls is one of intent and timing. Spearing is intentionally driving the helmet into a player in an attempt to punish him. It may be committed either by defensive or offensive players. Face tackling is driving the face mask, frontal area or top of the helmet directly into the runner. This can be only a defensive technique. Both tactics are condemned by all who are concerned with the safety of players and the perpetuation of football. (9-3-2k)

Situation: As A1 and B1 unpile following a scrimmage down: (a) A1 strikes B1 with his fist and immediately B1 swings but misses A1; or (b) B1 swings at A1 but makes no contact. *Ruling:* Personal fouls in both (a) and (b). In (a), the fouls will be administered in the order they occurred and A1 will be disqualified. (9-3-1; 9-4-1f)

Situation: Following the 2nd unsportsmanlike foul by the coach of Team B, the referee notifies him that he may no longer remain in the vicinity of the playing field and that he may not have any contact with his players, either direct or indirect, throughout the remainder of the game. The coach adjourns to the: (a) grandstand; or (b) press box; or (c) the team locker room. *Ruling:* Illegal in (a) and (b). Legal in (c). (9-7-1 Penalty)

Situation: With 1st and 10 from A's 40, A1 advances to B's 40 where he fumbles. A2 recovers and advances to B's 10 where he is at B's 38, and, during the advance by A2, B2 struck A4 at B's 26. *Ruling:* This is a multiple foul and the captain of A may accept either penalty or decline both and accept the result of the play. If A accepts the penalty for the foul by B1, it will be 1st and 10 from B's 25 because the basic spot is the spot of the fumble by A1. If A accepts the penalty for the foul by B2, it would be enforced from the end of the run which is B's 10. This would be the most advantageous to A and would result in 1st and goal from B's 5-yard line. The result of the play would be 1st and goal from B's 10. In any event, B2 will be disqualified. (9-3-1)

Situation: A1 breaks into the clear on his own 40-yard line. B1 and B2 move in to tackle A1. A1 veers into B1 and flagrantly contacts him with his helmet in an attempt to punish his opponent. A1 fumbles after making contact and B2 recovers on the 50-yard line. *Ruling:* Spearing foul on A1. Team B may retain possession by declining the penalty. A1 is disqualified from the game whether the penalty is accepted or declined. Disqualification is a separate procedure not subject to acceptance or declination of the penalty. A disqualified player must always be removed. (2-29; 9-3-2k)

BIBLIOGRAPHY

1. National Federation of State High School Associations. *Football Case Book.* Kansas City, Missouri 1983.
2. National Federation of State High School Associations. *Football Officials Manual.* Kansas City, Missouri 1982 and 1983.
3. National Federation of State High School Associations. *Football Rule Book.* Kansas City, Missouri 1983.
4. National Federation of State High School Associations. *Football Rules—Simplified and Illustrated.* Kansas City, Missouri 1977 and 1982.

6

Soccer

The Game

It has been clearly established that more people play and watch soccer than any other game. World Cup television audiences have been estimated at 500 million. Soccer in the United States is progressing well after several attempts to establish a foothold on the American sports scene. Contributing factors to this phenomenal growth have been the exceptional junior programs for boys and girls and the influence of foreign superstars that include Pele, George Best, Giorgio Chinaglia and Franz Beckenbauer.

The popularity of the game can be attributed to its fitness benefits, low expense requirements, and the adaptability to all body types—the quick, agile and wiry goalkeeper; the fast, aggressive, and proficient shooting forwards; and a defense led by highly conditioned halfbacks with superior ball control skills; and finally, the balance, toughness and patience of the fullbacks. The continuous action, involvement of all players, and limited injuries also add to soccer's attractiveness. Soccer and basketball have many similarities—restrictions on body contact, penalty kicks/free throws, and the movement and positioning of officials.

To sustain the growth of soccer, offficiating must continue to improve. Officiating associations must meet the challenge through exacting rules training and practical field evaluation.

Photo by UPI

Officials and Their Responsibilities

The suggested officiating unit for interscholastic and intercollegiate soccer is the three-person, diagonal system of control. The dual officiating system is still utilized in some leagues at the various levels of play. The use of a single referee is common in international matches and often practiced in the United States to limit expenses. The three-person diagonal and dual systems will be discussed in detail in the mechanics section.

Officials Uniforms and Equipment
The soccer official's shirt should be the solid black international shirt with white cuffs and collar. Black shorts with black footwear and black socks with white top complete the uniform. The whistle should be mounted on the forefinger. The official should also be equipped with a pencil, notebook, yellow and red cards and two watches.

Pre-Game Responsibilities
Officials should plan to arrive 30 minutes prior to game time. This will allow adequate time to check the field markings, goal nets, game ball, and consult with the time-keeper. A meeting with the coaches provides opportunities for introductions and rules coverage. A meeting with the captains for final instructions and the coin flip will precede a meeting with the two squads to clarify rules and to warn teams not to charge the goalkeeper. The official should assume the responsibility for checking the shoe cleats of the players and answer any questions they might have.

Game Responsibilities
The referee makes all the calls, keeps time and has complete control of the game. The referee will start and stop play according to the rules of the game, which include terminating the game in the event of extreme weather conditions, unruly spectators, or any other just cause. When a player is "cautioned", the clock will not be stopped but the coach will be notified. The referee shall enforce the rules and decide any disputed points. His or her duties include disqualifying a player for flagrant fouls or unsportsmanlike conduct, supervising all free-kicks and dropped balls, deciding whether or not a goal has been scored, supervising substitutions, stopping the game when a severe injury occurs, keeping non-players off the field, and deciding when and where ball is out of bounds after conferring with a judge. (9:377)

The referee must signal all fouls. Officials should carry a yellow and red card for purposes of signalling the warning and disqualification of players. When a player is disqualified, his team will play one man short. Finally, the referee must signal the timekeeper for all time-outs and when the clock is to be started again.

Line Judges
If a single referee is used, two judges will be approved by the referee. They will assist the referee by indicating when and where the ball went out-of-bounds. They will indicate where the ball left the field by play by raising a flag and calling out which team is entitled to the throw-in. This must be confirmed by the referee by pointing to the designated throw-in spot. The line judges will also assist the referee in determining whether a corner kick or goal kick should be awarded and whether an attacking player is offsides. It must be noted that a judge's signals are NOT an indication of an award. The final decision must always be made by the referee. The line judges will not have a whistle and must clearly understand their role of assisting the referee.

Ball Holders
The home team should provide ball holders to carry extra game balls and act as retrievers to avoid unnecessary delays during the game. Another option might be to leave an extra ball behind each goal.

Scorers and Timekeeper
Most games are scored and timed by the referee on the field. Time-out will be called and the clock will stop when a serious injury occurs, equipment repair is necessary, or a similar emergency exists. Timeouts vary with leagues. The clock does not stop for fouls.

Basic Penalties and Rulings

In determining fouls, the general rule dictates that the participants must PLAY THE BALL and NOT THE MAN. Deviations from this rule results in such violations as jumping, tripping, pushing, charging, high kicking, etc. It is critical to rule accurately whether a foul is intentional, in order to avoid placing the opponent at a disadvantage and to keep the game under control. To minimize flagrant conduct, a warning system is practiced. A yellow card is flashed by the referee to denote a warning or "caution" and a red card disqualifies the offending player.

SOCCER FIELD

Fig. 6.1 Soccer field. (By courtesy of
the N.F.S.H.S.A.)

Penalties

For purposes of clarification, we will examine only the most critical personal, non-personal and misconduct violations.

Major fouls. Direct free kick with opposing players at least 10 yards from the kicker at the spot of the foul. (A goal may be scored off this kick)

1. Kicking, Striking, Jumping and Tripping
   A player shall be penalized for kicking, striking or attempting to kick or strike an opponents. A player must be penalized for tripping— including throwing or attempting to throw an opponent by the use of the legs, or by low-bridging an opponent causing a fall or loss of control. The use of the knee in any way against an opponent is also a foul.
2. Holding and Pushing
   A player shall be penalized for holding or pushing an opponent with the hand(s) or with the arm(s) extended from the body and for impeding a player with the hand or any part of the arm extended from the body. Under no circumstances is a player permitted to push an opponent. (7:30)
3. Charging Illegally
   A player shall be penalized for charging into an opponent in a violent or dangerous manner.

Minor fouls. Indirect free kick with opposing players at least 10 yards from the kicker at the spot of the foul. (A goal may not be scored off this kick until another player touches the ball.)

1. Obstruction
   This is a non-contact intentional foul where a player not in possession of the ball or not attempting to play the ball, runs between the opponent and the ball, using the body as an obstacle.
2. Dangerous Play
   Dangerous play is defined as play of such a nature as to be likely to cause injury. Three common types of dangerous plays are high kicking, double-kicking ad lowering the head.
3. Misconduct
   Misconduct generally involves acts of unsportsmanlike play or constantly objecting to the referee's calls.

Penalty Kick. Direct free kick from the 12 yard penalty line awarded for a major foul committed by the defensive team in the penalty area. (A goal may be scored off this kick.) All other players must stand outside penalty box.

It should be noted that the ball must be kicked forward and the kicker cannot touch the ball again until another player touches or plays the ball.

Rulings

Kick-off. The game shall be started by a kick-off. The visiting captain shall choose one of the following two options and the home team has the remaining option.

1. To choose whether his or her team will kick-off or go on defense
2. To choose the goal that his or her team will defend

Substitutions. Substitutes may enter the game on dead ball situations. If there is not a scorer, the player should request substitution to the referee. The player shall remain outside the boundary line until the referee beckons to have the player enter the game. The basic substitution rule and substitution rules for injured players varies widely within the various soccer associations.

The drop ball. The ball is put in play by being dropped by the referee between two opponents. The best example might be a ball kicked out of bounds simultaneously by the opponent.

Ball in and out of play. The ball is out of play only when it has crossed completely over the goal or sideline on the ground or in the air and when play has been stopped by the referee.

Scoring. A goal is scored when the whole of the ball passes over the end line, between the goal posts and under the crossbar. This is the only means of scoring in soccer. One point is scored for a successful penalty kick from the penalty line or a successful kick from the field of play.

Handling. A player shall be penalized for intentionally handling the ball or touching the ball from shoulder to fingertips. Unintentionally handling the ball should not be penalized, but this varies with ruling associations.

Throw-in. A throw-in is performed by the player opposite the player who last touched the ball at the spot where the whole ball crossed the touch line. The ball must be delivered with both feet touching the ground on or behind the touch line. The release must be made with equal strength in both hands overhead.

Goal kick. A free kick made by the defending team from the goal area as a result of the attacking team causing the ball to go over the end line.

Corner kick. A Kick-in made by the attacking team from the corner arc on the opponents' end of the field. A corner kick is the result of the defending team last touching a ball crossing the end line.

Tie breaking procedure. The team that wins the penalty-kick tie breaker shall be declared the winner and credited with a one goal victory in the final score. (6:31)

Mechanics

The comparative size of the soccer field and the nature of the game challenges the conditioning of officials. By comparison, one, two or three soccer officials are responsible for field coverage up to 81,000 square feet while three to six football officials are responsible for field coverage of 57,600 square feet, including end zones.

The Diagonal System of Control

The most commonly used officiating system is referred to as the diagonal system. It is estimated that a referee working with two line judges may run from 6-8 miles per game. This system guarantees good calls on out of bounds, offsides, goal kicks, goal scoring and plays in the corners.

Diagram 1
The imaginary diagonal used by the Referee is the line A-B.

The opposite diagonal used by the Linesmen is adjusted to the position of the Referee; if the Referee is near A, Linesman L2 will be at a point between M and K. When the Referee is at B, Linesman L1 will be between E and F; this gives two officials control of the respective "danger zones", one at each side of the field.

Linesman L1 adopts the *Reds* as his side; Linesman L2 adopts the *Blues;* as *Red* forwards move toward Blue goal, Linesman L1 keeps in line with second last *Blue* defender so in actual practice he will rarely get into Red's half of the field. Similarly Linesman L2 keeps in line with second last *Red* defender, and will rarely get into Blue's half.

Diagram 1

Fig. 6.2 The relative positions of the
lead and trail officials for specific
game situations are as diagramed.
(Permission has been authorized
exceptionally by FIFA and is taken
from the FIFA publication *Laws of the
Game and Universal Guide for
Referees.*)

At corner-kicks or penalty-kicks the Linesman in that half where
the corner-kick or penalty-kick occurs positions himself at N and the
Referee takes position (see Diagram 4—corner-kick; Diagram 9—
penalty-kick).

The diagonal system fails if Linesman L2 gets between G and H
when Referee is at B, or when Linesman L1 is near C or D when the
Referee is at A, because there are *two* officials at the same place. This
should be avoided.

Diagram 2. Start of Game
Position of Referee at Kick-off—R. Position of Linesmen—L1 and L2: in
position with second last defender Players—O and ■. Diagonal followed
by Referee A-B. Referee moves to diagonal along line → according to
direction of attack. Ball-•.

Diagram 2

Diagram 4

Diagram 6

Diagram 9

Fig. 6.3 (Permission has been
authorized exceptionally by FIFA and
is taken from the FIFA publication
*Laws of the Game and Universal Guide
for Referees.*)

Diagram 4. Corner-Kick

Positions of officials the same no matter at which corner-area the kick is taken.

Referee (R) along line shown.

Linesman (L2)—in accordance with the instructions from the Referee the Linesman (L2) shall be near the corner flag or on the goal-line near the corner flag, to observe whether the ball is properly played; whether the opposing players are at proper distance (10 yards), whether the ball is behind the goal-line, or whether incidents have happened possibly hidden from the Referee.

Linesman (L1) in position for clearance and possible counter-attack.

Diagram 6. Goal-Kick

Referee (R) in midfield adjacent to central point of diagonal.

Linesman (L1) exercising watch over goal-kick, positioned in line with the penalty-area.

Linesman (L2) in position in line with second last defender pending a possible attack by side taking goal-kick.

Diagram 9. Penalty-Kick

Players O and ■ with the exception of the goalkeeper and kicker are shown outside the penalty-area and at least 10 yards from the ball—goalkeeper on goal-line.

Referee (R) is in position to see that kick is properly taken and that no encroachment takes place.

Linesman (L2) watches goalkeeper to see that he does not advance illegally and also acts as goal judge.

Linesman (L1) is in position should the goalkeeper save a goal and start a counter-attack.

Two Official System

The lead and trail method of field coverage is also effective. Depending on the position of the ball referees move up and down the sidelines to afford maximum coverage. The relative positions of the lead and trail officials for specific game situations are as diagramed.

Fig. 6.4 General field coverage.

The relative positions of the lead and trail officials for specific game situations are as diagramed.

Fig. 6.5 Positioning of lead and trail officials.

Hand Signals

Hand signals are the simple gestures used by the referee to indicate the foul and to point out the direction of play. The most common calls are as follows:

1. Throw-in: signal 2 hands overhead in throwing position and call out color
2. Corner kick: arm extended pointing toward corner
3. Advantage clause: opened hands, upward sweeping motion of the arms (no call on possible close call or violation to indicate debatable situation where offense might be placed at a disadvantage if called)
4. Direct kick: single forward underarm swing pointing to the direction of the kick
5. Indirect kick: single raised arm with palm open in a forward direction

Problem Calls

It should be noted that as players tire, fouls increase requiring even greater concentration by the officials.

Advantage Clause

Officials must guard against this violation by the defense wherein the offensive player breaks to the goal to gain the advantage, only to be fouled to offset that advantage. The infraction generally occurs when the offense is on attack. An example of such a situation would be intentionally holding an opponent from the rear in his or her solo move on the goalkeeper. The essence of the rule is to note the violation by the offending team without giving them any advantage by stopping the play immediately. The foul should be indicated by hand signal and by calling out "advantage" or "play on." In addition to the foul call, the referee will issue a warning by flashing a yellow card.

Playing the Ball

Often it is difficult to determine whether a player is legitimately playing the ball and not the opposing player. In the heat of the contest, this judgment call may be of great consequence to the outcome of the contest. For example, charging is an illegal action of a player who violently contacts an opponent from a dangerous angle; or while the opponent is off-balance or is not near the ball; or, through the use of the hip or in any manner designed to prevent the opponent from reaching the ball. Pushing off is a very common infraction in "heading" plays in congested areas. A player must not use his or her hands or arms either to hold an opponent back or push him or her away from the ball. The violation often occurs when the arms of the players become interlocked and the referee must be watchful for such infringements which may appear "accidental." (8:29)

Fig. 6.6 By courtesy of the N.C.A.A.)

Off-Sides

The off-side rule was introduced to prevent uninteresting plays and methods of attack. The purpose of the game is to score but, if a player or players are allowed to wait in front of the opponent's goal without restrictions, the game becomes dull. Since the off-sides rule provides for technical features of the game, it must be thoroughly understood, because when it is broken, attack stops immediately. (2:16)

An offensive player is off-sides when:

1. There are not two defenders between himself or herself and the opponents goal-line at the time the ball is played to him or her; and
2. Her or she is in his or her opponents' half of the field; and
3. The ball was last touched by a teammate; or
4. He or she is ahead of the ball when it was played to him or her. (3:12)

It is the position of the receiving player *when the ball was kicked* and not the position where he or she receives the ball that determines whether or not the receiver is offsides. A player in an off-side position shall not be penalized unless, in the opinion of the referee, he or she is interfering with the play or with an opponent, or is seeking to gain an advantage by being in an off-side position. (4:14) The most common off-sides infraction occurs when there is a clear pass to a teammate who has assumed a position inside the second defender illustrated by the following:

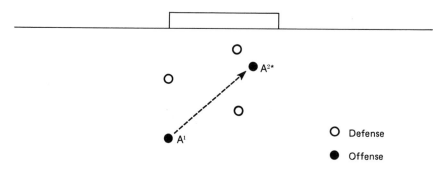

Fig. 6.7 Off-sides.
*A^2 is not off-sides until the ball is played by A^1 to A^2

It must be reiterated that an offensive player assuming this position, but not receiving the ball, does not constitute off-sides. This is illustrated as follows:

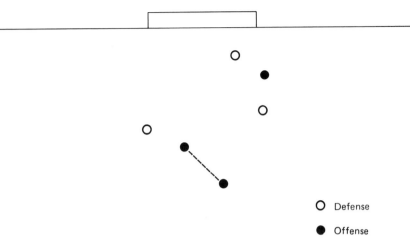

Fig. 6.8 Not off-sides.

Collision with the Goalkeeper

Whether the ball is loose or not, the goalkeeper may not be charged. "Blindsiding" the goalkeeper may result in serious injury to this key player. Both Federation and NCAA rules classify this as a dangerous play which will result in removal without warning of offending player who intentionally charges the goalkeeper in a possession of the ball. Incidental contact with the goalkeeper not affecting play should be ignored.

Miscellaneous Considerations

The referee must stay alert at all times as many soccer games are close and errors of omission can be consequential. An over-relaxed pattern of officiating in soccer can create these omissions. Other game concerns include substitutions and unnecessary conversation between opponents.

Delays on substitutions with the clock running can be used as a stalling tactic. Officials must be alert to offset this unfair advantage to the offending team.

There is considerable conversation between opponents during the course of a game. These "words" often create friction and may lead to complications late in the game. The referee may suggest that the coaches get together during a time-out or at halftime to rectify the situation before it has become aggravated. This is an effective means of resolving this problem as players tire near the end of the game and become more irritable. Talk between two opponents must be kept to a minimum by the appeal of the referee.

Officiating Evaluated by Coaches

What qualities do you appreciate in a soccer official?

1. Thorough knowledge of the rules with proper interpretations and intent
2. Punctuality
3. Consistency
4. Decisiveness
5. Always moving to get in the best possible position
6. Keeping the game under control

Miscellaneous Comments

1. Need for standard rules
2. Need for properly trained officials critical to game's success in the United States

Officiating Evaluated by Officials

What is the most difficult play to call in soccer?

1. Offside
2. Scoring
3. Advantage clause

What is the most difficult phase of mechanics in officiating soccer?

1. Position to make off-sides call
2. In a two official system, foul in partner's area when he or she is blocked out
3. Judging goal kick vs. corner kick on offensive side of the field in the dual system
4. Actually seeing the ball cross the line for a score when the goalkeeper has possession of the ball

Miscellaneous Comments

1. The discipline of the coach has a strong bearing on the behavior of the players. He will leave the discipline of the players to the referee.
2. A team official is one who would rather "miss a call" than give a partner poor trail coverage.

3. Total dedication to the officiating team working for the love of the game, not for the money.
4. Officials should take criticism without feeling personally maligned.
5. The game should be conducted with as little interference as possible. Constant whistling for questionable violations has a tendency to upset players, coaches and fans and cause the game to deteriorate.

Constructive Hints Summarized for Soccer Officials

- Control the game and be the boss. Show the players you mean what you say at all times.
- Know the rules, but don't be too technical.
- Be on top of all the plays. That's the only way the correct calls can be made.
- Don't anticipate or guess on any calls. If you are not in a position to see fouls plainly, and if there is any doubt in your mind whether they are fouls, don't call them.
- Every game is important to the player; he deserves a fairly officiated game.
- Never second guess your partner. When he calls a play, that's just what it is. (Discuss problems at halftime and after the game.)
- Make your decisions when at a dead stop. An official frequently loses his or her poise when calling and talking on the run.
- Never turn your head until the play is completed.
- Look directly at the offending player when you call a penalty on someone.
- Call your own plays. Never let the coaches or players call them for you.
- Never criticize any official. There will be days when you can't miss and there will be days when you can't seem to call them right.
- A smile and a pleasant manner will go a long way toward your success anywhere at any time.
- Do not let your voice or your tone be antagonistic.
- When the game is over, go up to your fellow official and walk off the field together. (5:6)

Play Rulings (7)

Situation: Team A arrives for the scheduled game to find that the scorers' and timers' table will be operating but no provision has been made to have both teams located on the same side of the field. *Ruling:* When a scorer and timer are used, both teams shall be on the same side of the field to facilitate substitution. (1-5-1)

Situation: The game ball is not satisfactory to the visiting team. The head referee's decision to use the visiting team's balls is protested by the home team. *Ruling:* The head referee shall choose 3 or more balls from those of both teams. (2-1-1)

Situation: The goalie goes down after making a save and remains motionless for a few seconds with the ball in his possession. *Ruling:* The official may stop play to determine if the goalie is injured. If after examining the goalie, it is determined that the goalie is able to continue play immediately and no attendants have come on the field, replacement is not mandatory and play will start with an indirect free kick. (3-3-3)

Situation: A1 is discovered wearing illegal equipment during the game. The referee removes A1 from the field with instructions to correct the equipment. After the equipment has been corrected, A1 attempts to reenter when Team B has possession of a throw-in. *Ruling:* A1 may reenter, but no substitutions may be made by Team A. If Team A had possession prior to the throw-in or the ball had gone over the goal line, A1 could reenter or the coach of A could substitute a new player. (3-3-4)

Situation: Player A1 is on the attack with the ball under control when fouled by B1. The ball moves sideways to player A2 who controls the ball immediately. *Ruling:* The official shall immediately either call the foul or signal "Play On," to indicate the foul was observed, but will not penalize Team B because to do so would give an advantage to the offending team, Team B. (5-3-1)

Situation: A penalty kick has been awarded as time expires. The penalty kick is taken but is deflected by the goalkeeper and is shot back into the goal by a member of the kicking team. *Ruling:* No goal. When the ball is contacted by any player other than the goalkeeper after the penalty is taken, the ball immediately becomes dead because time has expired. (14-1-5) (7-1-4)

Situation: B1 moves over the halfway line prior to the kickoff. *Ruling:* The official shall verbally warn the player and play is restarted. A caution may be given if the action is repeated. (12-8-1) (8-1-2)

Situation: The ball is in the area of the field as follows: *Ruling:* In (a), the ball is out-of-bounds; in (b) and (c), the ball is still in play. A ball on any part of a line is considered to be on the playing field. (9-1-1)

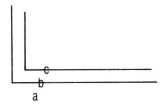

Situation: Player A shoots on the goal line and the: (a) ball rolls along the goal line; (b) goalkeeper, in front of the goal, fists the ball out into the field of play; (c) ball goes through the goalkeeper's hands into the net. *Ruling:* In (a) and (b), no goal, in (c), goal. (10-1-2)

Situation: A defender on Team B, with the goalkeeper out of position, heads the ball out, but in doing so falls into the goal. A2 gets the ball and passes it to A1 who has only the goalkeeper to beat. *Ruling:* The defender on Team B left the field during the normal movement of play, and since no advantage is gained, A1 is not offside. (11-1-2)

Situation: A1, who is in the air to head the ball, is approached by B1. (a) B1 goes up to head the ball simultaneously with A1; (b) B1 contacts A1 while A1 is in the air and B1 has both feet on the ground. *Ruling:* (a) Legal; (b) Illegal. Direct free kick. (12-4-2)

Situation: A1 takes a corner kick, which hits the goalpost and rebounds. A1 plays it again before it has been touched by another player. *Ruling:* Illegal: indirect free kick. (17-1-5) (13-3-2)

Situation: Extra time is allowed for a penalty kick to be taken. The goalkeeper deflects the ball to the goalpost, from which it rolls into the goal. *Ruling:* Goal, only the goalkeeper has played the ball and its hitting the post is incidental to the scoring of the goal. (14-1-6)

Situation: During the throw-in, the following happens: (a) A1 lifts the back foot from the ground while throwing the ball; (b) A1 takes a run up to the touchline and releases the ball with both feet on the ground; (c) A1 has one foot off the playing field and one foot on the touchline during the throw-in; (d) A1 throws to a teammate only 3 feet away. *Ruling:* (a) Illegal, award a throw-in to Team B; (b) Legal; (c) Illegal because the feet must be outside the field of play; (d) Legal. (15-1-3)

Situation: The placing of the ball for a corner kick is: *Ruling:* **(a) and (b) illegal; (c) and (d) legal. (17-1-3)**

a.

b.
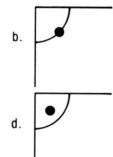

c.

d.

SOUTHERN CALIFORNIA SOCCER OFFICIALS ASSOCIATION

1976-1977 COACHES' EVALUATION OF REFEREES

GAME: .... (   ) vs. .... (   )

DATE: .... PLAYED AT ....

Name of Official	Preferred	Good	Satisfactory	Fair	Unsatisfactory
A.					
B.					

EXPLANATIONS ARE **REQUIRED** ON ALL UNSATISFACTORY RATINGS.

Please rate each referee below using the following scale:

  1—Outstanding   2—Satisfactory   3—Needs Improvement

A   B   **A   B**

.... Personal Appearance   .... Application of Advtantage

.... Physical Condition   Clause

.... Knowledge of Rules   .... Clarity of Signals

.... Ability to Keep up with   .... Decisiveness

         Play   .... Impartiality

.... Understanding with Other   .... Attitude toward Players

         Referee   .... Punctuality

CONSTRUCTIVE COMMENTS: _____

_____

_____

_____

_____

_____

Note: These reports will be used in the overall grading of referees, and it is important that they be RATED FAIRLY WITHOUT PREJUDICE, win or lose. Please mail reports back PROMPTLY.

PLEASE COMPLETE AND RETURN TO: SIGNED: ....

  SCSOA—Referee Reports   TITLE: ....
  531 11th Street
  Santa Monica, CA 90402   SCHOOL: ....

By Courtesy of the Southern California Soccer Officials Association.

BIBLIOGRAPHY

1. *FIFA Laws of the Game and Universal Guide for Referees with USSF Supplement.* New York: United States Soccer Federation, 1977.
2. *Illustrated Soccer Rules Guide.* Chicago: United States Soccer Federation, 1974. (By courtesy of D. J. Niotis)
3. Los Angeles Toros. *This is Soccer.* Atlanta: General Lithographing Company, 1967.
4. Matthews, Dave, Ben McGuire and Jim Peterson, *Officials Manual: Soccer.* Champaign: Stipes Publishing Company, 1972.
5. *NCAA Men's Soccer Rules.* Mission, Kansas: National Collegiate Athletic Association, 1983.
6. Soccer Rules. Kansas City: National Federation of State High School Associations, 1983.
7. Wade, Allen. *Association Football,* London: Educational Productions Publishing Company, 1970.
8. White, Jess R. *Sports Rules Encyclopedia.* Palo Alto: The National Press, 1966.

7

Swimming

The Game

The advent of increased numbers of pools in schools and private homes, coupled with Olympic attention to the sport, has enhanced the prominance of swimming in the world. Few other sports afford such a wide diversification of events for so many contestants.

Much the same as in track and wrestling, the swimming official rules on the athlete's physical technique in the performance of an event. Improper stroke technique should disqualify the contestant. The starter may have the inclusive responsibilities of judging the start, stroke and finish.

The official should realize that serious competitive swimmers and their coaches are highly dedicated. This is evidenced by swimmer's commitments to long hours of practice for nine to ten months per year during a good portion of their youth. Even the youngest competitors seem to realize that whatever success they may earn depends directly on the work and effort they put into it. Regardless of whether the swimmer is of novice or Olympics caliber, the goals and rewards remain largely personal. (1:21) Consequently, these swimmers deserve a dedicated effort on the part of the officials.

There is a great need for competent officials. Officiating in swimming has been and is primarily conducted by coaches, former swimmers and parents of swimmers. The quality and quantity of officials required demands that new "students" of swimming be developed to meet the needs of the sport.

Photo by Bob Coyle

Officials and Their Responsibilities

The most common working unit is composed of a paid starter/referee supported by a corps of volunteer officials. Since many swimming officials have little or no competitive swimming or diving background, it is imperative that either a rules clinic and/or extensive pre-meet officials meetings be conducted to assure competent officiating. It may be necessary to assign more than one responsibility per event to each official in a dual meet. In a championship meet, there should be only one assignment for a given event.

White clothing is recommended. This includes white slacks or shorts, shirt and tennis shoes.

Meet Manager

The organizational and administrative details are the responsibility of the meet manager and are generally assumed by the host assistant coach in dual meets. In championship meets, this assignment is generally the function of the athletic director. He or she typically delegates it to the host swimming coach. A meet manager does not serve as an active official. Many schools now employ a meet manager with a computer for printouts in championship meets.

Referee

The referee has complete jurisdiction over the meet. This official must enforce the rules and assume the responsibility for making all official assignments. The referee has the responsibility and authority to expedite the meet by assuring a minimum of delays.

Before the meet the referee shall:

1. See that all equipment necessary for the proper conduct of the meet is in the proper place and condition.
2. See that the pool is properly marked.
3. Assign officials to particular duties, reviewing with them the positions and responsibilities of each; and
4. Before championship meets, conduct a pre-meet conference with the starter and a captain from each team to review meet procedures and special instructions (4:12)

During the meet the referee shall:

1. Meet with the swimmers prior to each race to review lane assignments and starting instructions.
2. Check that each swimmer takes the proper lane, and signal the starter with a whistle that the starting commands may begin.

3. See that the meet progresses rapidly and that the results are announced properly; and

4. Assure that all competition is conducted according to rule. (4:13)

Starter

The starter has control over the contestants after they have been assigned to him or her by the referee. Before starting each heat, the starter must explain to each competitor:

1. The signal which is to be given to start the race.
2. The distance to be covered and where the race will terminate.
3. Stroke requirements; and
4. If necessary, call for "quiet at the start" (6:446)

In distance events, the starter shall signal by pistol when the leading swimmer has two lengths remaining.

Stroke Inspectors and Turn Judges

In championship meets, inspectors will be positioned on either side of the pool, dividing the responsibility for half the lanes, in order to observe the strokes of the competitors. Turn judges shall rule on proper turn techniques. It is common to have the same officials performing both duties. Violations in stroke or turn should be indicated by the official immediately raising his or her hand overhead with open palm. In dual meets, this responsibility is assumed by the starter.

Take-off Judges

A take-off judge is assigned to each relay team for the purpose of judging whether the second, third or fourth swimmers are still in contact with the starting mark when his or her teammate touches the end of the pool. A violation should be indicated by raising a hand when the last competitor is on the final length of the race.

Lane Judges and Timers

When automatic judging and timing equipment* is available, the results shown by such equipment will be considered primary and official. In case of malfunction, secondary information from a semi-automatic timing and judging device with one or more officials per lane or the prescribed

*Automatic Judging and Timing Equipment. A completely automatic device is one which automatically starts with the starter's pistol and stops when a contestant touches the finish pad. A semi-automatic timing device automatically or manually starts with the starter's pistol and stops when the lane judge presses a button when the swimmer in that lane finishes. Timing equipment must not interfere with the swimmer's starts, turns, or the function of the pool overflow system. (5:15)

ballot system should be used. **If neither the ballot system (see Judging on page 172) or automatic timing and/or judging device is used, judges are designated to pick the first three places. In championship finals, two lane judges and three timers should be assigned to each lane.** Many automatic timing systems are not sensitive on all surfaces. Consequently, a hand may break the finish plane but not touch the finish pad. This necessitates backup watches on each lane in championship meets. Three timers are assigned to each lane. In dual meets, three watches are assigned to each of the four middle lanes.

Clerk of the Course

The referee's most important aide is the clerk of the course. The clerk should check each swimmer into his or her assigned lane. The effectiveness of the clerk of the course will determine how well a meet will run. The clerk should make arrangements to have the name of each contestant announced before the event, in time to enable the swimmer to get to the proper lane at the desired time in a relaxed manner. (3:38) In relays and championships, it may be advantageous to provide chairs for succeeding heats to avoid delays.

Diving Judges

For dual meets, a minimum of three judges will evaluate each dive. The meet referee will serve as one judge. The home team is required to supply three judges if the visiting team does not exercise its option to supply one judge. Championship meets require a minimum of five judges. It is imperative that the judges assume a position that will afford them a profile view of the diver.

Scorer

In general practice this administrative responsibility is a function of the host school or club, regardless of the level of competition. The scorer is responsible for recording and scoring the meet. The referee should insist on an intelligent scorer for prompt, accurate and immediate posting of running scores. In dual meets, the referee also serves as scorer.

MEET SCORING

	Dual Meet	Championship Meet *
Individual Events	5-3-1-0	7-5-4-3-2-1
Relays	7-0	14-10-8-6-4-2-1

*When six swimmers qualify for the finals (college)

Announcer
The referee will assign the announcer, who usually doubles as clerk of the course, will announce each event, the swimmer in each lane, the results of each race, and the running score. If time permits, the pool and conference records in that event should also be announced. The team manager of the home team often serves as the announcer. For championship meets, the clerk and announcer responsibility should be filled by two officials. The announcer must keep the meet moving and interesting, which can contribute to the success of the meet.

Runners
To coordinate the immediate scoring of each event, runners carry the results recorded by judges and timers to the scoring table. This function is usually performed by students or non-competitors delegated by the team manager.

VARSITY SWIMMING

State University of
New York at Buffalo   vs.

Event	Contestants	Place	Score	Contestants	Place	Score	Time
400 yd. Medley Relay	1. ..... 2. ..... 3. ..... 4.			1. ..... 2. ..... 3. ..... 4.			
1000 yd. Free-style	1. ..... 2.			1. ..... 2.			
200 yd. Free-style	1. ..... 2.			1. ..... 2.			
50 yd. Free-style	1. ..... 2.			1. ..... 2.			
200 yd. Indiv. Medley	1. ..... 2.			1. ..... 2.			
1-meter Diving	1. ..... 2.			1. ..... 2.			
200 yd. Butter-fly	1. ..... 2.			1. ..... 2.			
100 yd. Free-style	1. ..... 2.			1. ..... 2.			
200 yd. Back-stroke	1. ..... 2.			1. ..... 2.			
500 yd. Free-style	1. ..... 2.			1. ..... 2.			
200 yd. Breast-stroke	1. ..... 2.			1. ..... 2.			
3-meter Diving	1. ..... 2.			1. ..... 2.			
400 yd. Free-style Relay	1. ..... 2. ..... 3. ..... 4.			1. ..... 2. ..... 3. ..... 4.			

Final Score   ....
Held at .... Date .... Referee ....

Fig. 7.1 Score sheet for
intercollegiate dual meet. (3:56)

Basic Penalties and Rulings

Fouls

1. Interference will result in the disqualification of the contestant who interferes with another swimmer. The race may also be ordered swum over if conditions were unfair. (e.g. lane line breaks apart).
2. Unsportsmanlike conduct will be penalized by the referee (disqualification).

Stroke Requirements

Freestyle. Freestyle events allow the greatest freedom because any stroke or combination of strokes may be used. Any part of the body may touch the wall in executing a turn, while the finish may be made by touching the wall with either hand or head.

Breaststroke. The breaststroke event calls for the swimmer to remain on the surface with a portion of the head above the water *except after the final arm pull prior to a turn and at the finish.* The International (FJNA) rulebook states that the breaststroke must be swum in a manner such that the arms move symmetrically and underneath the water, that the shoulders and arms lie in the same plane, and that the legs kick symmetrically and on the same plane in a "frog" or orthodox kick. (1:37)

Butterfly. In the butterfly, the hands must be recovered and brought forward out of the water. The undulation of the legs and feet in the kick call for simultaneous and symmetrical movements, as in a flutter kick. The touch is the same as that for the breaststroke. Infractions are most commonly called for breaking the legs apart in the dolphin kick.

Backstroke. This stroke must be executed on the back, including the touches. A hand touch is required at each turn and the swimmer's hips may not turn over beyond the vertical before the lead hand has touched the end of the pool.

The penalty for improper stroke technique is disqualification from the given event.

Entry Penalty
A male contestant may not swim more than three events including relays in collegiate dual meets, and three events, no more than two of which are individual events, in interscholastic competition. College women may

swim in four events, no more than three of which may be individual events in dual competition. A violation of this rule results in disqualification from the event in question and from further participation in the meet.

Mechanics

In the congested area of the pool deck, mechanics become especially important. All officials must confine themselves to their respective working areas. The starter must keep the sides of the pool clear for officials observing strokes, turns, take-offs and finishes. If possible, elevated stands should be situated on both sides of the finish to provide an unobstructed view for the judges. Dual meet timers should assume a position on either side of the finish to determine first place. Championship meet timers should be placed directly over their lanes at the finish. Finishes of many swimming races, especially in the shorter distances are decided by inches. It is therefore necessary to work continually for the best possible position in order to view the finish. In many pools it is advisable to have the area around the starting blocks and in the proximity of the scoring table roped off and restricted to officials only. Bright colored caps are recommended as a means of identifying the officials.

Starting Procedure

The starter should come equipped with a .22 caliber starting gun for indoor meets or a .38 caliber starting gun for outdoor meets. He or she should also have a second gun or a whistle for recalls.

This official must strive for an equitable start for all competitors, or a position where the heads and backs and feet of all swimmers can be viewed to determine whether they are steady on the mark. The starting sequence is as follows:

1. Sound whistle to alert timers and judges.
2. Command "take your marks".
3. Pistol shot or beeper if all swimmers are steady (no movement).
4. Second pistol shot or whistle if false start.
5. Signal to have the recall rope dropped to stop the swimmers; and
6. Restart race.

An experienced starter will repeat the command "quiet at the start" if there is undue noise and/or confusion before a race. The pistol should be cocked to reduce the chance of swimmers anticipating the starting

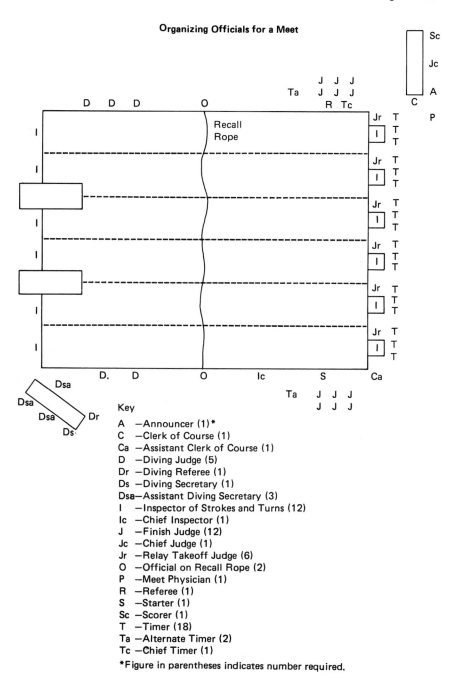

Fig. 7.2 Organization chart for
championship meet. (3:45)

gun. Furthermore, the starter should neither move the arm when firing the gun nor change facial expression. Finally, it is advisable to alter the timing of both the command "take your marks" and the pause between the command and the pistol shot. Veteran starters recommend dropping the inflection on the word "marks" and pausing at least one second between the command and the pistol shot.

Timing

Each watch should be tested prior to the race to determine its reliability. This can be accomplished by starting watches simultaneously by pressing the stems together to start and stop. Watches can also be checked by firing the gun to start and stop the watches. Watches off .2 seconds for the duration of the shortest race should not be used. A timer should familiarize himself or herself with the watch by taking the slack out at the stem, starting, stopping and resetting the watch. To avoid damage to the watches, the referee should prewind all watches and inform timers that this has been done. Cords for wearing the watches around the neck should be provided. Timers should be reminded to clear their watches before each race. This should be executed at the command of the head timer when he or she receives the ready signal from the starter. Each timer must take the slack out at

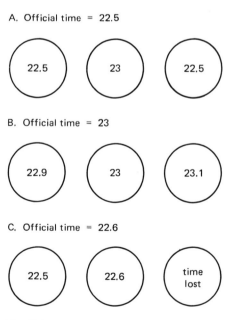

Fig. 7.3

LANE NO. ....   VALUE ....
        OFFICIAL TIME ....
EVENT ....
HEAT NO. ....
SWIMMER ....
TEAM ....
TIMERS ....
TIMERS ....
TIMERS ....
ALTERNATE ....
HEAD TIMER ....

Fig. 7.4 Timer's slip. (3:58)

the stem of the watch in preparation for the start, start the watch at the flash of the gun, take the slack out again as the swimmers approach the finish and stop the watch when the swimmer strikes or crosses the line of finish. The index finger is faster than the thumb and its use is recommended. How precisely the watch is started and stopped may determine whether the swimmer will place. when three watches are utilized, the official time is determined as follows:

Watches should be held horizontally and read vertically with the stem at a 12 o'clock position. It a watch's demarcation lines are faint, use a magnifying glass for accuracy. Following a race, *watches should not be cleared until the head timer has had the opportunity to verify and record an official time.* Timers must be prepared to get wet as they should be positioned low and directly over or to the side of the starting block to closely observe the touch of the swimmer.

Other suggestions for improved timing include:

1. Checking the watch after the start to assure that it is functioning (if not, notify the head timer who will designate an alternative timer).
2. Avoiding unnecessary movement of the arm or hand when starting and stopping the watch to assure accuracy.
3. Not being fooled by a false finish (lunge, headlift etc); and
4. If the hand is not centered on a tenth-second mark, reading it at the next highest or slower tenth.

Judging
In dual meets, a minimum of two judges should pick first place and one each for second and third places. If there is disagreement among the

LANE NO. .... PLACE ....
EVENT   ....
HEAT NO. ....
SWIMMER ....
TEAM   ....
JUDGE   ....

Fig. 7.5 Judge's slip. (3:58)

judges, the chief finish judge must follow numerical order. For example, if first and second place judges both select contestant A, the decision of the first place judge is final.

In championship meets, two judges are assigned to each lane. Positioned on opposite sides of the finish, each judge independently determines for the assignd lane where that contestant in the lane finished and records it on a card color coded for the given lane.

When three timers are assigned for each lane, they should be placed directly over their assigned lane at the finish. The official time will then be recorded on the coded card for the lane in question. Color coded numbered paddles will be utilized by judges to indicate the finish position of the lane assigned. The head timer will then record both time and place results for each lane.

Relay Take-off Judging
The method of judging relay take-offs is performed manually by the judge assuming a position on the right side of the swimmer allowing the judge to place the little finger of the left hand in light contact with the largest toe of the next swimmer. The take-off judge should concentrate on observing the touch of the incoming swimmer. If there is a "break" before the incoming swimmer touches, the judge's hand should be raised overhead to indicate the violation. When automatic equipment is used, back-up decisions are based on visual judgment.

Dive Judging
Preferably, one or more of the diving judges should have diving experience. If this is not the case, the judges of the dive must take it upon themselves to study the scoring procedures diligently. Each dive is categorized by a predetermined degree of difficulty. Points are awarded from zero to ten.

DIVING SCORING

Very Good 8.5-10
Good 6.5- 8
Satisfactory 5.0- 6.0
Deficient 2.5- 4.5
Unsatisfactory 0.5- 2.0
Completely Failed   0

Fig. 7.6

INTERSCHOLASTIC CHAMPIONSHIP DIVING

NAME ....   PLACE ....

DIVING

TEAM .... ORDER .... FINAL SCORE ....

Dive No.	Dive	Position	D. of Diff.	Judges' Awards 1 2 3 4 5	Total Award	Score
101	Forward Dive					⊠
5111	Forward Dive 1/2 Twist					
						⊠

Preliminary Total

201	Back Dive					⊠
401	Inward Dive					⊠

Semi-finals Total

301	Reverse Dive					⊠

(Diver's Signature)

Fig. 7.7 Diving score sheet for
interscholastic championship meet.
(3:57)

The judges must consider the starting position, approach, hurdle, take-off, execution and entry. Attention should be directed to the position announced for the dive-layout, pike or tuck. Judges must be able to discern whether the diver has taken a minimum of three steps and has executed the dive in the air, not on the board. After each dive, the whistle is sounded by the diving referee. The judges simultaneously flash their scoring awards using flip-type score-books. After all scores have been announced, the judges should close their scorebooks in preparation for the next dive. The score is computed by multiplying the total score of the judges by the degree of difficulty.

Diving judges must continually guard against being swayed by mediocre dives with exceptional entries and against being overly concerned about "staying together" in awarding scores.

Problem Calls

Close Finishes

Judges must secure an advantageous station along the finish in order to render a sound decision. An attempt should be made just before the finish to narrow down the field of swimmers contesting for the place being judged. The common problems of lunging, splashing and underwater touches emphasizes the need for electronic devices, especially in the freestyle and backstroke finishes. Unfortunately, many coaches encourage their swimmers to raise their heads and make a splash prior to touching the wall in a close race.

Rolling Starts

A legal start requires all contestants to attain their starting positions, remain motionless and wait for the starting gun. The starter should insist that swimmers assume the preferred position without delay. A rolling start is one where the swimmers persist in a slow downward movement in assuming their starting positions. For example, swimmers will begin to move with the "take your marks" command but will bend very slowly into the starting position, hoping they can be starting a recoil just as the gun is fired, gaining a split second advantage. (2:9) Extra motion may occur in the normal hang starting position or in the grab starting cantilevered position. When a swimmer or swimmers are moving, the "stand up" command should be used to obviate the need for calling a false start. When this is not possible, a false start must be charged to the swimmer(s) committing the infraction(s). Collegiate rules disqualify contestants with one false start in dual meets and two false starts in championship meets.

Starters must be firm in their efforts to assure an equitable start for all contestants. From age group swimming through university competition, starters must work for consistency. The command should be varied in timing and given in a calm, quiet voice to avoid exciting the swimmers and promoting false starts.

Effective starters will not hold swimmers if they go down to the starting position together.

Relay Take-offs

The most common infraction may be the relay take-off. Take-offs are difficult to judge since many touches are made underwater. If in doubt, don't call the infraction. Inexperienced judges tend to be water shy, an attitude which causes them to jerk away or close their eyes at the relay exchange. There is an understandable but unjustified reluctance to make such a crucial call. If the starter is working the meet alone, the touch and take-off cannot be judged from a distance with any confidence. Adequately staffed championship meets have a take-off judge assigned to each lane. As in close finishes, implementation of automatic timing devices would minimize this problem. Judges should be cautioned to avoid "reminder" taps or slaps when incoming swimmers touch. Regardless of age or experience a relay swimmer who "jumps" should be disqualified, since an advantage has thus been gained over those who have performed legally.

Stroke and Turn Infractions

Stroke infractions must be declared to the referee without delay. In keeping with the rules, the breaststroke is the most difficult to judge, with head position, shoulders position and symmetrical movements all to be considered. Regardless of their age, swimmers who are shown leniency are granted an unfair advantage and will fail to develop a competitive skill. Stroke infractions should be strictly enforced in age group and interscholastic swimming; they are almost non-existent in collegiate swimming. It is a good policy to develop uniform hand signals for stroke inspectors leading to disqualifications. Stroke technique is best observed from BEHIND the swimmers. If the inspector is not convinced that there is a stroke infraction, he or she should continue to watch the swimmer in question. When disqualifying a swimmer for a stroke infraction, it is important to explain the infraction to the swimmer in question after the race to avoid a reoccurrence. The swimmer is entitled to a tactful explanation by the starter or referee.

Miscellaneous Considerations

Volunteer Officials
In order to conduct an organized swimming meet, several officials are required. Championship meets require as many as thirty officials, a situation which presents a problem for small communities staging these events. An inadequate number of competent officials can result in inequities in judgment and the establishment of unreliable records. Due to financial circumstances, it is usually not feasible to provide a full complement of paid officials for dual or championship meets. Therefore, many responsibilities are assigned to volunteer officials. This creates a situation in which the host school or club must secure the services of interested individuals. Many leagues now require participating teams to staff one lane with timers and watches with the host team supplying all other officials. A clinic should be conducted prior to the meet date, or a pre-meet session should be conducted well before the scheduled hour of the meet. This meeting should instruct in how to use a stop watch, proper positioning at the start and the finish of the race, correct recording procedures and many other details. Successful meet directors recognize the importance of these volunteers and make it a point to keep them well informed on rule changes. Basic instructions should be attached to each official's clipboard. If a banquet is customary at the conclusion of the season, it is beneficial to invite the volunteer officials in order to properly recognize them for their service to the program.

Training Officials
Ideally a clinic or clinics should be scheduled on non-meet days to explain thoroughly the rules and to provide practice opportunities. Close (2:45) suggests three clinic phases: an hour and one-half lecture period, a one hour pool demonstration and practice officiating session, and a final hour devoted to a written test on the material covered in the lecture and demonstration/practice.

Appeal Procedure
Written appeals must be submitted to the referee within fifteen minutes of the final heat of that event. Appeals will be ruled upon by a games committee consisting of the referee, a representative of the host school and conference representatives.

Officiating Evaluated by Coaches

What qualities do you appreciate in a swimming official?

1. Completely familiar with the rules and applies them equally in all situations
2. Promptness
3. One who instills confidence in the athletes
4. Decisiveness
5. Willing to make the necessary disqualifications
6. Takes command of the contest without calling undue attention to himself/herself
7. Arrives equipped with guns, whistles, proper uniforms, rulebooks etc.

Officiating Evaluated by Officials

What is the most difficult situation to call in swimming?

1. Relay starts and finishes without electronic timing devices
2. Stroke violations
3. Finishes of close races where timers and finish judges disagree

What is the most difficult phase of mechanics in officiating swimming?

1. Judging relay take-offs
2. High enough positioning to observe the entire field of competitors at the finish
3. Developing a starter's command that does not invite false starts

PERFORMANCE RATING FORM FOR
SWIMMING AND DIVING OFFICIALS

Name of Official .... Capacity: .... Referee
Meet .... vs. .... Starter
                                            .... Finish Judge
Date .... Place .... Inspector of
                                                 Strokes and Turns
Signature of Rater .... Diving Judge
Position of Rater: .... Timer
    (Encircle one) Referee — Coach — Observing Official   .... Other ....
                   Other ....

Rating Scale for Duties Performed

Rating	Characteristic of Competency Desired for Officials at:
5—Superior	—National and regional level of championship competition
4—Good	—State championship and top-flight college meets
3—Average	—High school varsity, small college, and local championship meets
2—Fair	—High school junior varsity and junior high school meets
1—Poor	—Practice meets in schools and community organizations

Rating
(Encircle one)

Characteristic	Poor	Fair	Average	Good	Superior
Knowledge of the Rules	1	2	3	4	5
Displays accurate knowledge of the rules					
Renders proper interpretation of the rules					
Competency in Mechanics of Officiating	1	2	3	4	5
Assumes proper position and utilizes desirable movement patterns for specific duties					
Alert to total scene of contest and to cooperating and coordinating with other officials in performing duties					
Uses equipment properly, e.g., watch, gun					
Physical Attributes	1	2	3	4	5
Satisfactory physical condition					
Neat, tailored, and physically fit appearance					
Desirable Personal Qualities	1	2	3	4	5
Exerts positive control of responsibilities for supervising the contest					
Displays consistency and sound judgment in decisions					
Reflects confidence and poise, self-control, and calmness					

Total of
Key for Over-All Rating   Ratings ....

18 and over — 5	OVER-ALL
14-17 — 4	RATING ....
10-13 — 3	
7- 9 — 2	
4- 6 — 1	

Fig. 7.8 Performance rating form—
simplified version. (3:70)

Sample Officials' Certification Test

Check or fill in one (or more if more than one is correct)

Timer

1. Which finger is suggested for starting and stopping a watch?
   a. forefinger
   b. middle finger
   c. thumb
2. If you did not start or stop the watch accurately or if it did not function properly for some reason, you should
   a. call for an alternate timer
   b. record the same time as one of the other timers on your lane
   c. report "no time"
   d. estimate the correct time
3. What is the official time when three watches are used?
   a. the average of all three times
   b. the middle time if all differ
   c. two identical times

Finish Judge

4. In lane judging you pick the order of finish of:
   a. lst place
   b. the swimmer in your lane only
   c. lst, 2nd and 3rd place
5. Lane Finish Judges should stand
   a. at the end over the lane being judged
   b. at the side several feet away from the end
   c. at the side in a line with the end, preferably in a raised position
6. If you know that a swimmer has been disqualified what place do you award him?
   a. last place
   b. the same place as if he were not disqualified
   c. no place at all

Stroke and Turn Judge

7. A turn judge should be stationed
   a. on the deck in line with the end of the pool
   b. at the end over the lane being inspected
   c. in the stands at the side in a raised position
8. In butterfly, which of the following are rules violations?
   a. more than one kick after the start and each turn before the first arm stroke
   b. recover the arms underwater
   c. use frog kick
   d. switch from dolphin to frog kick and back to dolphin kick
   e. use flutter kick after start and turns
   f. take underwater arm pull after start and turns but recover over surface
   g. touch below the water line
   h. somersault into the turn
9. Judges of strokes and turns report infractions to the
   a. chief judge
   b. referee
   c. recording desk
   d. head lane timer

Relay Take-off Judge

10. A relay take-off judge should watch
    a. both the touch and the take-off
    b. only the touch
    c. only the take-off
11. When there has been a "break", the take-off judge should
    a. tell the other relay team members
    b. not tell the other team members
    c. raise his hand to indicate infraction
    d. report the infraction to the Referee
12. Before the touch on a relay, the following swimmer
    a. may be in motion
    b. may not be in motion

Starter

13. What does the Starter say after "Take your marks"?
    a. "Get set"
    b. "Go"
    c. nothing
14. Before the gun, a swimmer
    a. may be in motion but not moving forward
    b. must be perfectly steady
15. Who may call a false start?
    a. referee
    b. starter
    c. chief judge
    d. clerk of the course
    e. stroke inspector

Sample

Answers to Officials Certification Test

l. a 2. a,c 3. b,c 4. b 5. c 6. b 7. b 8. b,c,d,e 9. b 10. b 11. c 12. a 13. c
    14. b 15. a,b(2:60)

BIBLIOGRAPHY

1. Clark, Steve. *Competitive Swimming As I See It.* North Hollywood: Swimming World, 1967.
2. Close, Richard W. *Practical Swimming Officiating.* Stamford: Dolphin Aquatics, 1971.
3. Meyers, Carlton R. and William H. Sanford, *Swimming and Diving Officiating.* Palo Alto: National Press Books, 1970.
4. *Swimming and Diving.* Kansas City: National Federation of State High School Associations, 1983.
5. *1984 Men's and Women's Swimming and Diving Rules.* Mission, Kansas: National Collegiate Athletic Association, 1983.
6. White, Jess R. *Sports Rules Encyclopedia.* Palo Alto: The National Press, 1966.

8

Track and Field

The Game

Man has been running from the beginning of time. "Running for fun" has developed from an original context of running for survival. Track and field is considered an exacting sport full of challenges and a sport where the athlete must be self-reliant and absolutely on his or her own. The spectrum of competition ranges from children's match races to the Olympic Games.

Track and field is very satisfying to the individual as it is a natural activity and it provides a sense of achievement. (4:9) Ron Clarke (2:6) feels very strongly about the lasting benefits of track—the simple preparation, rigorous testing of his own ability, friends made and people met. Track and field undoubtedly contribute to the improvement of cardiovascular endurance which is a major component of physical fitness.

Track and field calls for a polished performance. The stop watch and tape measure can produce precise information regarding improvement and positive results. The track and field athlete competes not only against the athlete in the next lane, but also against the standards of time, distance and height. (3:10)

Track and field competition is unique in that several events progress concurrently. Due to the overlapping of events, there are understandable delays. Coupled with the challenge of individual effort, the contestants exhibit considerable tenseness. The referee and starter must make a concerted effort to keep both the coaches and competitors calm throughout the meet.

Photo by David S. Strickler

Officials and Their Responsibilities

As in swimming, the only paid official in most dual track meets is the starter/referee. The role of the referee is usually played by the host coach or athletic director. The numerous other volunteer officials required to conduct a meet are normally trained and supervised by the starter/referee.

The recommended clothing for the starter is a distinguishable red jacket, black trousers, white shirt with black tie and a red cap or hat.

Referee

The track referee has complete jurisdiction over the meet. The referee is responsible for insuring fair competition for all contestants.

Before the meet the referee shall:

1. See that all equipment necessary for the satisfactory conduct of the meet is in the proper place and condition.
2. See that the track is properly marked.
3. Assign officials to particular duties, reviewing the positions and responsibilities of each; and
4. Before championship meets, conduct a pre-meet conference with the starter and a captain from each team to review meet procedures and special instructions.

During the meet the referee shall:

1. Meet with the contestants prior to each race to review lane assignments and starting instructions.
2. Check that each contestant takes the proper lane and signal the starter that the starting signals may begin.
3. See that the meet progresses rapidly and the results are announced; and
4. Assure that all competition is conducted according to the rules.

The referee must be prepared to make decisions on any technical questions that arise during the meet. When there are no rules covering a dispute, the referee shall have the final judgment in the matter. (6:200)

Starter

The starter has control over the contestants after they have been assigned to him by the referee. Before starting each race, the starter should explain to each competitor:

1. The command and signal to be given to start the race.
2. The distance to be covered and where the race will terminate.

3. Relay exchange requirements; and
4. For races longer than one-quarter mile, signaling the last lap of the race.

The starter must have the ability to make fast, fair and firm decisions.

Inspectors

Spaced to best observe their assigned lanes, the inspectors should concentrate on runners changing course or impeding an opponent in an effort to pass. In relay races these officials must also determine whether the baton was passed in the prescribed passing zone. The chief inspector is responsible for three assistant inspectors and for reporting violations to the starter. Inspectors will also be responsible for disqualifying hurdlers in violation of the rules. The most common violation would be the hurdler trailing a leg to the side when going over the hurdle.

Clerk of the Course

The clerk of the course has the important task of seeing that the meet progresses according to the time schedule. This official is responsible for assigning contestants to their proper lane positions prior to each race and for placing all members of relay teams in their proper lanes. Before the start of each race it is recommended that the clerk of the course give the head finish judge a card with the names of the runners, their numbers, and the lanes in which they are running. The clerk should stay with the starter in dual meets and move to a designated check-in area for championship meets.

Finish Judges

The order of finish in all races is the responsibility of the head finish judge and the assistant judges. In dual meets there may only be three assistant judges, one assigned to pick each place. In championship meets at least two judges should be assigned to determine each place. The head finish judge must view each finish and be prepared to resolve any conflicts in placing as determined by the judges.

Field Judges

Each field event has a judge and one or more assistants. Each judge is responsible for conducting his or her competition according to the rules governing that event. The judge at each event is also responsible for the activities of assistants in marking and measuring legal throws or jumps. The head field judge, in turn, supervises the overall conduct of the field events. This includes weighing, measuring and inspecting all implements, checking the order of competition, and certifying any record made during the course of the meet.

Scorer
The primary responsibility of the scorer is to maintain running team scores as the results of the events become available. This should include a record of individual winners and their performances.

Announcer
Meet information should be provided to the contestants and spectators throughout the meet to maintain spectator interest. Announcements should be kept to a minimum in order to avoid interrupting and diverting attention from the competition. It is the responsibility of the announcer to give the 10 minute first call and the five minute second call for each event.

Marshall
The marshall is responsible for keeping the competitive areas clear, and barring all unauthorized spectators and athletes not competing in the event in progress off the track and infield. This makes possible the steady progress of the meet. A special cap or ribbon worn on the jacket should be used to identify the marshall.

Basic Penalties and Rulings

Lane Violations
Inspectors should be cognizant of the importance of their responsibility. A competitor must be disqualified who steps on or over the lane to the inside in races around the curve. Runners may also be disqualified for jostling, cutting across, or obstructing another competitor. Runners should not be allowed to cross into the next lane in a straightaway race. The "two strides" rule must be enforced in races which permit the runners to cross in front of each other. (4:123) A major concern is to note any action that causes another runner to break stride or lose momentum.

Relay Passes
The most important considerations are that the pass be made within the allotted zone of twenty meters, and that after making the pass, the runner does not veer out of the assigned lane, thus impeding an

opponent's path. From a technical standpoint, the baton must be passed within the zone although the runner may be out of the passing zone. If the baton is dropped in the passing zone, either runner may pick it up.

Hurdle Clearance

A hurdler should be disqualified who advances or trails a leg or foot outside a hurdle. The rules make it very clear that the contestant's entire body must go over the hurdle. A hurdler may also be disqualified for running out of the assigned lane and obstructing another hurdler or deliberately knocking down hurdles. Accidentally knocking down hurdles will not be penalized.

Events Using Circles—Shot Put, Discus, Hammer

In the shot put event, the shot must land within a 45 degree sector extending from the center of the circle. The shot must be put or pushed. Fouls should be called for throwing the shot and for letting the shot pass behind or below the shoulder. Basic rules call for the competitor not to touch the top of the toe-board or step out of the circle during the put. The contestant may touch the inside of the toe-board. The competitor must leave the rear half of the circle after the attempt. The measurement is from the nearest mark made by the shot to the inside circumference of the restraining circle.

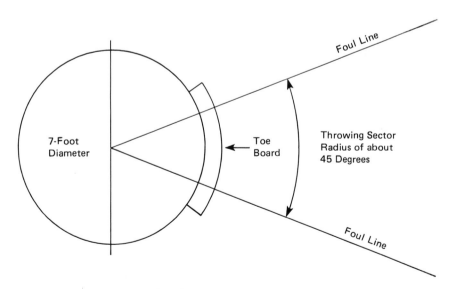

Fig. 8.1 Shot Put lay-out. (1:75)

The basic in-the-circle rules governing a legal discus and hammer throw measurement are the same as those for the shot put. The hammer throwing sector is the same as the shot put (45 degrees) while the discus sector is 60 degrees. The discus and hammer events utilize a ring instead of the toeboard used in the shot put.

High Jump

A legal jump is one in which a competitor jumps from one foot. A missed jump is recorded when:

1. The crossbar is displaced in an attempt to clear it.
2. Jumper passes under crossbar or touches ground with any part of the body extended beyond the crossbar; or
3. Jumper approaches the crossbar and leaves the ground (1:45).

A jumper is eliminated from competition when he or she misses three consecutive times at any height. If the event is tied, the winner will be determined by the fewest misses at the closing height or previous heights. A common misconception is that a jump is successful if the competitor leaves the pit before the crossbar falls off.

Pole Vault

The pole vault is one of the most challenging of all field events. A combination of speed, strength, endurance and coordination is required to succeed. A missed attempt is recorded when:

1. Bar is displaced by vaulter or pole.
2. Vaulter leaves the ground in an attempted vault and fails to clear bar.
3. Any part of the vaulter's body touches the ground beyond the plane of the stopboard; or
4. During the vault, the vaulter displaces his upper hand higher on the pole or moves his lower hand above his upper hand. (1:70)

Long Jump and Triple Jump

Both events utilize a wooden take-off board with the edge of the board nearest the pit referred to as the scratch or foul line. The triple jump is a three-ply action (5:231) that requires the competitor to make the first jump by landing on the same foot from which he or she took off, or hop; the second jump, or step, by landing on the opposite foot; and the third jump landing by preference. (7:75) The measurement in either event should be made at right angles to the foul line or from the closest point of entry to the front edge of the board. If necessary, to gain a right angle measurement, an extension of the scratch board may be made. A clipboard should suffice.

Fig. 8.2 Long jump measurement.

Foul attempts should be recorded when contestants step over the scratch line before the jump, run beyond the foul line extended or leave the pit out of control closer to the take-off board after landing in the pit. In the triple jump, a foul jump should be recorded if the trailing foot touches the ground.

For the safety of the contestant, it is strongly suggested that the landing pit not be more than thirty feet from the take-off board in the triple jump.

Javelin

A legal javelin throw must be made from behind the arc, and the javelin must fall within the sector. Foul attempts will be recorded for throwing outside the sector, touching any surface of the foul board, the run-up lines, or the area outside the foul board or the run-up lines. (7:79)

Mechanics

Starting

A pistol of not less than .32 caliber which can be cocked and has a flash clearly visible to the timers, must be used. For purposes of recall, the starter should have a second starting gun. The starter should repeat the race instructions to the participants and answer any questions that may be presented. Next, the head finish judge should be signaled that the race is about to begin. After receiving a return signal from the head finish judge, the starter should take a position to the side away from the bleachers and ten to fifteen yards ahead of the competitors in straight-away races. In staggered races, the starter should be positioned in lane 1 or 2, two to three yards, in front of the lead runner so that all runners can be observed.

In a calm and relaxed voice, the starter should bring the runners to the starting line by giving the command, "On your marks!" while pointing the free hand to the ground. The starter should then allow ample time for the runners to assume a comfortable position in the starting blocks. When all runners are motionless and have their fingers in position behind the starting line the starter should raise the free hand overhead in the same position as the gun hand and give the command "Set," requesting that all contestants assume their final positions. After an interval of approximately two seconds and when all participants are motionless, the starter should discharge the pistol. As soon as the participants leave the starting line, the starter's assistants should move the starting blocks to the infield. In races of more than 800 meters the commands are "Runners, take your marks" followed by the gun (for high school) and "Runners, set" and the gun (for college competition).

Timing
Before the meet, the head timer should check the watches for reliability as explained in the timing section of the swimming chapter. Before each event, the timer should complete the time slip, and then fill in the time immediately following the race.

In lap races, one timer should be designated to call split times for each runner.

The timer's slip should then be given directly to the head timekeeper, without discussion with the other timekeepers. The technique for timing is the same as that outlined in the chapter on swimming. A fully automatic timer utilizes a single electronic timer started automatically with the starter's gun and stopped by an electronic or optical device at the instant the first part of each runner's torso reaches the finish line. In the event of malfunction, this system is backed up with official timers. (7:61)

In championship meets, official pictures of all finishes may be taken. Utilizing the results of the automatic timer and the picture of the finish, the Chief Evaluator shall be responsible for the evaluation and interpretation of the finish place and time. (7:46)

Judging

Running events. Judges should be positioned in elevated stands approximately 15–20 feet back from the finish line on either side of the track. After completing the pre-race information on the finish slip, the judge should watch the race until the competitors are ten to fifteen yards from the finish line. The judge should then concentrate on the finish line and select his or her assigned place based on a torso finish. Even though the runners have been instructed to stay in their lanes and to turn around and face the judges at the end of the race, it is necessary for the judge to go immediately and obtain the name of the runner in question. The judge should then complete the slip and return it to the head finish judge who records the official results of the race.

Field events. The head field judge, event judges and measures should work together as a team to expedite the conduct of the field events. The head field judge must also ascertain whether the individual field judges have the necessary equipment to conduct the event. Along with the event scorecard, an instruction card that clearly outlines the basic rules of the event should be attached to the clipboard. An equipment list should be included on the instruction card, For example, the long jump list might include clipboard, pencils, tape, marking spike, shovel, rake, broom, leveler, red flag, traffic cones, ground markers for record efforts in the event etc.

After each attempt, the judge should verify the measurement and instruct the event assistants to prepare the area for the next competitor. To expedite matters, it is suggested that the judge announce the "on deck" competitor well before each attempt. A rule of thumb in measurement calls for measuring to the nearest quarter-inch under 100 feet and to the nearest inch over 100 feet. To ensure accuracy, a steel tape is highly recommended. At the conclusion of the event, the field judge should record the place order, enter the distances, and turn in the results to the meet scorer.

LONG JUMP

1. Six official entries (3 attempts)
2. Four advance to the finals (3 attempts)
3. Keep scratch line clean
4. Measure from point of entry to front edge of scratching line
5. Measure at right angles from the point of entry to the front edge of the scratch line extended (jumps entering extreme sides of the pit)
6. Falling back and out of the pit to gain balance is a foul jump

---

Fig. 8.3 Long jump instruction card.
(6:206)

Meet _____
Date _____
Place _____

Event _____

Competitors	Organization	Trials										Finals										Best Performance	Place
		1		2		3						1		2		3							
		ft.	in.	ft.	in.	ft.	in.					ft.	in.	ft.	in.	ft.	in.						

Place Winners

Head Field Judge _____
Field Referee _____
Official Scorer _____

Fig. 8.4 Sample score card for discus, shot put, javelin, and long jump. (6:206)

Meet Scoring
Dual meet scoring for individual events is 5-3-1 for the first three places. Relays in dual meets are scored 5 for first and 0 for second. In championship meets, scoring varies according to the number of teams entered.

Problem Calls

False Starts
False starts are sometimes the result of faulty starting techniques. Starters must be constantly aware that in short distance competition the runners are anxious and tend to anticipate the start. Regardless of the stature of the athlete, the false start must be called if there is a violation. Some starters have eliminated changes in body positions in starting signals because runners often react to the hand being raised on the "Set" command. A quiet, confident manner helps to relax the competitors so that they will not try to second guess the starter. The starter must be cautious not to hurry the commands and thereby invite false starts. If the starter is not satisfied with the final starting positions of the competitors in the blocks, the runners should be requested to "stand up"; in such circumstances, a false start should not be assessed. To protect the interests of all contestants, the starter must allow ample time for all runners to prepare for the next start without undue hurrying. One false start will disqualify a contestant in college and high school competition.

Starters seem to prefer verbal commands over whistle commands. (one whistle—to marks, two whistles—set and gun) The only problem with verbal commands is that they are often not heard.

Event Delays
It was previously suggested that first and second calls for the running events be given and that in field events the "on deck" or next competitor be announced. Contestants participating in two or more events at the same time should be encouraged to return to an event as soon as possible in order to receive their allotments of attempts. If the contestant has just completed a running event, the field event judge must ascertain that a reasonable recovery period be given before the competitor's next attempt. There is considerable difference of opinion as to how long the judge should wait for a contestant to return. Many judges feel that participants returning during a round in progress should go to the end of the order and then assume their original positions in the

next round. Regardless of the procedure adopted, a competitor should not delay the orderly progress of an event. The Track and Field Guide statement on the subject is as follows:

> In all field events, except the pole vault, a competitor shall be charged with an unsuccessful attempt if he does not initiate his trial within 1½ minutes after being called by the event judge. (7:67)

For the same reason that one athlete can score in two or more events that are running simultaneously, he or she should be required to finish these events in the prescribed amount of time. This constitutes an integral part of the competition.

Long Jump and Triple Jump Judging
Careful scrutiny of the toe and the end of the board, or the scratch line, is an important part of judging these events. This is a judgment decision that must be made quickly. A good practice would be to clear the area immediately adjacent to the board and pit, to eliminate the probability of contestants and spectators second guessing the judge. Scratch line foul calls should be made immediately after the contestant makes contact with the pit. If foul calls are made while the jumper is in the air, injury to the jumper may result. Contact with the surface in front of the board is not always visible. It is possible for the toe of the shoe to extend over the scratch line without marking the sand, dirt or runway in front of the board. Jumpers falling back and out of the pit behind their landing point in an attempt to regain their balance must be charged with a foul jump. The judge must also be alert to protect the jumpers from non-jumpers who may be warming up near the runway.

Relay Exchanges
Too often this fact of meet officiating is overlooked. Since meets may not be decided at the time of the relay, indifference in judging relay exchanges can be critical. Inspectors must observe the passes and rule accordingly. With only one inspector at each exchange position, it is very difficult to observe all the passes accurately.

Races 800 Meters and Up
Breaking to the inside at the 200 meter mark equalizes the competition for all lanes.

Blocks and Hurdles
In order to avoid delays following hurdle races and running events that require moving the hurdles and blocks respectively, the host coach must have reliable captains assigned to each responsibility.

Miscellaneous Considerations

Pre-Meet Duties
The referee and starter should arrive early to inspect the track, starting line, finish lines, relay passing zones, field event facilities and equipment. A meeting with both coaches should be conducted to clarify rules and answer any questions. The few minutes allotted for this meeting will usually pay dividends before the meet has ended.

Volunteer Officials
Finding reliable and capable volunteer officials is a most difficult problem for track coaches. Time must be devoted to the active recruiting of these volunteer officials. Experienced volunteer officials should be solicited each year and commitments secured when possible. A personal contact should be made to assure them that their services are important to the continuance of the sport. On the day of the meet, the coach should make every effort to refamiliarize these individuals with their responsibilities. The coach should also take time to review with the volunteer officials the instruction cards attached to each field event scorecard. Take nothing for granted; if there are rule changes, clarify these before the meet. Don't assume that even experienced volunteers have kept current on rule changes in any given event. Make provisions for questions before the meet. It is the responsibility of the coach to support these volunteers by moving around during the meet and tactfully

Fig. 8.5 Suggested placement of inspectors. (6:207)

assisting them. It should be noted that most volunteers wish to be timers and tend to avoid the field events. The host coach should be alert to the fact that these volunteers would like to watch the running events. To accomplish this, it is recommended that they be relieved periodically. The coach should make it a point to thank all volunteer officials at the conclusion of the meet.

Jury of Appeals

The coach has thirty minutes from the conclusion of the event to file a protest with the starter/referee who will make a ruling in a dual meet. In championship meets, a jury of appeals, usually consisting of the starter/referee, a representative of the host school and conference representatives, will make the decision following the trials in preparation for the finals.

Officiating Evaluated by Coaches

What qualities do you appreciate in a track and field official?

1. Punctuality
2. Willingness to accept responsibility
3. Hustle
4. Thorough knowledge of the rules
5. Fairness—all runners afforded on equal start
6. Personality—firm and exact but not harsh
7. Conscientious, calm and relaxed

Miscellaneous Comments

1. Before accepting a volunteer officiating responsibility, individuals should study the rules and keep up to date on rule changes.
2. Officials should be on hand during the warmup period to establish rapport with the competitors and ensure a prompt start of the event.

Officiating Evaluated by Officials

What is the most difficult situation to call in track and field?

1. Lack of meet management
2. Detecting a rolling start

What is the most difficult phase of mechanics in officiating track and field?

1. Finish judging without adequate elevated finish line stands
2. Starter's position for staggered races

Track and Field Officials Training Sessions

Candidates should be well versed and trained in the following aspects and areas:

1. Thorough knowledge of fouls and infractions, duties, dress and techniques.
2. Accuracy, quickness, and clearness in announcing fouls—the ability to make the correct decisions quickly and in an acceptable manner.
3. Ability to start various races satisfactorily, both straight and staggered; to judge correctly and inspect the races; to time accurately; and to discern track infractions.
4. Ability to correctly judge and rule on fouls in the field.
5. Knowledge of correct positions to judge the events and the ability to give both good verbal instructions and correct arm and whistle signals.
6. Proper attitude and demeanor for making quick and accurate decisions and for carrying out officiating duties to the smooth and correct conclusion of the meet and events.
7. Thorough knowledge of the written rules of all events and the official's duties. (4:121)

Situation Rulings (8)

Situation: A1 establishes a record in a preliminary heat or in preliminary trails in a field event but does not equal it in the finals, or does not qualify for the finals. *Ruling:* The record is allowed. (3-3-6, 10-5-1)

Situation: A1 is competing in the high jump wearing only one shoe. When confronted by the high jump judge, A1 states an infected blister would be aggravated if he were to be required to wear the shoe, and the judge permits him to compete without the shoe. When the coach of B1 protests to the referee, the referee upholds the decision of the high jump judge. *Ruling:* The referee is in error. No official, including the referee (4-2-2) has the authority to set aside a rule. (6-2-7, 2-3-1, 6-3-6)

Situation: A1, A2 and A3 draw lane 1, 2 and 3 and their competitors draw the outside lanes. Should the referee shift competitors? *Ruling:* If any school has more than one competitor in a race, it is best to draw by schools and to alternate teammates with competitors. However, if the draw is by individuals, each runner must start in the lane drawn. (4-3-2)

Situation: An inspector notes B1 impeding the progress of A1 by illegally crowding at the curve. *Ruling:* The inspector is required to signal the infraction by waving a red flag overhead. Following the race the inspector must report the infraction to the head inspector who will report to the referee. After hearing the evidence the referee shall make any decision regarding disqualification. (4-9-3)

Situation: The runners are in the "set" position and when the gun is fired, A1's starting block slips. *Ruling:* The start is considered to be unfair and the race is recalled. (7-1-2)

Situation: In one of the races, A1 is in forward motion after the "Set" position has been taken but the starter fires the gun. *Ruling:* The starter should recall the runners by firing the pistol a second time, and assess A1 with a false start. (7-7-6)

Situation: A1 and B1 reach the finish line at about the same time. A1 reaches forward to break the finish yarn with an extended hand or arm. *Ruling:* Under such circumstances, B1 should receive the benefit of any doubt as to who finished first. The referee has the authority to disqualify A1 if it is obvious the act was intentional. (7-2-2)

Situation: During the race, A1 accidentally uses one, or two, consecutive steps on or inside the curb. *Ruling:* No penalty should be enforced for such action, provided A1 promptly returns to the track. (8-7-7)

Situation: In a hurdle race, A1 loses his/her stride and runs around a hurdle or vaults in such a way that one leg trails to the side of a hurdle. *Ruling:* A1 should be disqualified. It is necessary that an attempt be made to clear each of the hurdles.

Situation: In the high jump, A1 hits the crossbar and it bounces on the supports but does not fall until after A1 has landed and has stepped out of the landing pit. *Ruling:* This is an unsuccessful trail. If a bar falls because of being hit by the jumper in his/her attempt, the position of the competitor at the time has no bearing. (70-4-3)

Pre-Meet Checklist

1. _____ CONFIRM DATE AND SITE OF MEET
   a. Check for conflicts of other local or regional events.
   b. Obtain necessary facility permits for location site.

2. _____ VERIFY INFORMATION TO BE INCLUDED ON OFFICIAL ENTRY
   FORM BROCHURE

3. _____ NOTIFY ARCO JESSE OWENS GAMES HEADQUARTERS OR
   REGIONAL COORDINATING AGENCY OF PARTICIPATION

4. _____ INFORM THE PUBLIC OF INTENT TO HOLD MEET

5. _____ DISTRIBUTE ENTRY FORMS—POST "SIGN-UP" POSTERS
   a. Develop system for receiving and recording entry forms.
   b. Notify participant when and where to report for registration
   day of meet.

6. _____ ASSIGN PERSONNEL TO WORK THE MEET
   a. Refer to "Statement of Duties."
   b. Send assignment letter.

7. _____ DEVELOP OPENING CEREMONY FORMAT
   a. Send letter of invitation to participating groups and
   participants.

8. _____ ORDER SUPPLIES FOR MEET
   a. Preliminary Meet
   b. Regional Championships

9. _____ SECURE NECESSARY EQUIPMENT FOR MEET

10. _____ PREPARE SCHEDULE OF EVENTS

11. _____ REVIEW FORMS

12. _____ CHECK AWARDS

13. _____ ARRANGE TO HAVE TRACK AND FIELD MARKED DAY BEFORE
    MEET

Fig. 8.6 Pre-meet checklist. (1981
Guide for Conducting Arco Jesse
Owens Games. Los Angeles: Arco
Jesse Owens Games, 1981.) (9:15)

Facility Checklist

_____ Availability—Restroom (male/female)

_____ Electrical Outlets _____ Power On _____

_____ High Jump Standards and Crossbars

_____ Grandstands

_____ Parking and Accessibility

_____ Maximum Number of Lanes

_____ Maintenance Personnel

_____ Lining of Track

_____ P.A. System

_____ Lighting (for Night Meets)

_____ Long Jump Pit(s)

The following Guidelines should also be kept in mind when selecting a site.

_____ The infield should be grass or tartan.

_____ If possible, track should be tartan or crushed brick (dust).

_____ The stands should be able to seat a minimum of 5,000 spectators and in many cases, more; and be separated by a barrier from the track.

_____ Concession facilities should be available for drinks and snacks (hot dogs, etc.).

_____ Night meets should have well-lighted facilities and good security.

_____ A portion of the stands should be able to be set aside as a "Bull Pen" or line-up area for participants. All participants will remain in this section until called by meet director or announcer for their event.

Fig. 8.7 Facility checklist. (1981
Guide for Conducting Jesse Owens
Games. Los Angeles: Arco Jesse
Owens Games, 1981.) (9:17)

Meet Director's Checklist

(For Use Day of Meet)

1. _____ Arrive 1-1/2 hours prior to start of meet
2. _____ Meet with Facility coordinator; unlock gates, restrooms, etc. Have P.A. System turned on and test system
3. _____ Telephone numbers of scheduled personnel
4. _____ Forms:

   _____ Completed worksheets and event cards
   _____ Supply of blank forms:
   - Relay event cards
   - Qualifying Heat Cards
   - Master Heat Sheets
   - Final Heat Cards
   - Awards Cards
   - Other _____

5. _____ Check equipment and supplies (refer to your pre-established list)
6. _____ Setup Field: (See Sample Field Lay-Out Chart on next page)

   _____ Tie up banners
   _____ Arrange Nerve Center and awards area
   _____ Affix Victory Stand Cover to front of awards stand
   _____ Display awards on table on the infield

7. _____ Post Signs:

   _____ Registration Desk
   _____ Parade Line-Up Area
   _____ Bull Pen
   _____ Field Events (Long Jump-Pit 1; Long Jump-Pit 2, etc.)
   _____ First Aid Station
   _____ Media/VIP area
   _____ Nerve Center
   _____ Free T-shirts distribution Center (Free iron-on decals)

8. _____ Hold Officials' Meeting
   - Distribute Officials' Caps, visors and sport shirts
   - Tell Officials about Post-Game Reception

9. _____ Hold Coaches' meeting
   - Distribute T-shirts for Participants
10. _____ Distribute Program containing Order and Schedule of Events
11. _____ Line-up teams/participants for "Parade of Athletes"
12. _____ Commence Opening Ceremonies (Refer to pre-established format)
13. _____ Announce that all Participants must take their seats in the stands
14. _____ Have all Officials take their stations
15. _____ Conduct Meet
16. _____ Closing remarks to participants and spectators
17. _____ Clean up field
18. _____ Move to Post-Game Reception

Fig. 8.8 Meet director's checklist.
(1981 Guide for Conducting Jesse
Owens Games. Los Angeles: Arco
Jesse Owens Games, 1981.) (9:40)

Organization of Track and Field Area for Meets

In case of multiple heats, you may wish to run dash from 1 and 2 toward center. If stands on both sides, you may wish to use 3 and 4 also.

Many cities have second microphone for announcer in the nerve center.

Fig. 8.9 Organization of track and field area for meets. (1981 Guide for Conducting Arco Jesse Owens Games. Los Angeles: Arco Jesse Owens Games, 1981.) (9:41)

Post-Meet Follow-Up

1. Prepare a Checklist:

The following checklist will insure the Meet Director that all necessary follow-up items have been completed, participants notified of next step in program and proper forms filed with Regional Coordinating Agency or National Meet Director. A brief description of these items follows the listing.

Post-Meet Checklist

1. _____ Prepare and distribute meet results to media outlets and participants.

2. _____ Send thank you letters to officials, track personnel and others connected with the meet's function.

3. _____ Hold an evaluation meeting.

4. _____ Verify eligibility of winners and notify them of next level of competition and requirements.

5. _____ Complete and send in required forms to register your team for next level of competition.

6. _____ Assume responsibility for your team at next level of competition.

7. _____ Respond in timely manner to information requests from Regional Coordinating Agency, National Meet Director or ARCO Jesse Owens Games Headquarters.

8. _____ Select chaperones to accompany Regional Team to Nationals.

9. _____ Accompany team to next level of competition. (4)

Fig. 8.10 Post-meet follow-up. (1981 Guide for Conducting Arco Jesse Owens Games. Los Angeles: Arco Jesse Owens Games, 1981.) (9:47)

BIBLIOGRAPHY

1. Bowers, Richard. *Track and Field Events: Fundamentals.* Columbus: Charles E. Merrill Publishing Company, 1974.
2. Clarke, Ron. *Ron Clarke Talks Track.* Los Altos: Tafnews Press, 1972.
3. Disley, John. The Young Athlete's Companion. Toronto: The Ryerson Press, 1962.
4. *1981 Guide for Conducting Arco Jesse Owens Games.* Los Angeles: Arco Jesse Owens Games, 1981.
5. Harkins, Dorothy. *Selected Track and Field Articles.* Washington: DGWS, AAHPER, 1972.
6. Jordan, Payton and Bud Spencer. *Champions in the Making.* Inglewood Cliffs: Prentice-Hall, Inc., 1968.
7. Thompson, Donnis H. *Modern Track and Field for Girls and Women.* Boston: Allyn and Bacon, Inc., 1973.
8. *Track and Field Guide.* Shawnee Mission: National Collegiate Athletic Association, 1980.
9. *Track and Field Rules.* Kansas City: National Federation of State High School Associations, 1984.

9

Volleyball

The Game

During the past two decades, the growth of competitive volleyball in the United States has been little short of phenomenal. Particularly noteworthy is the fact that this growth has taken place at all levels of play—professional, Olympic, intercollegiate, interscholastic, recreational and informal. Volleyball has become the first coed professional team sport.

From the official's point of view there are three particularly important aspects of volleyball: (1) the pace of the game can be explosively fast; (2) judgment on ball handling is the most crucial officiating responsibility; and (3) the approach to volleyball although highly competitive, is somewhat more amateurlike, and more sportsmanlike than any other popular American sport.

The volleyball official, therefore, must have lightning-quick reactions and very fine concentrative powers in order not to become absolutely overwhelmed by the speed of the action. The principles underlying ball handling decisions and volleyball in general must be fully understood. The fine spirit of this tremendous game must be exemplified at all times, which means being courteous but firm, being dedicated to the game, and officiating with an attitude of serving the players. The volleyball official must not be a tyrant nor a battle-hardened abiter.

The upsurge of volleyball popularity in the United States has produced as a by-product a serious problem—a distinct shortage of qualified volleyball officials. As the quality of competition improves, the

Photo by UPI

need for highly qualified officials is magnified. Players frequently serve as the best officials, but many of them wish to preserve their amateur standing or are not interested in officiating.

If the great sport of volleyball is to develop to its fullest in the United States, as it should, adequate means of producing qualified officials must be developed. At the more advanced levels of play, good officiating is absolutely essential. The game cannot be played at its best without consistency in ball handling decisions and other difficult judgment areas, and without poised, intelligent and courteous officiating.

Officials and Their Responsibilities

Volleyball officials include the referee, umpire, line judges, scorer and timer. According to the level of play, volleyball matches are officiated by any number of officials from zero to ten. A full complement of ten officials would include a referee, umpire, scorer, assistant scorer, timer, assistant timer and four line judges.

Officials Uniform and Equipment

Men and women wear a black and white or navy blue vertically striped short-sleeve shirt in combination with a black or navy blue skirt, culotte or slack for women and a black or navy blue slack for men. Athletic shoes and socks should be white. The referee and umpire should wear a whistle with a cord. The umpire should have a record of the teams' lineups and service rotation. (2:11)

Referee

The referee has final control and may overrule any other official, although considerable discretion is used in exercising this power. The referee takes a position on an elevated stand at one end of the net so that the line of vision is well above (two or three feet) the top of the net. One hand is placed on the net cable through the entire point to help detect illegal touches of the net.

The referee routinely causes the game to progress by blowing a whistle and beckoning the server to put the ball in play. The whistle is again sounded to kill the play when a rally has ended or a foul has occurred. Finally, a point is awarded, "side-out" declared, or a replay ordered, as the case warrants. The referee may rule on any action that occurs, but is particularly concerned about ball handling fouls, fouls at or above the net, player conduct fouls, and routine matters such as granting time outs.

COURT DIAGRAM

Fig. 9.1 Volleyball court. (By courtesy of the N.F.S.H.S.A.)

Before the match the referee:

1. Examines the playing site, checking particularly the four inch center line, the amount of clearance from boundary lines to walls or obstructions, and the height of the net.
2. Conducts a pre-match conference with the coaches and playing captains to cover pertinent rules and conduct the coin toss, the winner having choice to serve or receive or to take either side of the net. (If teams split the first two games of a best-of-three match or the first four of a best-of-five match, the referee conducts another coin toss immediately after the second or fourth game.)

Umpire

The umpire takes an out-of-bounds position near the end of the net opposite the referee and adjacent to the scorers' table. The umpire's chief responsibilities during play are to rule on situations which might be out of the referee's view and to concentrate particularly on play between the spiking lines. When the ball is served the umpire should view the entire receiving team from a position opposite the spiking line to check the serving order and for overlapping,* and to observe ball handling during the return of the serve. This official controls the entry of substitutes into the playing area and repeats the referee's point and sideout signals.

The umpire has a wide range of responsibilities during dead ball periods:

1. *Before the game,* to review the responsibilities of the scorer and timer and assist the officials as required; to check players' uniforms and equipment; and to check the correctness of each team's lineup.
2. *During timeouts,* to verify and place a check next to each team score; to communicate the number of timeouts remaining to the team calling the timeout; and, if either team delays following the timeout, to sound the whistle to hasten resumption of play.

When the ball is in play, the alert and competent umpire is mobile, constantly adjusting position as does the lead official in basketball. Mobility can improve the angle of vision and also remind the players of the umpire's presence. On the other hand, rapid action frequently frustrates effective movement. The intent of the umpire should be to emphasize mobility during the calmer moments of action and deemphasize it when the action is explosive.

---

*At the instant the ball is hit for a serve, adjacent players on the receiving team may not overlap front-to-back or side-to-side.

Line Judges

There may be two or four line judges, usually two in high school volleyball. Where two line judges are used they stand near the intersection of the sideline with the end line opposite the serving area. They should be close enough to their corners to get a goal, visual angle view of the boundary lines for which they are responsible—and far enough to allow free player movement. Like the umpire, the line judges should attempt to anticipate the movement of the ball and the players and vary their positioning accordingly, sometimes moving ten to fifteen feet. During game action they are concerned about three aspects of the playing rules: (1) Was the ball in or out of bounds when it struck the court? (2) Who last touched a played ball which landed out of bounds? (3) Was the entire ball in-bounds when it passed over the net? The line judges employ prescribed hand signals (see Figure 9.4)

Scorer and Timer

Volleyball rules place the scorer and timer opposite the referee and near the umpire. They are seated at a table far enough from the court so as not to impede the players' and umpire's movements.

The functions of the *scorer* are to record the score and operate the scoring device, to record all time-outs and substitutions, and to verify proper serving order to the referee prior to the start of and during a game. When there is an improper serving order, the scorer should sound a signal at the time the serve is contacted.

As is the case in basketball, volleyball scoring is complicated and, because of rapid-fire action, requires thorough training, alertness and reliability. The figure shows a sample high school scoresheet.

The *timer* is seated next to the scorer and operates the game timing device. Audio signals (usually a horn) are given to indicate playing time, timeouts, or the end of intermissions. The complexities of timing a volleyball match have been greatly reduced by the virtual elimination in recent years of time-restricted games in high school and college competition. At most levels of volleyball competition, however, the rules permit the termination of a game following eight minutes of ball-in play action. This practice is common in intramural and community recreation competition.

When the eight-minute game restriction is in effect, the timer starts the timing device when each serve is contacted and stops it when a whistle sounds and the ball becomes dead. If time runs out during ball-in-play action, the timer withholds the audio signal until the ball becomes dead. When, near the end of a period, a clock visible to the players is not available, the timer periodically should call out the remaining time in a loud voice during dead ball periods.

SAMPLE GAME

Visitor: *Liberty*

GAME 1	TIME OUTS ⊠⊠⊠ 3				FINAL SCORE	16		First
Player No.				Play		Referee's Verification *QR*		Visitor

5	1	2	3	–	–										✗ 13
6	R	4A	5A	XS 11/5	6	7	P–	15A	16A						✗ 2 ✗ 3 ⊗ 4
7 13 7	S 7/13	–													⊗ 17 ✗ 18
8	8	9	10A	R	–										✗ 19 ✗ 20
9	S 13/7	11A	–												✗ 21 ⊗ 22
10 21	12A	13A	14A	R	R	XT	–								⊗ 23 ⊗ 24

Coin Toss: Visitors choose to serve first.

Score V-H

Visitors Serve: V 5 serves and scores first three regular points (1,2,3). Fourth serve develops into side-out. 3-0
Home Serve: H 11 serves, side-out. 3-0
Visitors Serve: V 6 serves, replay called (no attempted serve). V 6 serves two straight aces for points four and five. Next play is an opponent's substitution (H 11 is replaced by H 5 — XS 11/5). V 6 next two serves are for regular points (6,7) before a penalty on the Visitors awards the serve to the Home team (P —). 7-0
Home Serve: H 12 serves three straight points before Visitors (opponent) calls time out (XT). H 12 then serves points four, five, and six, with points five and six being aces. Next serve is a side-out. 7-6
Visitors Serve: V 13 replaces V 7. V 13 serves, side-out. 7-6
Home Serve: H 13 serves two straight regular points (7,8). Next serve is called a replay (R). Next play a penalty is called on Visitor (opponent), awarding point to Home team (P 9). *NOTE: A penalty on Home would have been denoted by P —.* Visitors call time out (XT). Home calls time out (T). H 13 serves one more regular point (10) before side-out. 7-10
Visitors Serve: V 8 serves three straight points (8,9,10), the last point being an ace. Next serve develops into a replay. Next serve develops into side-out. 10-10

Key: ⬚1 Point   ⬚– Side Out   ⬚P– Penalty Side Out
⬚2A Ace Point   ⬚P8 Penalty Point Awarded

Fig. 9.2 Sample game visitor. (By courtesy of the N.F.S.H.S.A.)

SAMPLE GAME

Home: *Independence South*

Serve	GAME 1		TIME OUTS 2 3				FINAL SCORE *14*						Referee's Verification *JR*
Home.	Player No.						Play						
X ⊗	*11 5 33*		–	*5/33*	*14*	–							
Z 14				*5*									
X 15	*12*		*1*	*2*	*3*	*X/T*	*4*	*5A*	*6A*	–			
X 16													
⊗ 17	*13*		*7*	*8*	*R*	*P9*	*X/T*	*T*	*10*	–			
⊗ 18													
X 19													
⊗ 20	*14*		–										
⊗ 21	*15*		*11*	*12*	*13A*	–	*XS 10/21*	–					
X 22													
X 23													
X 24	*16*		–										

Home Serve: H 14 serves, side-out.   10-10

Visitors Serve: Visitors substitute V 7 back in for V 13 (S 13/7). V 9 serves ace (point 11). Next serve, side-out.   11-10

Home Serve: H 15 serves three straight points (11,12,13) with the last of the three points being an ace. Visitors substitute V 21 for V 10 (XS 10/21). Next serve, side-out.   11-13

Visitors Serve: V 21 serves three straight aces (points 12,13,14). Next two serves develop into replays (R,R). Home calls time-out. Next serve, side-out.   14-13

Home Serve: H 16 serves, side-out.   14-13

NOTE: With each complete service rotation (all six players serve) a different color pencil or ink should be used to begin the next rotation (i.e. first complete rotation — black; second complete rotation — red; third complete rotation — green). In sample game player V5 served points 1,2,3, and a side-out in the first rotation (black ink). Her first serve the second time around was a side-out (red ink or in this case the shaded area).

Visitors Serve: V 5 serves, side-out.   14-13

Home Serve: Home substitutes H 33 for H 5. H 33 serves one point (14). Next serve, side-out.   14-14

Visitors Serve: V 6 serves two straight aces to win game. Record final score in appropriate boxes.   16-14

X- Opponent   [TS 2/3] Opponent   [X1] Opponents
[R] Replay   S- Substitution   Substitution   T - Time   Time Out
                                                        Out

Fig. 9.3 Sample game home. (By courtesy of the N.F.S.H.S.A.)

Basic Penalties and Rulings

A volleyball *game* is played to 15 points, with a two point margin needed to win. (Exception: games may be limited to eight minutes of ball-in-play action, but the game must still be won by two points.) A volleyball *match* consists of two out of three games in high school and three of five under NAGWS. The teams change sides of the net for each game. If the teams split and a final (third or fifth) game is necessary, a coin toss is conducted immediately after the second or fourth game in order to determine which team serves and the respective sides of the net for the final game. The teams remain on the same side of the net for the entire final game.

Only the serving team can score a point. If the servers' opponents win a given "point," it is termed "side-out" and the serve goes to the other team. When a serve touches the net, it is a side-out. A ball in play, other than a served ball, remains in play if it touches the net. After the serve, each team may touch the ball no more than three times in returning the ball to their opponents. A single player may not play the ball twice consecutively, with the exceptions of (1) the block and (2) following simultaneous contact by teammates or opponents.

Service
The server must be behind and to the right ten feet of the end line when the ball is contacted. A depth of at least six feet should be provided for the server. The ball may be hit from the hand or from a toss.

Ball Handling
The ball must be contacted cleanly and crisply by a body part or parts above and including the waist. It may not be double-hit by a single player, and it may not be thrown. Service returns *must* be cleanly hit, while a degree of discretionary leniency is granted on "sets," blocks at the net and, more recently, spike returns.

When any of the above rules are violated, the penalty is either side-out or point for the serving team. The volleyball official's job is simplified by this uniformity of penalties (either a point or side-out).

The practice of providing an assistant scorer and an assistant timer is specified in high school rules and is becoming more common. When present, these assistants are seated respectively next to and outside the official scorer and the official timer whom they are assisting.

Fouls at the Net
At the moment the ball passes over the net, it must be within the sidelines.

Net fouls have liberalized and now permit a player to cross the center line with the foot/feet as long as:

1. a part of the foot/feet remains on or above the center line.
2. the player does not touch the net; and (exception—no foul if touched only by the player's hair)
3. the player does not interfere with the play of the opponent.

Miscellaneous Rulings

1. *A game shall be forfeited* when (1) either team has fewer than six players before the match or (b) a team refuses to play when directed to do so by the referee.
2. *A player, coach, or substitute may be warned, penalized* (point or side-out) *or disqualified for unsportsmanlike acts.* Only the referee may assess these penalties. Such measures may be taken for a number of reasons, such as attempting to influence an official's decision, disrespect, objecting to a decision, etc. Considerable discretion is required, since disqualification is never mandatory for any act.
3. *The points made by a team should be cancelled* during the time of play when a player (a) was serving out of turn; (b) has entered a game for the fourth time (a player may enter a game only three times); or (c) has reentered a game in a position different from his or her first position in that game, relative to other players. Such violations also should be penalized when discovered via point or side-out. Alertness to these violations will alleviate the need to cancel points.
4. *The referee should rule a replay* when the circumstances warrant. Such circumstances include: double fouls, an official's mistaken whistle, a foreign object entering the court, a ball "held" above the net by opponents, a player injury, or conflicting line calls which the referee cannot resolve.

Mechanics

Positioning
Placed on an elevated stand, the referee gains a greatly advantageous but immobile view of play. Prior to the serve, the umpire moves slightly along the sideline towards the receiving team to determine that no overlapping is occurring. At the moment of the serve and throughout the point, the umpire stays with the net (not behind the standards) to check on net fouls and foot faults while the referee goes visually with the ball.

The goals of the line judge(s) are to remain well away (three to ten feet) from the boundary lines and to anticipate the action and move quickly to the most advantageous position which will not interfere with player action. Given *two* line judges, these officials are constantly jockeying for a position to call either the end line or the sideline for which they are responsible. Given *four* line judges, each line judge is assigned one of the end lines or one of the sidelines and therefore needs to move only to avoid interfering with player action.

Use of the Whistle

The referee's whistle controls all volleyball action. It tells the server when to serve and sounds the end of a rally, killing the play. The umpire's whistle and, occasionally, those of line judges, can also kill the play for cause. A well officiated volleyball match is characterized by frequent and definite hand signals and whistle soundings, *not* by verbal commmunication among officials, players and coaches.

There is an art to the use of the whistle in volleyball. The experienced and capable volleyball official varies use of the whistle according to the circumstances. When the action is fast and hectic before a large crowd, it is sometimes necessary to sound the whistle repeatedly with short, sharp blasts. When a ball is clearly out of bounds or a served ball hits the net only the mildest whistle is needed. The referee's whistle directing the server to serve should be of diminished intensity—loud enough to gain the attention of all players, but no louder. New officials are cautioned to hold their whistles out of their mouths when conversing with players, coaches or other officials.

Hand Signals

Decisive and clear hand signals are very important to the success of a volleyball official. Good hand signals tend to eliminate the necessity for unneeded verbal communication and excessive use of the whistle. When conversation and whistling can be reduced, the game becomes more the *player's* game than the officials'.

There are three requisites to effective hand signaling in volleyball. First, *know all the signals,* so that each can be used appropriately; second, execute the signals decisively, yet not dictatorially; and third, choose the right moment to exercise the signal, so that it need not be repeated or explained. There is an exact moment when all players and spectators normally look to the referee or umpire—whoever sounded the whistle.

Teamwork Among Officials

As mentioned before, the referee has the authority in volleyball to overrule another official. Obviously, this authority should be exercised

Fig. 9.4 (By courtesy of the
N.F.S.H.S.A.)

with discretion. Players and coaches as well as the other officials, become confused and irritated if the referee overrules fellow officials too frequently or without apparent reason.

The pregame discussion among members of a team of officials serves to establish the proper understanding for the particular match to be officiated. In a championship match where the umpire and line judges, as well as the referee, are experienced and knowledgeable, very few cases of overrulings by the referee would be expected. On the other hand, at lower levels of volleyball competition the referee is often the only member of the crew who really knows and understands volleyball rules and mechanics. In such circumstances, it may be necessary for the more experienced person not only to step in but to set the stage for doing so before the match. Generally, the referee should avoid overruling any decision by another official when the other official had a good view. The referee should use great discretion in overruling the umpire on ball-handling decisions and net fouls.

Given an experienced referee/umpire crew, an observer would notice that the two would establish and maintain eye contact with each other whenever possible—that either would anticipate calls out of the view of the other and make the appropriate rulings. The referee controls the "flow" of the game. Neither official tries to over call the other. If during a match one official, either referee or umpire, feels her/his partner has lost concentration or is not calling tightly enough the partner can be brought fully back into the match by the one official making an obvious call that is normally the partner's call to make.

Beyond the "referee may overrule" aspect of volleyball officials' teamwork lies the other normal aspects of officiating teamwork; a willingness to communicate with one another, a general attitude of support for one another, a collective capability to rule and signal decisively. The relative lack of movement by volleyball officials, however, eliminates much of the necessity for teamwork found in such sports as basketball, football, baseball, and water polo. One other important aspect of volleyball officiating teamwork involves a close check between the umpire and the scorer and the timer to ascertain that no errors have been made in either scoring or timing.

Problem Calls

Ball Handling Decisions The most difficult responsibility of volleyball officiating is to maintain consistency in decisions relative to ball handling fouls. The basic principle for ruling on borderline ball handling situations can be stated in the form of a question: "Did the ball *visibly come to rest* on the player's body part(s) at contact?" Experienced volleyball officials and observers have found that certain hand-ball contact positions often result in the ball coming visibly to rest at contact. Thus, the official should be mentally prepared to signal a ball handling foul when:

1. The ball contacts the fingers and the hand in a spread-fingered "underhand" position, whether the player is facing the net or away from it.
2. Two hands are used to "throw" the ball from one side of the player's head to the other; or
3. A player attempts to return a hard driven spike or serve by means of the normal two-handed "overhand" volleyball pass.

These three contact positions quite often produce ball handling fouls, but it is critical that a referee actually observe a ball handling foul rather than anticipating one as a result of a player's position. The principle of ball handling fouls must take precedence. Each ball handling decision made by the effective volleyball referee results from a judgment regarding whether or not the ball visibly came to rest.

The current trend in volleyball officiating, caused primarily by international volleyball influence, is for the referee to be quite strict in whistling down improper ball handling used in returning a serve or spike but to be less strict in ruling on ball handling errors occurring on bumps and second touches. (The second touch is usually the "set-up" touch. There is considerable worldwide disagreement regarding the strictness of interpretation on third, or "attacking" touches.) No other single interpretations can influence the course of a volleyball match as will ball handling judgments.

Overlapping
With the development of more complex offenses, overlapping is becoming more and more difficult to detect. Switching is occurring both before and after the ball is served. See the play rulings at the end of the chapter.

Counting Touches
The basic rules on touches are that each team is entitled to just three (and no more) touches of the ball each time a ball in play comes to their side of the net, and that one player may not touch or be touched by the ball twice in succession. These apparent straightforward rules frequently become complicated during the normal course of a match. For the players and coaches, touch rule interpretations provide a basis for

fairness. For the officials, however, these interpretations require a thorough understanding of the rules, experiences, concentration and alertness—especially when the action is skilled and rapid.

Question 1: *When is play on the ball NOT COUNTED as one of a team's three touches?*

Answer: When the play involves a *block* or *simultaneous touches by opponents.* The touch following the block or simultaneous contact counts as the first touch of three permissible touches.

Question 2: *When is it legal for a player to play the ball TWICE IN SUCCESSION?*

Answers:

1. Following *simultaneous contacts by opponents;* (The ball may next be legally played by a player involved in the simultaneous contact on whose side of the net the ball falls—and *counts as the first touch.*)
2. Following *simultaneous contacts by teammates;* (The ball may next be legally played by either teammate and *counts as the second touch.*)
3. Following a *block.* (A "block" by definition must be above and close to the net and not executed with a downward swing of the arm or hand. A player(s) involved in a block may legally play the ball next as a *first touch.*)

Question 3: *During a single attempt to play the ball, when is it legal for a player to be contacted by the ball twice in succession?*

Answers:

1. Following a *block;* (The multiple-contact block does not count as a touch and may be followed by another touch by the same player, which counts as *a first touch.*)
2. On *one attempt to play a spiked ball not already touched,* provided the ball does not rebound from one forearm or hand to the other forearm or hand. (This counts as *one touch*—the next touch must be by a different player.)

The referee who works advanced levels of volleyball competition is challenged by the fact that the above interpretations come into play frequently. Furthermore, they occasionally occur *in combination with each other* as a part of a single game action. Further complicating such situations are the possibilities of net violations or center line violations. These complications can cause the referee and umpire to divide their attention and perhaps to miss an action that calls for a decision. The referee should *concentrate primarily on the ball,* utilizing peripheral vision and feet of the net to determine whether or not other violations have occurred.

Reaching Over the Net to Block

Players may reach over the net to their opponent's side while attempting to block a *ball traveling toward the net* so long as they do not interfere with the play of a setter. A foul should be called if the ball is contacted by the blocker while moving parallel to or away from the net.

Determining Net Violations

It is frequently very difficult for the referee or umpire to determine whether or not the net has been touched while the ball is in play. When two to six opposing players are very close to the net and the action is explosive, net violations can easily be missed or ruled against the wrong team. No net violation may be called if the *force of the ball* causes the net to brush a player.

The well qualified volleyball official has the capability, developed through experience, of directing vision to the ball while applying discriminating peripheral vision to the net zone. The learning officials on the other hand, must rely more on feel of the net supplemented by a constantly shifting direct observation until such time as his or her peripheral vision becomes more discriminating and reliable. The referee's hand-feel of the net cable can serve as a secondary check, but there is no substitute for actually seeing the contact with the net. Volleyball officials must avoid the temptation to "guess" on net contact fouls; they should call only those net fouls about which they are certain.

Balls Passing Over the Net from Out of Bounds

Volleyball rules stipulate that the ball becomes dead and point or sideout is ruled if the ball passes over the net from one side to the other *completely outside* the vertical tape markers or *not entirely within* the net antennas. The addition of net antennas in recent years has helped the officials tremendously to make this call accurately and consistently. Nevertheless, the prescribed positions of volleyball officials make this decision difficult especially when there are only two line judges. Official rules imply that the line judges should call such fouls. In actual practice, the referee and umpire also call them even though their angle of vision is poor.

There is no problem when these shots are directed precisely at or away from a line judge behind one of the corners of the court. The best solution to this problem call is anticipation on the part of the line judges—a readiness to move to the precise spot where they will have a perfect angle of vision. A line judge is free to anticipate this call and to drastically alter court position when a second touch is misdirected out of bounds. The referee should instruct line judges about this difficult decision before the game, urging them to anticipate and to *move.* If, during the contest the line judges *are* anticipating and gaining good position, the referee and umpire should leave this call to the line judges as much as possible.

Officials' View of Action Is Screened by Players

Quite often the referee or umpire is unable to see the actual touch of the ball at the precise moment of the touch because an intervening player has screened the vision of the official. Fortunately, either the referee or the umpire usually has an unobstructed view when a fellow official is screened. Two guidelines apply to such situations: (1) the proven officiating maxim that *you must call only what you see, not what you guessed to have happened,* and (2) the referee and the umpire should accept the fact that occasionally one of them will be screened out and the call must be made by the other. A predetermined gesture can be used whereby one official can communicate to the other, ''I was screened out—that is your call to make.''

Miscellaneous Considerations

Pregame Conference

It is specified in the rules that the officials should discuss their particular approach to the match. At this meeting such items as signals, positioning, the authority limits of line judges, and helping each other when screened, can be reviewed. Questions on particular rules and rule interpretations can be raised, analyzed and agreed upon. The emphasis in these pregame officials' conferences is upon establishing teamwork and consistency within the officiating crew. The referee should take the lead, but, according to the dictates of his or her personal approach, should involve each official in the discussion.

Officiating Evaluated By Coaches

What qualities do you appreciate in a volleyball official?

1. Confidence
2. Commanding presence
3. Consistency
4. Businesslike

Miscellaneous comments

1. A coach looks for an official who possesses a high tolerance for stress and pressure.

2. A referee should be capable of making a quick and fair decision to prevent delays in the game.
3. Officials must be cognizant of current rule interpretations.
4. A good official with a degree of showmanship and fine personality can convey to the crowd moments of finesse, daring and explosiveness.

Officiating Evaluated by Officials

What is the most difficult play to call in volleyball?

1. Observing a spiked ball touch blocker
2. Ball handling violations
3. Touching of the net or ball by spikers and blockers

What is the most difficult phase of mechanics in officiating volleyball?

1. Officiating stand not elevated enough to allow full view of the total play
2. Concentrating on top portion of net during a spike attempt
3. Player's back to officials when playing the ball, blocking the vision of the official

Miscellaneous comments

1. A quick reaction time and keen sense of the game is required.
2. There is a definite need for formal volleyball officiating associations.
3. A good referee subtly controls the game, blends into the flow of the game.
4. Officials must make their rulings in a non-accusing manner—be matter-of-fact rather than "HA! I caught you!"
5. Crucial is the ability to make a subjective call based on an accurate knowledge of the skill involved.

Play Rulings

Situation: Team A forfeits to Team B with the score: (a) Team A-13 and Team B-14; or (b) Team A-4 and Team B-4 *Ruling:* in (a), Team B wins 14-13; in (b), Team B wins 15-0. (1-5-2)

Situation: A player enters the game wearing (a) a small stud earring; (b) a medical tag taped to the body under the shirt. *Ruling:* (a) Illegal; (b) Legal. *Comment:* If a player requires the wearing of a medical tag or religious medal; it is to be taped to the body under the uniform. Chains, etc. shall not be worn. (4-1-5)

Situation: The referee notifies the coaches the pre-match conference is to start. The coach of Team A (a) sends the playing captain but does not attend personally; (b) sends the assistant coach and playing captain; (c) attends with the playing captain but leaves before the coin toss is conducted; (d) sends the team manager and the playing captain. *Ruling:* (b) and (c) are Legal; (a) and (d) are Illegal. *Comment:* The coach or assistant coach shall attend the pre-game conference (5-3-1)

Situation: A ball landing near an end line is called "in" by one line judge and "out" by the other line judge. The referee: (a) sees the ball land; or (b) does not see the ball land. *Ruling:* In (a), the referee shall call the play as he or she saw it. In (b), the referee may give preference to the line judge closest to where the ball landed, or declare a replay. (5-3-3)

Situation: The umpire stops play and calls a net foul. The referee disagrees and declares a replay. *Ruling:* The referee may overrule a decision made by another official when, in the referee's judgment, an erroneous call was made. (5-3-3)

Situation: During a play at the net, the referee cannot determine whether a back line player, who was in front of the spiking line, returned a ball higher than the top of the net. *Ruling:* No call shall be made unless the official can clearly determine a foul has been committed. (5-3-3)

Situation: Immediately after the referee gives a visual and audio signal for the serve, the umpire blows the whistle for a substitution. The server holds up on her serve hearing the second whistle. *Ruling:* Official's time-out. The referee verbally informs the umpire the substitution was out-of-order and gives a new visual and audio signal for the serve. (5-2-3)

Situation: Prior to the beginning of the first game, an official notices several players wearing jewelry. *Ruling:* The official may remind these players the jewelry must be removed prior to the game. Any player discovered wearing jewelry after the first serve is contacted shall be penalized for unnecessary delay. (5-4-1)

Situation: A team has only 6 players one of which is injured during the first game and unable to play. *Ruling:* The team may play with 5 players, and the position of the injured player shall remain open throughout the game, which means the team shall rotate an extra position when it is the injured player's turn to serve. (6-1-2)

Situation: The receving team is in the following positions at the instant of the serve:

RULING: (a) Illegal, RF and CF are overlapping;
(b) Legal;
(c) Illegal, CF and CB are overlapping.

Situation: The receiving team is set up as follows:

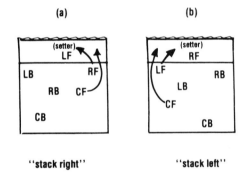

"stack right"   "stack left"

Ruling: (a) and (b) Legal.

Situation: CF on the receiving team claims RF on the serving team, who is standing close to the net but not jumping or waving, is intentionally screening her view of the server. *Ruling:* This is not intentional screening. *Comment:* No player on the receiving team is entitled to a specific position on the floor. If a player on the receiving team cannot see the server, that player should move. If, after that player moves, the serving team's player moves to take another position which blocks that player's view of the server, the referee shall call intentional screening. (12-2-PEN #1) (6-4-1)

Situation: Eight minutes before the scheduled starting time of a match, Team A (the serving team) presents its roster and lineup to the scorer. Then 5 minutes before the match, Team A presents 2 additional names for the roster. *Ruling:* Team B will serve first, leading 1-0. (7-2-Penalty)

Situation: LF on Team A steps completely across the out-of-bounds extension of the centerline: (a) to hit the ball to teammates; (b) as a result of momentum from the play of the ball on Team A's side of the centerline; or (c) in order to get out of the way of a play by a teammate. *Ruling:* In each case, it is a foot fault, and a point or side-out is awarded to Team B. (9-11-4) (9-3-1)

Situation: A back line player jumps from behind the spiking line, contacts the ball above the top of the net and in front of the spiking line, and lands in front of the spiking line. The ball is returned. *Ruling:* Legal. (9-3-3)

Situation: RF on Team A spikes the ball for a point after which he: (a) steps over the centerline; (b) touches the net. *Ruling:* No foul in (a) or (b). *Comment:* The ball must be in play for a net foul or foot fault to occur. (9-4-3)

Situation: LF on Team A contacts the ball on the sideline and returns it to the middle of the playing area of Team B by turning his wrist during contact. *Ruling:* This is a legal hit unless the official actually sees the ball remain in contact with LF's hand while the hand is turning. (9-5-1)

Situation: CF on Team A blocks a spike which sends the ball straight into the air over Team A's court. CF plays the ball next. *Ruling:* This is a legal play and CF's play is the team's first hit. (9-6-2)

Situation: LB on Team A saves a spiked ball so it deflects off her hand to: (a) her shoulder; (b) her biceps; (c) her other hand; (d) a forearm. *Ruling:* (a) and (b) Legal hit; (c) and (d) Illegal, double hit. (9-6-2)

Situation: There is simultaneous contact by Team A's spiker and Team B's blocker on a ball which is: (a) moving parallel to the net directly over the net; (b) moving toward the net on Team A's side of the net; (c) moving parallel to the net on Team A's side of the net. *Ruling:* (a) Legal; (b) and (c) Illegal. *Comment:* The offensive team must have the first opportunity to contact the ball if there is a player in the area. (9-7-2)

Situation: LF on Team A spikes the ball, but at the instant the ball hits the floor on Team B's side of the court, the spiker contacts the net. *Ruling:* Double foul. (9-11-2) *Comment:* Team B's failure to return the ball is a foul, as is the net foul by LF. Because they occur at the same instant, the proper call is double foul and a replay. (9-10-1) (9-8-2)

BIBLIOGRAPHY

1. National Federation of State High School Associations. *1983-84 Volleyball Rule Book* Kansas City, Missouri, 1983.

10

Wrestling

The Game

Wrestling is one of the oldest forms of sport and combat dating back to 300 B.C. and the Stone Age Man. (2:3) Prehistoric man relied on strength and endurance to provide for himself when at peace and in combat. In 1927 the NCAA organized the Wrestling Rules Committee which proved to be the greatest step ever taken toward developing amateur wrestling in America. (5:4)

The sport of wrestling is distinct in that it pits man against man in physical combat. Wrestling, one of the most strenuous sports, involves 6 to 8 minutes of consistent action testing the contestant's speed, agility, balance skill, endurance, strength, timing and conditioning. In contrast to other sports where boys of greater height and weight have an advantage, a boy of any body type can participate in wrestling with good results. (5:8)

Wrestling is one of the most difficult sports to officiate because the actions of the wrestlers are quick and are accompanied by constantly changing positions. In wrestling, an official may warn a contestant visually or verbally of a potential injury situation if his whistle is not readily available. The judgment of the referee has profound influence on the outcome of the match and the meet.

Photo courtesy of the Long Beach Independent Press Telegram

Officials and Their Responsibilities

Wrestling is somewhat unique, in that the referee works alone in most dual meets. Mat judges are generally provided in semi-finals and championship meets to assist the referee.

Officials Uniform and Equipment

The wrestling referee should wear a short-sleeved, knit shirt with black and white 1 inch stripes, full length black trousers with black belt, black gym shoes and white socks. The referee should also have a silver coin or colored disc and a whistle.

Referee

The referee has full control of the meet and his decisions are final. The referee's primary responsibilities include checking the wrestlers to avoid health and safety hazards, clarifying the rules, awarding points for competitive maneuvers, penalizing for infractions of the rules and, finally, declaring a winner. To minimize injuries, the referee should be constantly alert to detect illegal holds. Since a wrestler has only six to eight minutes to prove his superiority over his opponent, the referee must dedicate himself to the orderly progress of each match.

Pre-meet responsibilities. The referee should arrive one hour before the meet, dressed in official attire, and ready to officiate. He should get the coaches together and clarify his interpretation of the rules as needed. The contestants must be inspected for grooming, which would include fingernails, hair and general cleanliness. Just before the meet, the referee should call the two captains to the center of the mat to conduct the coin toss for choice of position in split or tie matches and remind the wrestlers of new rules he intends to enforce. When a match is to start, the referee should call the first two contestants to the center of the mat, where they shake hands and are given brief instructions:

1. They are not to stop wrestling until the referee blows his whistle.
2. They are to do most of their wrestling near the center circle of the mat. (5:249)

After the match. As in other sports, the referee should make it a point to leave for the dressing room immediately after the final match. The referee should not comment on the meet to spectators, press, coaches or athletes.

Mat Judges

The judges' main function is to assist the referee on any action on the mat. This could include stalling, illegal holds, technical violations, and even disagreeing with a fall called by the referee. (7:11)

Match Timekeeper

The timekeeper is responsible for keeping the overall time of each match, time-out for injury, calling out the time remaining and for signaling the referee, contestants, and spectators at the end of each period. The end of the period should be signaled by tapping the referee's shoulder or sounding a buzzer. The practice of throwing in a towel to signify the end of the period should be strongly discouraged. The assistant timekeeper is responsible for recording the time advantages of the contestants on a second clock.

Scorer

The scorer should work closely with the timekeeper and record the points scored as signaled by the referee. The scorer is also responsible for recording the down positions during the course of the match. The team score is the scorer's final responsibility.

Basic Infractions, Penalties and Rulings

Illegal and Potentially Dangerous Holds

The referee must be alert and in position in order to stop an illegal hold or potentially dangerous hold. He should anticipate the injury potential of these holds and attempt to prevent or block them before they reach the danger point. Whenever possible, an illegal hold should be prevented, rather than called.

Table 10.1

Illegal Holds

hammerlock above the right angle	twisting hammerlock
front headlock without the arm	full nelson
headlock without the arm	straight scissors and over-scissors
strangle holds	body slams
twisting knee lock	key lock
overhead double arm bar	full back suplay from a rear standing position
bending, twisting or forcing the head, or any limb beyond its normal limits of movement	locking the hands behind the back in a double arm bar from the neutral position
	any hold used for punishment only (6:33)

Table 10.1 *Continued*

Potentially Dangerous Holds		
double wristlock		
chicken wing		
guillotine, when being applied with the limb forced beyond normal range of movement	toe hold split scissors	(6:37–38)

Unnecessary Roughness
Intentional striking, gouging, kicking, hair pulling, butting, elbowing, or an intentional act which endangers life or limb should be penalized. A wrestler lifting his opponent off the mat is responsible for his safe return to the mat. If he drops his opponent forcefully, he should be penalized.

Conduct of Contestants
Penalties will be administered for:

1. Misconduct by either wrestler.
2. Abusive or unsportsmanlike conduct.
3. Flagrant misconduct; and
4. Unnecessary roughness (7:24)

Conduct of the Coaches, Team Personnel and Others
Unsportsmanlike conduct by the wrestlers, coaches, and spectators will result in the removal of the offenders from the wrestling area at the request of the referee. Coaches are restricted to the bench while the match is in progress. If not curtailed, such action could provide an unfair advantage to a contestant. In addition, it is disconcerting to the referee.

Technical Violations
Penalties will be administered for the following:

1. Delaying the match
2. Assuming an incorrect starting position
3. Going out of the wrestling area
4. Grasping of clothing; and
5. Interlocking or overlapping the hands, fingers or arms around the opponent's body
6. The figure 4 scissors
7. Leaving the wrestling area (7:24)

The collegiate infraction penalty table is essentially the same as the interscholastic penalty chart. The college summary of technical

PENALTY CHART

Infractions	Warning	First Penalty	Second Penalty	Third Penalty	Fourth Penalty	Rule
Illegal Holds	No	1 Pt.	1 Pt.	2 Pts.	Disqualify	7-1
Technical Violations	No	1 Pt.	1 Pt.	2 Pts.	Disqualify	7-3
False start or incorrect starting position		A caution is given for the first offense and for each infraction thereafter there is a 1-point penalty. (Does not count toward disqualification.)				
Stalling	Yes	1 Pt.	1 Pt.	2 Pts.	Disqualify	7-6
Misconduct of Contestants and Unnecessary Roughness	No	1 Pt.	1 Pt.	2 Pts.	Disqualify	7-4-1
Misconduct of Coaches	No	Deduct 1 Team Point	Remove from premises on second penalty. Removal is for duration of dual meet or tournament session only.			6-6-5
Unsportsmanlike Conduct - Contestants, Coaches and Non-participating Personnel	No	Deduct 1 Team Point	Remove from premises on second penalty. Removal is for duration of dual meet or tournament session only.			7-4-2 7-5-1
Flagrant Misconduct - Contestants	No	Disqualify on first offense and deduct 1 team point. Remove from premises for dual meet or tournament session. Contestant is eliminated from further competition in dual meet or tournament.				7-4-3
Flagrant Misconduct - Coaches and Non-participating Personnel	No	Remove from premises on first offense and deduct 1 team point. Removal is for the duration of the dual meet or tournament.				7-5-2
Greasy Substance on Skin, Improper Grooming, Objectionable Pads and Braces, Illegal Equipment or Uniform.	No	Disqualify if not removed or corrected in allotted time (2 min.).				3-1-3 to 5

Note 1—Disqualification due to technical violation, illegal hold, stalling or misconduct of contestants and unnecessary roughness does not eliminate a contestant from further competition in tournaments. Disqualification for unsportsmanlike conduct eliminates a contestant or coach from the tournament session only. Disqualification for flagrant misconduct eliminates a contestant from further competition in the tournament and a coach is removed for the duration of the tournament.
Note 2—Points for unnecessary roughness, grasping clothing or locking hands, are awarded in addition to points earned.
EXAMPLE OF INFRACTIONS—Wrestler "A" in the first period locks hands—penalty, 1 point. Second period, he uses illegal hold—penalty, 1 point. Later in second period he is warned for stalling. In third period, he is called for stalling again—penalty, 2 points. Later in the third period he locks his hands—penalty, disqualification.

SUMMARY OF TECHNICAL VIOLATIONS

Delaying Match (7-3-1)
Assuming Incorrect Starting Position (7-3-2)
Going Off Wrestling Area (7-3-3)
Grasping Clothing, Etc. (7-3-4)
Interlocking Hands (7-3-5)
Figure 4 Body Scissors (7-3-6)
Leaving Mat Without Permission (7-3-7)

Fig. 10.1 Wrestling penalties. (By courtesy of the N.F.S.H.S.A.)

violations is increased to include stalling, holding legs, false starts and starting positions, and coaching an injured contestant.

Mechanics

The most important concern for the referee is to move constantly to secure the best possible position to observe and protect the wrestler in dangerous situations. Not moving diminishes the effectiveness of the referee, encourages illegal holds and possible injury to the competitors.

Major High School Differences

High School	College
APPEARANCE—No facial hair allowed.	Mustache is allowed.
COACHING INJURED WRESTLER—No rule.	Unsportsmanlike conduct.
OPTIONAL OFFENSIVE STARTING POSITION—No rule.	Can choose to use modified version of international start.
RIDING TIME—No riding time.	One point for one minute or more accumulated time advantage more than opponent.
FALL—Two seconds.	One second.
WEIGHT CLASSES—98 [44.5kg], 105 [47.6kg], 112 [50.8kg], 119 [54.0kg], 126 [57.2kg], 132 [59.9kg], 138 [62.6kg], 145 [65.8kg], 155 [70.3kg], 167 [75.7kg], 185 [83.9kg], unl.	118 [53.5kg], 126 [57.2kg], 134 [60.8kg], 142 [64.4kg], 150 [68.0kg], 158 [71.7kg], 167 [75.8kg], 177 [80.3kg], 190 [86.2kg], unl.
LENGTH OF MATCH—Three two-minute periods.	First period, three minutes; second and third periods, two minutes.
CONSOLATION MATCHES—Three periods; first, one minute, second and third, two minutes.	Three two-minute periods.
SIGNALING FOR STALLING—Same as college except do not stop match for warning offensive wrestler. Stop to warn in neutral. Stop to penalize in all positions.	Stop match when warning and penalizing in all situations except when warning or penalizing the defensive or neutral wrestler.
NUMBER OF MATCHES—No wrestler shall compete in more than four full-length matches in any day.	No similar rule.
WEIGHT ALLOWANCE—Allowance of two pounds [0.9kg] added to growth allowance beginning on December 25. An additional pound is added on February 1 and March 1 for a net allowance of four pounds [1.8 kg].	Three-pound [1.4kg] allowance in November and December, two pounds [0.9kg] in January, one pound [0.5kg] in February, except qualifying tournaments which are scratch weight.
WEIGH-IN—Shoulder-to-shoulder weigh-in within a maximum of one hour and a minimum of one-half hour before the time a dual meet is scheduled to begin.	Maximum of five hours and minimum of one-half hour unless otherwise mutually agreed upon. (Contestant must face away from the dial or weight indicator of the scale.)

Fig. 10.2 (By courtesy of the N.C.A.A.)

MAJOR HIGH SCHOOL DIFFERENCES

COMPETITION—A wrestler weighing in for one weight class may be shifted to a higher weight, provided it is not more than one weight class above that for which his actual stripped weight qualifies him.

A contestant may wrestle any weight class above the one for which he weighed in except unlimited weight class contestants, who must weigh a minimum of 177 pounds.

SWEAT BOX—The use of sweat box or similar heat devices for weight reduction purposes is prohibited.

No similar rule.

UNLIMITED WEIGHT CLASS—Unlimited class contestants must weigh a minimum of 184 lbs. [83.6kg].

Contestants must weigh a minimum of 177 lbs. [80.3kg].

ILLEGAL HOLDS—Any Salto or suplay in which a contestant goes to the top of his head from the standing position is illegal.

Straight back suplay and overscissors are illegal.

OVERTIME—Is a completely new match and warnings and penalties are not accumulative from match to overtime period. Criteria will determine winner if OT ends in a draw.

Same—Injury time carries over.

NEUTRAL STALLING—When a wrestler continuously avoids contact and plays the edge of the mat. When the wrestler steps out-of-bounds, it provides a sequence of: 1. Warning visually, and 2. Penalizing.

Stalling warning will be given one wrestler at end of first period of regulation time if no points have been scored or no stalling warning has been given.

DELAY OF MATCH—Treated as a technical violation.

Treated as stalling.

Fig. 10.2 cont.

The referee should stay far enough away from the wrestlers to avoid blocking the view of the other officials and spectators. It must be remembered that wrestlers may change positions so fast that several points may be awarded in a few seconds. The "away" position of the referee affords the best possible position to see both men and also the off mat limits. This position also allows the referee sufficient area to avoid exposing himself to wrestlers coming over on top of him.

Wrestling Area

The wrestling area should be no less than 24' square in high school and 32' square for college with a 10' diameter circle. An alternate wrestling area should be a circular area of not less than 28' in high school and 32' in college with the same 10' diameter circle.

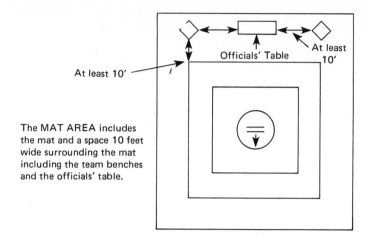

The MAT AREA includes
the mat and a space 10 feet
wide surrounding the mat
including the team benches
and the officials' table.

Fig. 10.3 Wrestling match lay-out
(7:9)

Weigh-In Procedure

Officials should arrive one hour before the match to conduct the weigh-ins. Otherwise the weigh-in would be administered by the host coach, a situation which could result in the disqualification of a wrestler and determine the outcome of the meet. The coach should not be placed in such a vulnerable position. In the absence of the referee, both coaches shall supervise the weigh-ins.

Failure to make weight will render a given wrestler ineligible to wrestle in that weight class. A contestant not able to make weight may enter the weight class next highest. Both interscholastic and intercollegiate rules allow for weight allowance provisions for dual and tournament competition. Interscholastic wrestling also has a growth allowance provision.

While Wrestlers Are on Their Feet

The referee sounds a whistle to start the match. He should face the scoring table with the contestants, scorers, and timers in full view. The referee should keep moving from one side to the other to get a clear view of both sides of the action, keeping a safe distance to avoid interfering with the progress of the match. The referee should watch for wrestlers intentionally backing off the mat and for stalling techniques; he should be alert to the enforcement of illegal starting position and action in collegiate competition.

Table 10.2   Weight Classes

High School	College
98	118
105	126
112	134
119	142
126	150
132	158
138	167
145	177
155	190
167	UNL
185	
UNL	

OFFICIAL WEIGH-IN SHEET

Date_____ Time_____

Auburn University	Weight Class
	118
	126
	134
	142
	150
	158
	167
	177
	190
	UNL

Signed by ....

Fig. 10.4 (5.220)

When Wrestlers Are On The Mat

The referee must be alert while the wrestlers are down on the mat, since positions are subject to quick changes. When the wrestlers become entangled, it is difficult to tell who has the advantage; especially along the edge of the mat. The referee should continue the match in the referee's position, at the beginning of the second and third periods; when the contestants go off the mat with one wrestler having the advantage, and, if the match is stopped because of an injury or an illegal hold when one wrestler has the advantage. In high school wrestling the official should assume a position in front of the wrestlers, facing the scoring table, when continuing the match from the referee's position or on the mat. The referee should enforce the following requirements for the man in the down position:

1. Are his hands, knees and feet parallel to each other?
2. Are his hands at least one foot in front of his knees?
3. Are his hands flat on the mat?
4. Is he sitting still?

A brief description of the referee's position by Hopke and Kidder (1:43) is as follows: The wrestler must be on both hands and knees with hands at least 12″ in front of knees. In collegiate wrestling, the contestant must keep both knees on the mat even and behind the rear starting line. The heels of both hands must be on the mat in front of the forward starting line. (6:13) The weight of the wrestler's body should be back with the hands touching the mat lightly, fingers pointing ahead and elbows slightly bent. This position will allow for a fast reaction of the bottom man. The referee should encourage a head-up position prior to the signal to begin wrestling. The referee should enforce the following requirements regarding the top man's position:

1. Is his hand flat on the stomach of the opponent?
2. Is his hand in the position on his opponent's elbow?
3. Does his leg touch the opponent's leg?
4. Is his head in a legal position?
5. Is his knee outside of the parallel line of the hand, knee or foot? (5:250)

It should be noted that current rules call for the knee on the nearest side to be down on the mat in high school rules and one knee to be down on the mat in college rules.

When the referee is satisfied that the contestants have assumed their proper position, he should raise his hand to indicate to the wrestlers and the timer that the match is ready to begin. The referee continues the match by sounding his whistle and bringing his arm down sharply. The referee should remain close to the contestants at all times to block illegal holds, to determine when the wrestlers go off the mat, to award points for takedowns, escapes, near falls and falls. Most important, the referee should be in a position to prevent possible bodily injury to competitors.

Mat Judging

Mat judges are normally employed during semi-final and final championship matches. The mat judges should sit or kneel outside the wrestling area and observe the action from that vantage point. When a judge has an opinion different from the referee, he should raise his hand to gain the attention of the referee. When both judges disagree with the referee, the referee will stop the match and conduct a conference with the mat judges. This conference will be held on the edge of the mat in front of the timers-scorers table. Following the majority decision of the three officials on the situation in question, the scorers' table will be informed of any scoring change and the match is resumed.

Whistle Use

The whistle should be in good working order and available for immediate use. The whistle should be used only when required to start and stop the action, and then forcibly.

Hand Signals and Awarding Points

Hand signals are important to convey decisions to the scoring table, and coaches, spectators, such as points scored, illegal holds and timeouts. Effective use of signals can alleviate the need for discussions during the match. The referee should point to the wrestler who has gained the advantage and at the same time, holding his other hand above his head, indicate the number of points to be awarded with his fingers extended upward. Verbal statements should accompany hand signals for clarification. This aids in keeping the wrestlers, scoring table, and spectators informed as to what has happened when it happened. Referees should not assume that the points signalled are recorded. They should follow up by checking the scoreboard. If not thus recorded, the match should be stopped immediately and the scoring be rectified.

Protest

Section 20. Committees can be appointed at tournaments to hear all protests. Coaches only may protest errors in recording points or match results and nonjudgemental errors in the application of the rules. The coach must inform the official scorer and the referee of his intent to protest the bout before the boutsheet is removed from the scorer's table. The referee will note this intent to protest the bout on the boutsheet and will notify the opposing wrestler not to leave the area until the matter is settled. These protests must be filed with the tournament committee in writing within a 10 minute period following the bout. (6:32)

Problem Calls

Calling Near Falls and Falls

Two point "near-fall" requirements are satisfied if both shoulders or scapula of the defensive wrestler are held momentarily within four inches of the mat or less, or when one shoulder or scapula is touching the mat and the other shoulder is held at an angle of 45 degress or less from the mat. A three point near fall is awarded if these requirements have been held continuously for five seconds.

Novice officials are too anxious to award points for near falls before the defensive wrestler escapes or time expires. Don't confuse pauses as new starts on move for new point awards. (exception would be if opponent stops motion—then new point award is possible). Premature awarding of points could lead to duplication of awards. Each situation must be continuous and taken to its conclusion before the points are awarded.

The fall is the final outcome of a well-wrestled chain of maneuvers. (4:69) In order to call a fall, the referee should be down on the mat "in the middle of the action" where he can see the scapulae in contact with the mat. When blocked out by the entangled wrestlers, it is permissible to feel under the shoulders of the wrestler on your blind side to determine contact with the mat. A one second count by the referee is required for a fall in college and a two second count in high school. As soon as the fall requirements are satisfied, the referee should raise one hand and quickly strike the mat with his palm. There is a tendency to lean towards the near-fall call. The one second college fall requirement implies anticipation of this call.

Edge of the Mat Calls

If one wrestler has an "advantage" position, the match should continue as long as the supporting parts of either wrestler remain within the boundary lines of the wrestling area. Wrestling should continue if a *fall is imminent,* as long as both shoulders of the defensive wrestler are within the boundary lines. Consistency in judgement on the part of the referee is imperative. Vacillation in this situation may destroy the confidence of the wrestlers and coaches.

Fig. 10.5 (By courtesy of the
N.F.S.H.S.A.)

```
┌─────────────────────────────────────────────────────────────┐
│                    SUMMARY OF SCORING                         │
│                                                              │
│         Dual Meet                        Tournament          │
│                                                              │
│  Fall ................... 6 pts.   Fall ................. 1 pt. │
│  Forfeit ............... 6 pts.    Default .............. 1 pt. │
│  Default .............. 6 pts.     Forfeit ............. 1 pt.  │
│  Disqualification ...... 6 pts.    Disqualification ...... 1 pt. │
│  Decision                          Advancement              │
│    (by 12 or more pts.) .... 5 pts.  Championship Bracket .... 1 pt. │
│    (by 8 thru 11 pts.) ...... 4 pts. Consolation Bracket .... 1/2 pt. │
│    (by less than 8 pts.) ..... 3 pts. Decision              │
│  Draw ................. 2 pts.       (by 12 or more pts.) .... 3/4 pt. │
│                                      (by 8 or more pts.) ..... 1/2 pt. │
│                                                              │
│                      Individual Match                        │
│  Takedown ............ 2 pts.   Near-Fall ............ 2 or 3 pts. │
│  Escape ............... 1 pt.   Time-Advantage .......... 1 pt.  │
│  Reversal ............. 2 pts.     (Maximum for 1 full minute)  │
└─────────────────────────────────────────────────────────────┘
```

Fig. 10.6 (By courtesy of the
N.C.A.A.)

Interlocking Hands
The detection of which wrestler's hand is interlocked is sometimes difficult to determine when the wrestlers are down on the mat. Too often a wrestler is penalized for interlocking hands when he actually has his opponent's hand. The referee should be certain before making this call. The situation is most common when the wrestlers are executing the standup maneuver. Interlocking hands or gripping the clothing also occurs frequently during an escape or reverse maneuver.

Stalling
Stalling determinants should be clearly understood. Each wrestler must be working to improve his position or pin his opponent. The bottom man must make a legitimate attempt to gain control. Stalling on the top man is more difficult to call. Stalling penalties should be proceeded by a warning and strictly enforced. Since the stalling rule presents a judgment problem, the rule has been minimized in importance through the years. Consistency is the key in this ruling.

WRESTLING MEET

Date .... vs. .... Place ....

Won by .... Score .... to ....

Weight Class	Contestants	Up or Down	Man'ver Points	Period First	Second Period	Third Period	Time Adv.	Match Points	Team Score	Meet Our	Score Their
118		U D	Man'ver Points								
		U D	Man'ver Points								
126		U D	Man'ver Points								
		U D	Man'ver Points								
134		U D	Man'ver Points								
		U D	Man'ver Points								
142		U D	Man'ver Points								
		U D	Man'ver Points								
150		U D	Man'ver Points								
		U D	Man'ver Points								
158		U D	Man'ver Points								
		U D	Man'ver Points								
167		U D	Man'ver Points								
		U D	Man'ver Points								
177		U D	Man'ver Points								
		U D	Man'ver Points								
190		U D	Man'ver Points								
		U D	Man'ver Points								
H.W.		U D	Man'ver Points								
		U D	Man'ver Points								

Fig. 10.7 Sample wrestling
scoresheet. (5:216)

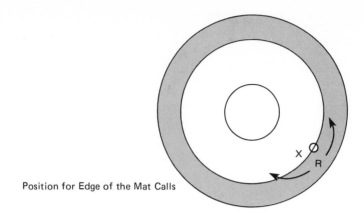

Position for Edge of the Mat Calls

Fig. 10.8 Position for edge of the mat
calls.

Miscellaneous Considerations

Tournament Seeding
In order to balance competition, two outstanding wrestlers in a weight
class should be placed in the upper and the lower half of the tournament
bracket. When numerous contestants are of equal ability, a draw for
bracket position should be conducted. Criteria for selecting seeding
includes defending champion status, an exceptional dual meet record
and won-loss record against common opponents.

Overtime Procedure
In tournament competition, if the match ends in a tie, three extra periods
of one minute will be conducted to determine the winner. There is no
carryover of penalties and warnings from the match to the overtime
session. In the event of a tie in the overtime, each contestant will be
evaluated using an established list of wrestling techniques criteria to
determine a winner.

Injury Circumstances
An injured contestant may be awarded up to maximum timeout of two
minutes, which is cumulative throughout the match, including the
overtime. There shall be no limit to the number of timeout periods which
may be taken in any match, but the total timeout shall not exceed two
minutes. If, at the expiration of the timeout, the injured wrestler is able
to continue wrestling, the match shall be resumed as if the contestants
had gone out of bounds. Only the referee may call such timeouts. (6:46)

Officiating Evaluated by Coaches

What qualities do you appreciate in a wrestling official?

1. Takes full authority (but not arrogant without it).
2. Sticks with calls, does not back down or change rulings (calm and deliberate).
3. In control of match at all times.
4. Hustle—was in best possible position to make the correct calls and protect wrestlers.
5. Alertness.
6. Consistency in enforcing rules, making calls and utilizing proper mechanics.
7. Was reserved in making quick decisions.
8. Talked to wrestlers to prevent injuries and penalties.
9. Firm, knowledgeable answers to questions on rules and has concern for the safety of the wrestlers—not confusing interscholastic with intercollegiate rules.
10. Inconspicuous during the match.

Miscellaneous Comments

1. Referee must gain the respect of the wrestlers during the pre-match conference.
2. Outstanding official was a former wrestler and is presently a coach with a good understanding of wrestling techniques, strategy and rules.
3. Many ex-wrestlers are poor mechanically due to "old-hat" attitude and tendency to be overtly friendly with wrestlers before the match.

Officiating Evaluated by Officials

What is the most difficult situation to call in wrestling?

1. Subjective calls which often bring disputes
2. Takedown without control
3. Edge of mat calls
4. Change of position or control as time expires

What is the most difficult phase of mechanics in officiating wrestling?

1. Scoring points while continuing to observe the action
2. See a pin in a cradle situation
3. Calling falls in fast changing situations (half nelson with bridging and twisting)

4. Falls when the shoulders are covered "front and back" and reversals on the edge of the mat

Miscellaneous Comments

1. Many coaches are lacking in rules knowledge making it difficult for them to accept the rulings of the referee.
2. Wrestling officiating is one of the most difficult sports to officiate because you are on your own to make all decisions.
3. Officials working both high school and college meets must be cognizant of the constantly changing rules differences

Situations and Rulings (8)

Situation: During a tournament match, wrestler had three penalties called on him. The match goes into overtime and A uses an illegal hammerlock. The referee disqualifies him and awards the match to B. *Ruling:* This is incorrect procedure. The overtime is a completely new match which is separate from the competition which resulted in the tie, with all the scoring, penalties and warnings which occurred during the regular match cancelled. Consequently, one point is awarded to B.

Situation: At the weigh-in prior to a dual meet, Team A's 145 pounder is ½ pound overweight. Team B's 145 pounder is also ½ pound overweight. Both coaches agree that since both boys "balance out", why waste the time making weight and permit time to compete. May this be permitted? *Ruling:* No. In all dual meets, net weight shall be required. No overweight is permitted, nor should it be requested.

Situation: The coach, contestant, manager or trainer leaves his restricted area and approaches the mat area for the purpose of coaching, directing or encouraging his wrestler. Is this a violation? If so, what is the penalty? *Ruling:* Yes, the coach is expected to set an example of admirable conduct. The present wrestling guide provides that all personnel other than actual participating contestants be restricted to an area at least 10 feet from the actual mat area during a match. Coaches are restricted to team benches except during time-outs or the end of the match. Officials are instructed to penalize promptly. First offense, deduct 1 team point, second offense remove from premises.

Situation: A, who allegedly had injured his elbow during a practice session reports to wrestle with a bulky, loose fitting pad on his elbow. *Ruling:* If, in the referee's opinion, the wearing of such an item would prevent the opponent from applying normal holds, he will direct the wrestler to remove the pad before wrestling. If the wrestler is injured to the extent that he cannot continue without this equipment, the match shall be forfeited to his opponent.

Situation: A has B in a pinning hold and B's head supported by A's elbow extends outside the wrestling area. B's head does not come in contact with the line or the area outside the wrestling area. Can a fall be awarded? *Ruling:* As long as the shoulders of B are inside the wrestling area, A may be awarded a fall.

Situation: A has B in a pinning situation. B deliberately crawls or bridges off the mat. Can referee award A near-fall and a penalty point since B deliberately crawled off the mat? *Ruling:* No. If near-fall points have been earned and are awarded, no penalty points can be given.

Situation: A is injured because of illegal action of B. B is penalized by the referee for the illegal hold. At the completion of the three minute injury time allowance, A is unable to continue. The referee awards the match to A. Is this correct? *Ruling:* Yes. Once the referee has penalized a contestant for an illegal hold and the opponent has been injured by that hold, the referee has no recourse except to award the match by default to the injured contestant. There is always the possibility that some coaches can and do take advantage of such a situation, and even though a referee may feel that the injured participant could continue, it is not his responsibility to make that decision.

Situation: A applies a Chicken Wing and Half Nelson on B and immediately places B into a pinning situation. The official stops the match and awards B a penalty point, claiming that the Chicken Wing was used as an illegal twisting hammerlock. The coach of B points out that the Chicken Wing is not listed as an illegal hold. *Ruling:* The ruling was correct. The Chicken Wing is legal as long as the pressure is applied perpendicular to the long axis of the body. When the pressure is parallel to the long axis of the body it is illegal.

Situation: From a neutral position, A in attempting a takedown, lifts B from the mat, and: (a) brings him to the mat with force or: (b) brings him forcibly to the mat so the upper half of his body contacts the mat before any other part of the body. B does not appear to be shaken up in either case. *Ruling:* A slam in both (a) and (b). Whether B is injured is no criterion in determining the slam. The slam is defined as lifting and bringing the opponent to the mat with unnecessary force. It is entirely possible for a slam to occur without a boy being injured.

Situation: Contestants are in a neutral position. A applies a legal headlock on B and takes him to the mat. Both contestants are on their right sides approximately parallel with each other, B's right shoulder is touching the mat and his left shoulder is within two inches of the mat. A maintains this position for approximately 10 seconds and the period ends. The referee awards no points. Is the referee correct? *Ruling:* Yes. Bringing a man to the mat with nothing more than a headlock cannot be considered a takedown and even though B's shoulders are in a near-fall position, since no takedown is awarded, near-fall points cannot be given. It must be understood also that a simple headlock would not be considered a pinning combination, and although a "fall" could occur, near-fall points should not be given in this or similar situations. A plain headlock affects only the near shoulder of the opponent and has little or no effect on the far shoulder. If and when contestant A adjusts his position and / or pressure within legal limits to the extent that B's far shoulder is endangered, then a takedown and / or near-fall may be considered.

BIBLIOGRAPHY

1. Hopke, Stephen L. and Worden Kidder. *Elementary and Junior High School Wrestling.* Cranbury, NJ: A. S. Barnes, Inc., 1977.
2. Keen, Clifford P. and Charles M. Speidel and Raymond H. Swartz. *Championship Wrestling.* Menasha, Wisconsin: George Banto, Inc., 1976.
3. Keith, Art. *Complete Book of Wrestling Drills and Conditioning Techniques.* W. Nyack, NY: Parker Publishing Co., Inc., 1976.
4. Perry, Rex and Arnold Umbach. *Wrestling.* New York: Sterling Publishing Co., 1976.
5. Umbach, Arnold W. and Warren R. Johnson. *Successful Wrestling.* Dubuque: W. C. Brown Co. Publishers, 1972.
6. *1984 NCAA Wrestling Rules.* Mission, Kansas: National Collegiate Athletic Association, 1983.
7. *Wrestling Rules.* Kansas City: National Federation of State High School Associations, 1983.
8. *Wrestling Rules Case-Book.* Los Angeles: Southern California Wrestling Officials Association, 1976.

Index